Screening Youth
Contemporary French and Francophone Cinema

Edited by
Romain Chareyron and Gilles Viennot

EDINBURGH
University Press

Edinburgh University Press is one of the leading university presses in the UK. We publish academic books and journals in our selected subject areas across the humanities and social sciences, combining cutting-edge scholarship with high editorial and production values to produce academic works of lasting importance. For more information visit our website: edinburghuniversitypress.com

© editorial matter and organisation Romain Chareyron and Gilles Viennot, 2019, 2021
© the chapters their several authors, 2019, 2021

Edinburgh University Press Ltd
The Tun – Holyrood Road
12 (2f) Jackson's Entry
Edinburgh EH8 8PJ

First published in hardback by Edinburgh University Press 2019

Typeset in Monotype Ehrhardt by
Manila Typesetting Company

A CIP record for this book is available from the British Library

ISBN 978 1 4744 4942 7 (hardback)
ISBN 978 1 4744 4943 4 (paperback)
ISBN 978 1 4744 4944 1 (webready PDF)
ISBN 978 1 4744 4945 8 (epub)

The right of the contributors to be identified as authors of this work has been asserted in accordance with the Copyright, Designs and Patents Act 1988 and the Copyright and Related Rights Regulations 2003 (SI No. 2498).

Contents

List of Figures   v
Notes on Contributors   vi

1. Disparate Lives: Representations of Youth in French and Francophone Cinema   1
   Romain Chareyron and Gilles Viennot
2. Un Vrai 'Teen Film' Français? The Contemporary Adolescent Genre in French Cinema   18
   Gemma Edney
3. Childhood and Gender Panic in *Ma Vie en rose* and *Tomboy*   33
   Jeri English
4. Bargaining the Body: Love, Death and Rites of Passage in Three Films by François Ozon   47
   Ericka Knudson
5. Repetition and Difference: The Representation of Youth in the Films of Céline Sciamma   62
   Karine Chevalier
6. Mia Hansen-Løve, Postfeminism in France and the Melancholic Girl   81
   Fiona Handyside
7. Frames of Desire and Otherness: Queer Bodies Caught *in-between* France and the Maghreb   99
   Walter S. Temple
8. 'A Child of the Ruins': Youthful Disaffection and the 'Making Of' the Terrorist   115
   Maria Flood
9. Gender and Representations of the *Banlieue* in Abd Al Malik's *Qu'Allah bénisse la France!* and Sylvie Ohayon's *Papa Was Not a Rolling Stone*   136
   Jocelyn A. Wright

10 (Re)Framing Youth and Identity in the Classroom in
   Être et avoir and *Entre les murs* 152
   Aubrey Korneta
11 Young Love and Everyday Freedom: Abdellatif Kechiche's
   La Faute à Voltaire and *La Vie d'Adèle* 173
   Kathryn Chaffee
12 Anthem for (Doomed) Youth: War, AIDS and the Queer
   Autobiographical Cinema of André Téchiné 188
   Claire Boyle
13 'Je veux promouvoir le vivre-ensemble': Youth and
   Friendship in *L'Auberge espagnole*, *Les Poupées russes* and
   Casse-tête chinois 206
   Ben McCann
14 Catherine Breillat's Maiden Trilogy 222
   Juliette Feyel
15 Dismembering and Remembering Childhood in
   Bruno Dumont's *P'tit Quinquin* 234
   Elizabeth Geary Keohane

Index 251

Figures

6.1	Clémence in *Father of My Children*	83
6.2	Camille in *Goodbye First Love*	84
6.3	Pamela in *All is Forgiven*	84
8.1	A youthful *bande à part*	121
8.2	Bahta performs authority in a police uniform	124
8.3	Directorial gestures of control and manipulation	130
8.4	Bahta's final incarnation, in a jacket marked 'Picasso'	132
11.1	Adèle's first view of Emma in downtown Lille	181
11.2	Adèle writes in her diary after meeting Emma for the second time	183
15.1	P'tit Quinquin slyly shows his dislike of the *gendarmerie*	236
15.2	One of the priests lays his hands on P'tit Quinquin	238
15.3	Van der Weyden shows a flicker of disapproval at the laying of hands	239
15.4	Carpentier does tricks in the police car	239
15.5	The children gather at the scene of the Bhiri shooting as it unfolds	241
15.6	Mohammed points a gun out of the window of the Bhiri household	241
15.7	The helicopter swoops down to hover over the children	242
15.8	Ch'tiderman	242
15.9	The mysterious *motard*	243
15.10	Aurélie sings at the first victim's funeral	246
15.11	Aurélie sings at the talent show heats	247
15.12	One of the murder victims as she is found on the beach	247
15.13	*Saint Sebastian comforted by an Angel* (*c.*1630) by Gerard Seghers	248

Notes on Contributors

The Editors

Romain Chareyron is Assistant Professor of French in the Department of Languages, Literatures and Cultural Studies at the University of Saskatchewan. Before coming to Saskatoon, he held teaching positions at the University of Kansas and Washington State University. His areas of study include: the representation of gender and sexuality in contemporary French cinema; the reworking of the genres of horror and pornography; the connections between auteur cinema and societal issues, such as immigration, racism and poverty. His current research focuses on the representation of disability in French cinema.

Gilles Viennot is Assistant Professor of French in the Department of World Languages, Literatures & Cultures at the University of Arkansas. His areas of study include: contemporary French literature (with an emphasis on Michel Houellebecq); the connections between neoliberalism, technology and family; as well as cinema and TV shows.

Contributors

Claire Boyle is Lecturer in French at the University of Edinburgh, where her teaching interests encompass French cinema, thought, literature and culture. Her research centres on explorations of selfhood and subjectivity in twentieth-century and contemporary French and francophone literature and film. Her interest in self-writing led to the publication of her monograph, *Consuming Autobiographies: Reading and Writing the Self in Post-War France* (2007). Latterly, and as part of her broad interests in the cultural inscription of subjectivities, her research focus has shifted to personal testimony and expressions of selfhood in French and francophone cinema. One strand of her research concerns queer testimonies in French cinema, which flows from a long-standing engagement in her published work with queer French cinema, theory and literature. She has published widely on these topics, including in journals such as *Modern & Contemporary France*, *French Studies*, *Paragraph* and *Esprit créateur*.

Kathryn Chaffee is a PhD student in the Department of French and francophone Studies at the University of California, Los Angeles. Her research and teaching interests encompass a variety of topics related to twentieth and twenty-first-century French literature and cinema, early modern philosophy, and French critical thought. She is the author of 'Adèle as Subject in Pursuit and Object Pursued: Narrative Structure in Abdellatif Kechiche's Blue is the Warmest Color' in *Revue CELAAN: Regards sur les films d'Abdellatif Kechiche*, Vol. 12, No. 2 (Spring 2016).

Karine Chevalier is Senior Lecturer in French and Film Studies (University of Roehampton, London). Her main research interests lie in the field of French cinema, visual arts and aesthetics, francophone postcolonial studies as well as filmmaking. She has published two monographs on memory from both imaginative and cultural perspectives (*La Mémoire et l'Absent. Nabile Farès et Juan Rulfo de la Trace au Palimpseste*, 2008; *La Mémoire et le Présent. Daniel Maximin et Salman Rushdie du Masque au Chaos*, 2010) as well as numerous articles about cinema: 'Le cinéma français face à la violence: du New French Extremism à une violence intériorisée' (2016), 'On ne naît pas déraciné, on le devient. La représentation de l'Autre dans le cinéma de Tony Gatlif' (2017) and 'Les gueules cassées ou l'éthique de l'écran crevé: du masque au visage cinématographique' (2018).

Gemma Edney is a PhD candidate in Film Studies at the University of Exeter. Her thesis explores the relationship between music and girlhood in contemporary French cinema, bringing together film studies, feminist theory and musicology to examine how music can bring us into contact with a young female subjectivity. Her other research interests include film sound studies, teen film aesthetics and digital media. Recent publications include 'Language Barriers? Songs, Nostalgia and Adolescence in Lisa Azuelos's *LOL* (2009)' (2017), and the Introduction to special journal issue 'Femmes Créa(c)tives: Women's Creativity in its Socio-Political Contexts' (with G. Alessandroni and S. Daroczi, *L'Esprit Créateur*, 2018).

Jeri English is an Associate Professor of French and of Women's and Gender Studies at the University of Toronto, Scarborough. Her research areas include feminist theories on gender and sexuality, French cinema, twentieth and twenty-first-century French women writers and the philosophy of Simone de Beauvoir. She has published articles and given papers on Rachilde, Annie Ernaux, Violette Leduc, Marguerite Duras, Marie Darieussecq, Camille Laurens and Simone de Beauvoir. Her current research project examines the reproduction and subversion of heteronormative tropes of femininity and masculinity in science fiction films.

Juliette Feyel holds a PhD in comparative literature and is an affiliated researcher of the University of Paris-Nanterre. She is the author of an essay entitled *Georges Bataille, une quête érotique du sacré*, 2013). Her research focuses on the representation of the body, corporal experiences and gender issues in English and French literature and cinema.

Maria Flood is Lecturer in Film at Keele University. Her PhD from the University of Cambridge focused on historical, memorial and aesthetic absence in French and Algerian cinema and she was awarded a Mellon Postdoctoral Fellowship in Cornell University in 2014. She has published widely on francophone film, world cinema and political violence. Her monograph, *France, Algeria and the Moving Image: Screening Histories of Violence* was published in 2017. She is currently working on a British Academy-funded project on the representation of radicalisation, affect and gender in contemporary world cinema.

Fiona Handyside is Senior Lecturer in Film Studies at the University of Exeter. She is the author of *Sofia Coppola: A Cinema of Girlhood* (2017) and *Cinema at the Shore: The Beach in French Cinema* (2014).

Elizabeth Geary Keohane is a Lecturer in French at the University of Glasgow. She has previously published on areas including travel writing, the imaginary voyage, sex tourism and text-image relations in journals such as *French Studies*, *Convergences francophones* and *Studies in Travel Writing*. She recently published an article on André Gide in the *Routledge Encyclopedia of Modernism*.

Ericka Knudson, Preceptor of French at Harvard University, teaches courses on French media and film. Her research interests include French New Wave cinema and modernity (articles in *Théâtre, levain du cinéma, théâtre, destin du cinéma*, 2013, *Regards cinématographiques sur le XVIIIe siècle*, 2009), youth in contemporary world cinema (*Thinking through the Child Protagonist in Films from Around the World*, with David Campos, in progress), as well as strategies for developing curriculum that is inclusive ('Films for Inclusion: LGBT perspectives in the French language classroom', in progress).

Aubrey Korneta is currently a guest faculty member at Sarah Lawrence College. She received her PhD from New York University's Department of French Literature, Thought, and Culture in 2017, and her dissertation is entitled 'Writing (in) the School: Codes. Constraints. Emancipation?' Her research focuses on twentieth to twenty-first-century French and francophone literature and film, with a particular interest in autobiography and memoir, postcolonial literature, and the representation of education, youth and identity formation.

Ben McCann is Associate Professor of French Studies at the University of Adelaide. He is the co-editor of *Michael Haneke: Europe Utopia* (2011) and *Framing French Culture* (2015) and the author of *Ripping Open the Set: French Film Design, 1930-1939* (2013), *Le Jour se lève* (2013), *Julien Duvivier* (2017) and *L'Auberge espagnole: European Youth on Film* (2018). He is currently writing a book on the interface between French and Japanese cinema.

Walter S. Temple is active in the fields of French and francophone literary and cultural studies, and second language acquisition. His research interests include twentieth to twenty-first-century French and francophone studies, French and North African cinema, diaspora studies, and L2 pedagogy. His research in literary and cultural studies highlights how a diverse archive of works by French and North African writers (and filmmakers) elucidates various modes of otherness (*l'altérité*). Central to his scholarship is what he defines as the narrative process of 'rewriting' as it relates to redefine territories of desire and melancholy.

Jocelyn A. Wright is a PhD candidate in French Studies at the University of Texas – Austin. Her dissertation, '*Beur, blanc, black*: The *Banlieue* Talks Back in Novels, Films and Graphic Novels', examines representations of the French *banlieue* in autobiographical and autofictive novels, films and graphic novels published between 1999 and 2015 and produced by persons who grew up in the *banlieue*. With an eye to the specificity of each medium, this multimedia project analyses how the authors leverage the unique creative possibilities of each genre to challenge the mythology of the *cité* as an urban ghetto.

CHAPTER 1

Disparate Lives: Representations of Youth in French and Francophone Cinema
Romain Chareyron and Gilles Viennot

Si l'adolescence est bel et bien le champ d'âge le plus intéressant, le plus vulnérable, le plus fragile, le plus dangereux dans la vie d'un être, elle est également faite de disgrâce et d'harmonie: c'est un tandem de contraires. (Egloff 2007: 15)

The initial impulse for this collection originated from one simple observation: while the topic of youth has informed a great variety of productions over the years,[1] little work has been done from an academic perspective to investigate this trend in a French and Francophone context,[2] and to analyse the polymorph entity that is youth and its many cinematic avatars. Our interest in this topic stems from a similar observation to the one made by Timothy Shary in his introduction to *Youth Culture in Global Cinema*, namely that little has been done to analyse the ways youth has been portrayed by adults, and what these portrayals might reveal to us from a social, cultural or ideological point of view: 'numerous studies and books have been written on the negative and positive effects of media on youth . . . yet nearly not as much time or effort has been expended in examinations of how youth are represented by the media' (Shary 2007: 3). What this comment suggests is that there might be a stronger interest in youth and the media when the former is understood from an economic point of view, that is, when it can benefit the latter. The ways film can help us get a better, more nuanced and true-to-life understanding of the complexity and struggles of youth have been somehow overlooked, which is even more blatant when one looks at the topic of youth in a French or Francophone context.

How do film directors approach youth today? Are there discernible narrative and aesthetic patterns at work throughout these films that could help us to navigate the intricacies of youth and its various portrayals? How do films about youth inform the viewer about some of society's most sensitive issues? These are some of the questions we had in mind when we launched this project and that inform the chapters in the collection. However, before we bring our attention to the different chapters, we thought it was important to spend some time revisiting the genre of the 'teen film', as it constitutes the backdrop against which our approach to youth narratives is based, as well as the source of inspiration – both from the point of view of storytelling and *mise en scène* – for many of the directors whose films are analysed in the different chapters that constitute the collection. Observing the evolution of the 'teen film' will enable us to better understand its socio-cultural foundations which, in turn, will serve to bring out the particular status of films about youth in French-speaking films.

Before we do so, we need to offer some terminological explanations, as well as discuss the scope of this collection in more detail, so that the reader can have a better grasp of the way we considered discussing the topic of youth in French and Francophone cinema. Firstly, we deliberately chose the word 'youth', rather than 'teenage years', 'childhood' or 'adolescence' because of its semantic flexibility. Indeed, choosing the word 'youth' gave us the possibility to encompass all the aforementioned age groups and eliminated the risk of creating artificial – and often counter-productive – boundaries between these different stages of life, which would have been too restrictive for the purpose of our collection. While a great number of chapters are focused on characters about to leave adolescence to enter adulthood – with a particular focus on the process of coming of age – we still thought that opening up the scope of the study would allow us to offer a more accurate illustration of the complexity and ambiguity characteristic of youth, the latter being first and foremost defined by its ever-changing nature.[3] In so doing, we make Daniel Sibony's comments on youth ours, when he declares '. . . the adolescent is not an animal whose life starts at 12 and ends between the ages of 16 and 20. Neither is it an entity that can be neatly circumscribed . . . Being an adolescent is in itself a process . . .' (Sibony 1991: 11 – our translation).[4] Different terms have been used to designate films based on youth and their targeted age group: 'teen film', 'youth cinema', to name just two. For the purpose of this collection, and due to our more comprehensive approach to youth, we will use these terms in an interchangeable manner in the course of this introduction.

Secondly, we want to mention that this volume intends to study films *about* youth, rather than films aimed at youth. As a result, we have put aside mainstream productions that are specifically directed at a teenage or adolescent audience, and tend to offer a more polished and often caricatured image of youth.[5] While some of the films analysed in this volume have been box office hits (we are mostly thinking here about Cédric Klapisch's trilogy), what informs the portrayals of youth discussed throughout the collection is the director's take on the topic and a general desire to have youth be in conversation with today's societal concerns, so that this particular time in one's life is not perceived as an idealised realm remote from 'real life' considerations. Speaking on a metaphorical level, we can say that these films understand youth as a 'sound box', where internal struggles collide with contemporary concerns, and this interaction of an external reality with 'specific social, cultural, political circumstances' (Thévenin quoted in Egloff 2007: i) often appears as amplified and distorted, due to the elusiveness and instability inherent to this stage of life.

Lastly, and maybe more importantly, as the reader will notice from the chapters, the majority of them address the topic of youth and its various representations in a French context. While respectively born in Tunisia and Morocco, filmmakers Abdellatif Kechiche and Abdellah Taïa, whose films are featured in this collection, live in France. Their ties with French culture are all the more significant, in that their films are either set in France or benefit from French funds for their production.[6] The same comments apply to French rapper-turned-director Abd Al Malik, whose film *Qu'Allah bénisse la France* is analysed in one of the chapters, who is of Congolese origin, but was born in Paris and spent most of his childhood in Strasbourg. Of all the directors mentioned in this collection, only Tunisian director Nouri Bouzid (who directed *Making Of*) operates outside the boundaries of French cinema. Because of their respective history, France and Tunisia have experienced a significantly different development in terms of their film industries and their relationship with film genres. Since the set of formulas that defines a genre has strong ties with the economy as well as with the sociocultural standards of a given society, the comments we are about to make about youth cinema in France, its history and its various representations might not necessarily find the same echo in other countries of the francophone world. However, it is our hope that these comments might help to cast new light on the works of these directors and establish cross-cultural dialogues between these countries regarding their cinematic treatment of youth.

While discussing the history and evolution of Tunisian cinema is beyond the scope of this introduction, it is, however, beneficial for the reader to get a general sense of some of the distinguishing features of this cinema. Indeed, for many years, Tunisian cinema struggled to establish a strong and singular cinematic culture. Unlike its Algerian neighbour, Tunisia never benefited from the involvement of the State in the production and distribution of its films. Partly because of that, a unified film industry never blossomed in the country, so that 'output in Tunisia is largely the work of dedicated individualists . . .' (Armes 1996: 667). Another reason for this erratic output could be that, for several decades, Tunisian cinema struggled to find its own voice, as it suffered from the overwhelming presence of Egyptian cinema throughout the Arab world, and the influence of its constitutive key genres: the melodrama, the social drama and the historical epic (see Armes 1996: 662–5). Since the mid-1980s[7] though, Tunisian cinema seems to have found a new creative impulse, with films engaging the audience with questions about national identity, the growth of political Islam and the dangers of an authoritarian State.

Based on these comments, it will be interesting to observe how each country responds to the challenges posed by youth and its cinematic representations, but also how each country's sociopolitical concerns are problematised within their portrayals of youth.

Delineating Youth Cinema in a Non-American Context

When researching the topic of youth and its relationship with cinema, the first thing that stands out is how 'teen film' as a genre finds its roots in American culture. While we will not use this introduction to offer a survey of the birth and evolution of the 'teen film' in America,[8] it is nonetheless crucial to have a clear understanding of the strong ties between the visual and narratives tropes that have come to define this film genre and the culture within which these tropes emerged. In his article 'Teen Films: The Cinematic Image of Youth',[9] Timothy Shary offers a comprehensive overview of the evolution pertaining to the representation of youth in US cinema,[10] and how these evolutions reflected the changes that were taking place within American society:

> The deep and compelling history of films about youth informs us of more than the changing social conditions and perceptions of young people, it gives us a special appreciation for how successive generations have endured the conflicts of claiming identity and seeking recognition for their actions. This endurance was seen most visibly in teen films after WWII as young people restively entered the Cold War era their parents created, and then again in counter-culture films of the '60s, and most recently at the turn of the millennium as youth face a future that will be far more fast-paced and removed from the traditions and mores of their parents' generation. (Shary 2012: 577)

In addition to this affinity between youth narratives and American culture, another distinctive feature of the American 'teen film' lies in its economic impact. Indeed, the Hollywood film industry realised early on how it could benefit from catering to a younger audience, and thus dedicated an entire segment of its production to teen movies, which we are reminded of by Timothy Shary in his introduction to the edited collection *Youth Culture in Global Cinema*, when he writes that 'Hollywood's appeal to youth is essentially for profit, since young people constitute such a high portion of the moviegoing audience' (Shary 2007: 2). In this particular case, we are talking about films *about* youth and *for* youth.[11] This gave way to a highly codified universe with emblematic characters and well-delineated plot developments.[12]

When placed in a French-speaking context, it is especially interesting to notice that, whether as a genre (films about youth) or from an economic perspective (films for youth), 'teen films' have never enjoyed the same status they have in America. While some films about youth or for youth have been box office hits,[13] this never translated into the establishment of a proper genre within French production, as these films were not considered through their possible generic affiliation, but rather as isolated events without any thematic or aesthetic similarities to connect them. This lack of a cohesive body of films centred on youth and with established narrative and visual codes is noted by Olivier Davenas when, writing about the sub-genre of the 'high-school movie', he says the following:

> When looking at the highly codified genre of the American high-school movie, one can only notice that there is no such equivalent within European film production. This extremely delineated film genre never took form in countries such as France or the UK, even though it is possible to notice some recurring thematic or aesthetic tropes specific to each country [such as] the naturalistic approach and the attention paid to characters' psychological development found in French films. However, these recurring aspects are not exclusive to films portraying youth, as they can also apply to a much wider range of productions. (Davenas 2012: 8–9 – our translation)[14]

France's reluctance to consider a film through the lens of genre can be traced back to the emergence of the New Wave, in the late 1950s, and the primacy it gave to the figure of the film director as auteur. Discussing the intricate nature of the concept of 'film genre' as well as its complex relationship with French cinema is beyond the scope of this introduction.[15] However, we can say that with New Wave's criticism of *cinéma de la qualité*,[16] which it considered to be a purely commercial enterprise with little depth and bloated film techniques, a new generation of directors called for a renewed perception of what the art of filmmaking should truly be about: the expression of a filmmaker's unique point of view on the complexity of life. The New Wave's call for creativity and subjectivity, in terms of subject matters and *mise en scène*, is by definition at odds with the requirements and limitations imposed by generic conventions. As Andrew Tudor reminds us in this very concise, yet extremely instructive definition of film genre: 'The very existence of a set of conventionalized genre parameters constrains movies towards a norm. A genre is a relatively fixed culture pattern . . . By its nature, its very familiarity, it inclines towards reassurance' (Tudor 1974: 180–1).

By choosing to favour intimate portrayals of characters experiencing love, loss and longing, and pondering over the nature of life, over more mainstream and, supposedly, less worthy productions, the directors of the New Wave instigated a long-lasting divide within French cinema between auteur cinema and a more commercial type of cinema, often denigrated by critics. This divide remains today and continues to inform the way films are classified, which prevents the development of strong and viable film genres,[17] as noted by Olivier Davenas:

> This strange phenomenon of resistance observed in various film industries throughout Europe, and at odds with the overall stranglehold of American culture, is partly due – in France at least – to the ever-present influence of the New Wave . . . the heavy presence of the auteur still looms over the artistic process and is rooted in France's philosophical approach of art, making it particularly difficult for films to comply with generic requirements. (Davenas 2012: 8–9 – our translation)[18]

With this in mind, we will now discuss how some French and francophone directors are managing to navigate the idiosyncrasies of French cinema to bring us singular depictions of youth that bypass the straitjacket of auteur cinema while retaining some of its founding principles (an emphasis on the singularity of the director's vision, a focus on realism, as well as on intimate descriptions of individuals or groups, often intermingled with socio-economic concerns). This will allow us to bring out some of the narratives and visual strategies these directors display in their works to try to reconcile two seemingly antithetical points of view: that of the youth portrayed on screen and that of the adult behind the camera.

Capturing the Inexpressible

> The study of youth is by necessity inexact and incomplete. (Lewis 1992: 2)

As a narrative art, film has the power to impact on our understanding of youth, either enforcing preconceived ideas about this age group or challenging them, and forcing us to look at them anew. As mentioned previously, youth is first and foremost 'defined' by its unstable and elusive nature. Any attempt at capturing youth on screen should thus be respectful of its 'shapelessness' and refrain from superimposing onto its representation 'a pre-packaged identity that subverts the natural emergence of an authentic self' (Thévenin quotedd in Egloff 2007: ii). As our discussion about the emergence of 'teen films' in American culture pointed out, the success and longevity of this genre rest on its well-delineated and predictable narrative structure, as well as on easily identifiable visual and thematic tropes. However, what the films analysed in this collection have in common is that they offer new ways of considering youth, as this formative stage in a person's life is no longer depicted as a stable or uncomplicated process, but is instead portrayed as 'an epigenetic process' (Egloff 2007: 24) that happens gradually, through added layers of significance. In so doing, these films restore the need for authenticity that is vital for any truthful portrayal that wishes to seize youth in all its contradictions. It is in their ability to distance themselves from some of the clichés often attached to the genre that the films discussed in this collection find their common ground. In these films, characters are not forced to fit any preconceived idea pertaining to what 'youth' is or should be, as the process of coming of age that is central to most youth narratives is not considered as immutable or interchangeable. Instead, what could be called the 'process of youth' is described as something unique to each individual, and based on his or her own life circumstances.

Indecisiveness, ambiguity and the lack of clear boundaries are what inform the various portrayals of youth put together in this collection. These concepts are expressed through characters whose opacity governs the entire narrative (François Ozon), characters embarked on a personal journey towards self-knowledge (Mia Hansen-Løve, Cédric Klapisch, Céline Sciamma) or self-acceptance (Olivier Ducastel and Jacques Martineau, Abdellah Taia), and also characters trying to claim a different life for themselves (Laurent Cantet, Sylvie Ohayon, Abd Al Malik). The complexity of youth can also be rendered visually, some directors using the feeling of 'in-betweenness' that characterises youth (the 'not yet an adult, but no longer a child' phase) as the leitmotiv for their *mise en scène* (Bruno Dumont), sometimes carrying the identity crisis and the feeling of inadequacy felt by youth to a point of no return (Catherine Breillat).

Youth in Contemporary French and Francophone Cinema: an Overview

The different chapters in this volume constitute many snapshots of what it means to be an adolescent today, while highlighting the breadth and richness of French and francophone cinema, and the energy and talent of a young generation of filmmakers. While it is not our intention to offer a definite or exhaustive appraisal of what defines youth cinema – as it would be detrimental to the principles of fluidity and indeterminacy that characterise youth – we can nonetheless sketch some guiding principles that seem to inform some of the films being made today that take youth as their main narrative and/or aesthetic device.

The number of chapters that tackle the questions of gender and sexuality underscore their primal significance in contemporary youth narratives. As exposed by Walter S. Temple, Jeri English and Kathryn Chaffee, coming to terms with one's desires and managing the fine line between society's demands and one's personal freedom are central themes in French and francophone cinema. Some directors choose to deal with sexuality from a more psychological angle, using it to convey the upheavals that are integral parts of the process of coming of age. A more forthright approach to female desire and a foray into the darker side of intimacy where death looms are some of the ways these directors operate, as Ericka Knudson and Juliette Feyel's chapters set out to demonstrate.

However, it would be a misguided conception to believe that sexuality and gender take centre stage when it comes to the representation of youth in film; youth also appears to be the ideal vehicle for directors to reflect upon today's society and some of its most sensitive issues. In a French context, the question of identity in connection to ethnicity, education and socio-economic status informs a significant number of youth-centred narratives, a phenomenon that Aubrey Korneta, Elizabeth Geary Keohane, Jocelyn A. Wright and Karine Chevalier analyse in their chapters. As Maria Flood and Claire Boyle's chapters rightfully highlight, youth can also be a conduit for directors to discuss events of great magnitude that are not limited to youth, but affect people worldwide.

Some directors take a more philosophical approach to their depiction of youth, with narratives that place a greater emphasis on the indecisiveness and loneliness inherent to the process of 'becoming'. With a particular focus on the passing of time, the loss of ideals, and the importance of interpersonal relations to reach a better knowledge of self and others, these films offer an understated yet poignant testimony of what it means to be coming of age in the twenty-first century, as Ben McCann and Fiona Handyside's chapters aptly point out.

Gemma Edney's 'Un vrai "teen film" Français? The contemporary adolescent genre in French cinema' will serve as the introductory chapter to this volume, as the author chooses to discuss the genre of the 'teen film' in a French context. In this chapter, Edney asks the question of whether there is such a thing as a French 'teen' film. In an attempt to answer this question, she observes how the French production of films whose narrative is based on the depiction of the lives of teenagers is divided into two main streams: the first one does not specifically aim at a teenage audience and generally falls under 'auteur cinema'. Critics, she argues, usually favour this type of production, as it offers a more realistic portrayal of the lives of teenagers. The second one, which borrows more evidently from its American counterpart, is usually directed towards a broad audience and does not tend to attract critics' attention. In her chapter, the author suggests that a more encompassing approach that does not operate such an arbitrary divide could help us to get a clearer idea of what a French 'teen pic' might actually represent.

Jeri English's 'Childhood and Gender Panic in *Ma Vie en rose* and *Tomboy*' examines the intersection between youth, family, gender identity formation and sexuality in Alain Berliner's *Ma Vie en rose* (1997) and Celine Sciamma's *Tomboy* (2011). English posits that while these two films portraying transgender children adopt wildly contrasting styles – Berliner uses a bright colour palette that reflects the main character's whimsical world, while Sciamma opts for a more realistic approach – they echo each other in the emphasis they place on the importance of the gaze in the construction of each character's gender identity. Focusing on the significance of the gaze at a diegetic and extra-diegetic level, English's chapter examines how the main characters' determination to embody a new gender identity triggers a 'gender panic' in their immediate surroundings, as their exploration of gender constructs does not remain within the confines of their respective homes. English explains that the family in both films is portrayed in a dualistic manner, as allowing a certain degree of freedom regarding gender nonconformity, while also reinforcing gender binaries when the situation gets out of control.

In her chapter called 'Bargaining the Body: Love, Death and Rites of Passage in Three Films by François Ozon', Ericka Knudson explores the French director's take on the cinematic trope of the *femme fatale*. She argues that while Ozon is indebted to some prominent New Wave directors such as Jean-Luc Godard and Éric Rohmer in his depiction of young female heroines, he further experiments with the cliché of the *femme fatale* to incorporate more contemporary considerations about the position of women in French society. According to Knudson, Ozon's *mise en scène* of the female body echoes New Wave's portrayals of ambiguous female characters who used their body to gain power over male characters, which corresponds to the newfound sexual freedom France underwent in the 1960s. However, the author suggests, Ozon's specificity lies in the fact that his female heroines are never punished for their sexual freedom, as it is perceived as a rite of passage, and offers his characters greater self-awareness and leads them towards adulthood.

Karine Chevalier's 'Repetition and Difference: The Representation of Youth in the Films of Céline Sciamma' offers a comprehensive approach to the director's triptych, *Naissance des pieuvres* (2007), *Tomboy* (2011) and *Bande de filles* (2014), by focusing on the ways the girl characters in Sciamma's films go through a process of differentiation and repetition – through clothes, hairstyles or gestures – necessary to their individuation. In this chapter, the author aims to show how Sciamma's films can be situated between two genres: that of the American 'teen movie', with its codes and conventions, and that of the French auteur film, where adolescent characters are forced to confront the real world. Chevalier thus explains that the 'in-betweenness' that characterises Sciamma's films allows the director to reassure the audience with the perpetuation of some familiar tropes, while introducing more personal elements in her narratives, as her films deal with contemporary issues such as post-colonialism, female homosexuality and gender nonconformity.

Fiona Handyside's 'Mia Hansen-Løve, Postfeminism in France and the Melancholic Girl' analyses the theme of girlhood as represented in what she calls the director's 'young girl trilogy', namely *Tout est pardonné* (2007), *Le Père de mes enfants* (2009) and *Un Amour de jeunesse* (2011). She discusses how the director's films crystallise a particularly French inflection of a postfeminist discourse more usually associated with American media production. Her chapter observes how Hansen-Løve's films explore girls coming of age in which their ability to be educated, work, travel, love and explore is taken for granted. However, the author says, her heroines differ from the textual and thematic models offered by Hollywood, as her trilogy develops a melancholic pattern of girlhood, since her 'girls' are systematically portrayed as being profoundly alone, brutally let down by men and unable to be supported by other women. This specific pattern, the author states, is at odds with the fun and sparkle of mainstream girl culture promoted by Hollywood in its portrayals of girlhood.

In his chapter, 'Frames of Desire and Otherness: Queer Bodies Caught *in-between* France and the Maghreb', Walter S. Temple chooses to explore the questions of identity and immigration in connection to queer desire and belonging among French and Maghrebi youth. Through his study of Olivier Ducastel and Jacques Martineau's *Drôle de Félix* (2000) and Abdellah Taïa's *L'Armée du salut* (2013), Temple offers a transnational exploration of the difficulties faced by gay youth in both Western and Arab cultures. In his chapter, the author sets out to examine the confluence of the French and North African cultures in a transnational and bicultural context in order to bring to light a number of current debates fuelled by questions of immigration, identity and otherness. Temple's analysis aims at revealing the complementary nature of these two films in regards to the portrayal of the queer youth subject. Indeed, as Temple posits, in either case, these northern and southern bodies coincide in 'foreign' territories, inciting discourse on the fragile parameters that define constructs of sexuality, masculinity and national identity in a twenty-first century Franco-Maghrebi context.

Maria Flood's '"A Child of the Ruins": Youthful Disaffection and the "Making Of" the Terrorist' sets out to discuss terrorism and the process of radicalisation in connection with the dissatisfaction of youth as portrayed in contemporary Maghrebi cinema, focusing on Nouri Bouzid's *Making Of* (2006) and Nabil Ayouch's *Les Chevaux de Dieu* (2012). Flood's chapter proposes an examination of the links between terrorism and youthful dissatisfaction in neo-liberal society, focusing on the figure of the male terrorist drawn into fundamentalist violence. The films' novelty, Flood states, lies in the fact that they invite the spectator to encounter the terrorist as a humanised and vulnerable young man and not as an utterly unscrupulous agent of violence, as is often the case in Western depictions of terrorism. Flood's intent in this chapter is to show how contemporary Maghrebi cinema can offer a re-examination of the role that youthful disenfranchisement in global neo-liberal societies plays in the radicalisation of young men.

Jocelyn A. Wright's chapter 'Gender and Representations of the *Banlieue* in Abd Al Malik's *Qu'Allah bénisse la France!* and Sylvie Ohayon's *Papa Was Not a Rolling Stone*' compares two filmic portraits of youth in the French *banlieue* of the 1980s. While both films are based upon each director's own autobiography, Wright's chapter aims to show the very different depictions of life in the *banlieue* that result from these adaptations. Wright's analyses reveal the aesthetic and thematic differences between these two works. In so doing, the author's text reappraises Carrie Tarr's (2005) distinction between *beur*-authored *banlieue* films and white-authored *banlieue* films, with Tarr stating that the former provides a more sympathetic portrayal of the *banlieue*, as *beur* directors supposedly have a more personal approach to the topic. Wright posits that rather than one's ethnicity, it is gender that tends to play a significant role in terms of how childhood in the *banlieue* is characterised.

Aubrey Korneta's '(Re)Framing Youth and Identity in the Classroom in *Être et avoir* and *Entre les murs*' offers a discussion on the representation of the French education system and reflects on its role in shaping youth identity through a cross-analysis of two successful works that use school as their setting. Korneta states that while these two films present some similarities, they also offer some strikingly different perspectives on youth in the context of a classroom. Korneta's argument is that, while Nicolas Philibert's documentary *Être et avoir* is primarily interested in reasserting the importance of learning, knowledge and community as cornerstones of democracy, Laurent Cantet's *Entre les murs* presents a more complex – and perhaps, realistic – vision of the challenges faced by the French education system today. Through an analysis of the politics of space and language deployed in each work, Korneta demonstrates that Philibert's attempt to capture 'universal' values is not always successful, while Cantet's film raises important questions regarding the question of French identity and the role played by education in shaping it.

Kathryn Chaffee's 'Young Love and Everyday Freedom: Abdellatif Kechiche's *La Faute à Voltaire* and *La Vie d'Adèle*' discusses the theme of freedom in connection with the representation of blossoming love stories in two of the director's films. While both films deal with contemporary and sometimes highly sensitive topics in French society (homosexuality and immigration), Chaffee's chapter sets out to demonstrate that Kechiche's films are never overtly political, as the director is more interested in fixating on intimate moments of young love and everyday life, implying that his notion of freedom is to be found in the quotidian rather than through obvious political stances.

In 'Anthem for (Doomed) Youth: War, AIDS and the Queer Autobiographical Cinema of André Téchiné', Claire Boyle chooses to cast light on two of the director's films that have received little scholarly attention: *Les Roseaux sauvages* (1994) and *Les Témoins* (2007). Her chapter explores Téchiné's representation of youth in conjunction with questions of sexual identity, futurity and becoming. Both narratives take place against the backdrop of two traumatic moments in late-twentieth-century French history (the Algerian War of Independence in *Les Roseaux sauvages*, and the outbreak of the AIDS epidemic in *Les Témoins*), leading the author to discuss how, while certain thematic and aesthetic continuities straddle the two films, they also offer opposing portrayals of the experience of coming of age. Boyle also discusses how, while certain thematic and aesthetic continuities are found in the two films, they also offer opposing portrayals of the experience of coming of age. While *Les Roseaux sauvages* shows the young protagonists' resilience in the face of death and national trauma, *Les Témoins* testifies to the brutal arrest of youthful birthright that is the process of becoming.

Ben McCann's '"Je veux promouvoir le vivre-ensemble": Youth and Friendship in *L'Auberge espagnole* (2002), *Les Poupées russes* (2005) and *Casse-tête chinois* (2013)' explores the complexity and life-affirming power of friendship in Klapisch's widely popular trilogy. In this chapter, the author discusses how these films perpetuate the director's long-lasting preoccupations with the fraught relationship between individuals and community and the need for universal acceptance and tolerance. The chapter looks at the evolution of friendship across the trilogy, noticing how the familiar rhythms of the coming-of-age genre are enriched with contemporary considerations about identity in a European and global context.

Juliette Feyel's 'Catherine Breillat's Maiden Trilogy' discusses the director's exploration of female sexuality by analysing three of her films that deal with a young girl's coming of age: *Une Vraie jeune fille* (1976), *36 Fillette* (1988) and *À ma sœur!* (2001). The author reveals how, in these films, Breillat revisits the codes of mainstream teen movies, infusing them with her distinctive brand of brutal intimacy and unsentimental depiction of sexuality, thus shedding a crude light upon her heroines' darkest desires. In her defence of Breillat's thematic and aesthetic approach, Feyel argues that the director's confrontational style does not aim to objectify women, but instead conveys the loss of personal integrity due to puberty's hormonal upheaval. She thus maintains that the three films' blunt addressing of the loss of virginity in no way indicates a misogynistic view on Breillat's behalf, but instead fuels a drive to subjugate men.

In her chapter, 'Dismembering and Remembering Childhood in Bruno Dumont's *P'tit Quinquin* (2014)', Elizabeth Geary Keohane explores Dumont's unique take on childhood, as it is portrayed in an unsavoury and irreverent manner by the director, in an effort to blur the lines between childhood and adulthood, while exploring questions about French identity, life in provincial France, and the construction of masculinity and femininity. By focusing on various film techniques, Geary Keohane analyses how Dumont seamlessly blends adult situations with the child protagonist's perception of these events, often to comic and jarring effects. In so doing, the author argues, Dumont's film is not only one about children, but also one which uses the motif of childhood to shape both its narrative techniques and its style.

Notes

1. Early on in the history of French cinema, youth has been used as the privileged vehicle by directors to tackle questions of identity, freedom, rebellion and self-affirmation, while experimenting with the narrative and visual possibilities of the medium. Jean Vigo's highly controversial *Zéro de conduite*, initially released in 1933, was subsequently banned from French cinemas until 1945, due to its polemical portrayal of youth, the adult world as well as the school system. François Truffaut's *Les 400 coups* (1959) represents another

landmark in world cinema, as the director's fictionalised retelling of his rebellious years as a teenager is also associated with the birth of the New Wave and auteur cinema. In more recent years, a new generation of directors has been using youth as its main narrative and aesthetic device to offer a renewed perception of the complexity of coming of age while negotiating questions of ethnicity, racism and social alienation (Mathieu Kassovitz's *La Haine* (1995); Abdellatif Kechiche's *L'Esquive* (2003)), gender and sexuality (Abdellatif Kechiche's *La Vie d'Adèle* (2013); André Téchiné's *Quand on a 17 ans* (2016); Robin Campillo's *120 Battements par minute* (2017)), and more generally speaking the very process of coming of age in the twentieth century (Noémie Lvovsky's *La Vie ne me fait pas peur* (1999)). One of the most recent examples of the richness and vitality of youth-based narratives in French cinema is the success – both at the box office and with critics – of Thomas Cailley's *Les Combattants* (2014) that attracted around 400,000 spectators (<http://www.jpbox-office.com/fichfilm.php?id=14455>; last accessed 31 October 2018) and garnered the awards for Best First Feature, Best Actress and Best Promising Actor at the 2015 César Awards.

2. The only full-length book to address the question of youth in French cinema is Egloff, (2007). Other significant contributions to the field are: Boutang and Sauvage (2011) and Davenas (2013). However, unlike Egloff's these books do not solely focus on French representations of youth, as they also include American productions within their analytical framework.

3. The instability that characterises youth is a phenomenon that most of the literature on the topic agrees on. As Jon Lewis notes in his introduction to the study of teen films and youth culture: 'Youth is fragmentary and fleeting, transitional and transitory . . . youth culture has proven to be an elusive target' (Lewis 1992: 2).

4. 'L'adolescent n'est pas un animal qui naît vers 12 ans et disparaît vers 16 ou 20 ans. Ce n'est pas une entité que l'on peut cerner, objectiver, traiter . . . L'adolescent est un processus . . .' (Sibony 1991: 11)

5. A good example of this trend is the recent film adaptations of René Goscinny and Jean-Jacques Sempé's children books *Le Petit Nicolas*. The two adaptations (*Le Petit Nicolas*, Laurent Tirard 2010, and *Les Vacances du Petit Nicolas*, Laurent Tirard, 2014) were box office hits, attracting respectively 5,500,000 (<http://www.jpbox-office.com/fichfilm.php?id=10600>; last accessed 31 October 2018) and 2,500,000 spectators (<http://www.jpbox-office.com/fichfilm.php?id=14010>; last accessed 31 October 2018). These films perpetuated the idealised vision of childhood made popular by the cartoonists, as they offer a harmless and outdated representation of youth in the 1950s.

6. All of Kechiche's films are set in France. Taïa's first (and, to this day, only) film, *L'Armée du salut*, that is discussed in one of the chapters is a French–Moroccan–Swiss production.

7. In his book *New Tunisian Cinema: Allegories of Resistance*, Robert Lang defines the birth of what he calls 'new Tunisian cinema' as coinciding with

the release of Nouri Bouzid's *Man of Ashes*, in 1986. For more information regarding the history of Tunisian cinema, see Lang (2015).
8. Some of the most recent contributions to the topic of American 'teen films' include Shary (2005); Driscoll (2011); Smith (2017).
9. For more information, see Shary (2012). It is to be noted that, in his study of teen films, the author more particularly focuses on the last twenty years of the 20th century, which roughly corresponds to the time where, as mentioned by Shary, 'youth cinema' started being considered as a film genre.
10. Interestingly, Shary notes how the birth of cinema, in the 1890s, is almost concomitant with the landmark work of American social psychologist G. Stanley Hall and his two-volume publication on 'youth' as an area of academic research. As stated by Shary: 'That the proliferation of cinema and the founding of youth studies coincide within the same historical generation may not be indicative of a cause-and-effect relationship; however, the relationship between cinema and youth is significant . . .' (Shary 2012: 578).
11. The two most successful franchises belonging to this trend are the *Harry Potter* and *Hunger Games* series. The eight instalments in the *Harry Potter* series grossed near 8 billion dollars worldwide (<https://www.boxofficemojo.com/franchises/chart/?id=harrypotter.htm>; last accessed 31 October 2018), while the four instalments in the *Hunger Games* series grossed near 3 billion dollars worldwide (<https://www.boxofficemojo.com/franchises/chart/?id=hungergames.htm>; last accessed 31 October 2018).
12. When discussing some of the narrative conventions to keep in mind when writing a coming-of-age scenario, Jule Selbo makes some insightful comments that can help us to get a better understanding of what could be called the 'invariable elements' of the genre. She writes: 'The coming-of-age genre requires the building of three-dimensional characters. Characters often struggle with the *gray* areas; those characters with moral certitude may come to understand that an absolute "right" or an absolute "wrong" may not exist. Personal integrity is all. Coming-of-age characters may never have been tested for personal integrity, they may never have asked themselves the *big* questions regarding love, morality or personal responsibility. Successful coming-of-age narratives center on storylines that force the protagonist to face big questions and find themselves in the answers' (Selbo 2015: 292).
13. In recent years, the three most popular films that could be labelled as belonging to 'youth cinema' would be *Les Choristes* (Christophe Barratier, 2003) that attracted over 8,500,000 spectators in France alone (<http://www.jpbox-office.com/fichfilm.php?id=1043>; last accessed 31 October 2018), *Neuilly sa mère!* (Gabriel Julien-Laferrière, 2009), with over 2,500,000 spectators (<http://www.jpbox-office.com/fichfilm.php?id=10874>; last accessed 31 October 2018) and *La Famille Bélier* (Éric Lartigau, 2014), with 7,400,000 spectators (<http://www.jpbox-office.com/fichfilm.php?id=14660>; last accessed 31 October 2018).

14. 'Force est de constater qu'il n'existe pas d'équivalents européens au genre très balisé du *high-school movie* américain. En Grande-Bretagne comme en France, un tel genre n'a jamais émergé comme catégorie nettement définie, même s'il est possible de relever certaines récurrences thématiques ou esthétiques selon la nation considérée . . . un naturalisme formel et une grande attention portée à la psychologie des personnages dans les films français. Toutefois ces récurrences peuvent se rapporter à un ensemble bien plus vaste d'œuvres cinématographiques et pas uniquement aux films traitant prioritairement de l'adolescence' (Davenas 2012: 8–9).
15. For further information regarding the concept of 'film genre', see Grant (2007); Geraghty and Jancovich (2008). For further information regarding film genre in a French context, see Moine (2005).
16. In his seminal text 'Une Certaine tendance du cinéma français', initially published in *Les Cahiers du cinéma* in 1954, François Truffaut discusses what he sees as the pitfalls of French cinema in the early 1950s and offers new avenues cinema could explore to escape the limitations imposed by the domination of 'psychological realism' in films. The full text is available at <http://www.newwavefilm.com/about/a-certain-tendency-of-french-cinema-truffaut.shtml> (last accessed 20 August 2018).
17. The two main exceptions are the comedy and the *polar*, or detective story, that have enjoyed continuous success over the years.
18. 'Ce curieux phénomène de résistance des cinémas nationaux dans un contexte général d'impérialisme culturel américain tient beaucoup, en France, à la persistance . . . de l'héritage de la Nouvelle Vague . . . la figure surplombante de l'auteur et la suprématie du style emblématiques de la philosophie française de l'art s'accommodant fort mal de la soumission d'une œuvre à des impératifs génériques' (Davenas 2012: 8–9).

Works Cited

Armes, Roy (1996) 'The Arab World', in G. Nowell-Smith (ed.), *The Oxford History of World Cinema*, New York: Oxford University Press, pp. 661–7.

Boutang, Adrienne and Célia Sauvage (2011), *Les 'teen movies'*, Paris: Librairie philosophique J. Vrin.

Davenas, Olivier (2012), *Teen! Cinéma de l'adolescence*, Montélimar: Les Moutons électriques.

Driscoll, Catherine (2011), *Teen Film: A Critical Introduction*, Oxford and New York: Berg.

Egloff, Karin M. (2007), *Les Adolescents dans le cinéma français: Entre deux mondes*, Lewiston, NY: The Edwin Mellen Press.

Geraghty L. and M. Jancovich (eds) (2008), *The Shifting Definitions of Genre. Essays on Labeling Films, Television Shows and Media*, Jefferson, NC and London: McFarland & Company, Inc.

Grant, Barry Keith (2007), *Film Genre: From Iconography to Ideology*, London and New York: Wallflower.
Lang, R. (2015), *New Tunisian Cinema: Allegories of Resistance*, New York: Columbia University Press.
Lewis, Jon (1992), *The Road to Romance and Ruin. Teen Films and Youth Culture*, New York and London: Routledge.
Moine, Raphaëlle (2005), *Le Cinéma français face aux genres*, Paris: Association de Recherches sur l'Histoire du Cinéma.
Selbo, Jule (2015), *Film Genre for the Screenwriter*, New York and London: Routledge.
Shary Timothy (2005), *Teen Movies: American Youth on Screen*, London and New York: Wallflower.
Shary, Timothy (2007), 'Introduction. Youth Shock Culture', in T. Shary and A. Seibel (eds) *Youth Culture in Global Cinema*, Austin: University of Texas Press.
Shary, Timothy (2012), 'Teen Films: The Cinematic Image of Youth', in B. K. Grant (ed.), *Film Genre Reader IV*, Austin: University of Texas Press, pp. 576–601.
Sibony, Daniel (1991), 'Le Cinéma révèle l'adolescence comme un processus, une dynamique nécessaire et subversive de la vie sociale, "pas hors la loi"', in A. Lefèbvre and P. van Meerbeeck (eds), *Sage comme une image. Adolescence et cinéma*, Bruxelles: De Boeck Université, pp. 11–20.
Smith, Frances (2017), *Rethinking the Hollywood Teen Movie: Gender, Genre and Identity*, Edinburgh: Edinburgh University Press.
Tarr, Carrie (2005), *Reframing Difference: Beur and Banlieue Filmmaking in France*, Manchester: Manchester University Press.
Tudor, Andrew (1974), *Image and Influence*, London: Allen and Unwin.

CHAPTER 2

Un Vrai 'Teen Film' Français? The Contemporary Adolescent Genre in French Cinema

Gemma Edney

This essay explores the contemporary adolescent genre in French cinema, asking if, when 'teen movies' are so heavily situated in the American context, and given the French cultural establishment's efforts to avoid a *culture américanisée*, it is possible to have a truly *French* 'teen movie'. Following a discussion of the difficulties in defining the teen genre as a whole, and a brief exploration of the genre's American roots, this essay examines the recent rise in adolescent films in France, asking if there is a certain French specificity evident in these films and therefore what, if anything, makes a teen film *à la française*. Upon an examination of recent film releases, it is possible to identify two distinct types of French 'teen' films, both of which share similarities with and also differ from their American counterparts: this chapter explores these similarities and differences in order to go some way to creating a taxonomy of the French teen film. As such, this essay offers a broad, introductory overview of the contemporary French adolescent genre and what it means to make a 'teen movie' in France today.

What is a 'Teen Movie'?

The existence of a specific 'teen movie' genre has never been disputed: since the emergence of the teenager as a cultural consumer in the 1950s, the generic label has been willingly adopted and applied to films with apparent ease, and there have been various critical works devoted to the genre itself.[1] However, despite this apparent simplicity, we, as scholars, have consistently run into difficulties defining exactly what a 'teen movie' *is*. What does a teen movie look like? What links films together to classify the genre as a whole? The difficulty in answering these questions can be traced to two main factors:

1. Breadth of genre
   While 'teen movie' is used as a generic label, the genre in fact encompasses a whole host of sub-genres, such as the 'teen slasher', the 'high

school movie' and the rom-com, to name but three. As Adrienne Boutang and Célia Sauvage write in *Les Teen Movies*, 'le *teen movie* est une catégorie très large, englobant un ensemble de sous-genres cinématographiques hétéroclites, qui n'ont en commun que leur focalisation sur une classe d'âge spécifique' (Boutang and Sauvage 2011: 11). The sheer breadth of genres that can be classified as 'teen movies' thus makes it increasingly difficult to lay down and define generic conventions: lots of teen movies take place in a high school setting, for example, but not all of them do; by the same token, some films that are set in a high school are not *teen* movies.

2. The difficulty of defining 'teen'

   The second difficulty facing scholars of the teen genre is the ambiguity in the term 'teen' itself. Catherine Driscoll notes how not all films about teenagers (i.e. individuals between the ages of 13 and 19) are classed as 'teen movies', and some films with non-teen characters (such as college movies) are (Driscoll 2011: 2). While the word 'teen' may be an age-specific term, it actually denotes a much more fluid period of time. Indeed, as Boutang and Sauvage observe, adolescence, rather than signifying simply the pubescent period between childhood and adulthood, 's'est transformée en une catégorie sociologique informe, allant de 12 à 40 ans' (Boutang and Sauvage 2011: 11). This difficulty in defining the period of adolescence or 'teenage-hood' consequently makes it increasingly difficult to define the teen film genre: how is it possible to define a 'teen' genre if it is impossible to definitively understand what a 'teen' is?

It is thus difficult to pin down a set definition for a 'teen movie'. Nevertheless, despite these difficulties, some authors have attempted to identify certain defining characteristics of the 'teen movie' in order to provide a concrete starting point for the study of the genre. Driscoll's outline of certain narrative conventions that are present in teen movies is perhaps the clearest and most comprehensive, though still fairly generalising:

> There are certainly narrative conventions that help define teen film: the youthfulness of central characters; content usually centred on young heterosexuality, frequently with a romance plot; intense age-based peer relationships and conflict either within those relationships or with an older generation; the institutional management of adolescence by families, schools, and other institutions; and coming-of-age plots focused on motifs like virginity, graduation, and the makeover. (Driscoll 2011: 2)

While this list certainly covers a lot of ground, it still remains, as Driscoll herself acknowledges, quite generalist and variable: there are many films that would fit this list that would not necessarily be categorised as 'teen movies', and some films that are classified as teen movies that do not fulfil all of the criteria.

The importance of audience is also an ambiguous factor in the defining of a film as 'teen': does a teen movie need to be made specifically *for* teens? Driscoll notes how the majority of scholarship on teen movies seems to make the assumption that they are aimed at a specifically 'teen' audience, though exactly who might be included in such an audience is still unclear (Driscoll 2011: 3). Indeed, teen movies are often cited as examples of popular culture that, as well as *representing* teens, also attempt to 'construct dominant ideals of [teen] behaviour' (Henderson 2006: 146). Teen films thus provide an ideal example of identity construction and social behaviour for their intended audience members. Some, however, suggest that a film does not have to be specifically aimed at a teen audience in order to be classified as a teen movie: Boutang and Sauvage argue that as long as films are 'situés dans des univers adolescents', they can be 'soit . . . *pour adolescents*, soit . . . *avec* adolescents' (Boutang and Sauvage 2011: 9–11). Thus, it seems that, with the breadth of genres encompassed by the teen film category, and the difficulties in pinning down what is meant by the term 'adolescence' in general, there are few universal defining features of the genre, except perhaps a generic concern with adolescence and its representation.

Despite this lack of clear defining features, there is one thing on which many scholars, either directly or indirectly, seem to agree: teen movies are somehow inherently American. Driscoll writes how American teen films are among the 'most widely recognized' in the genre (Driscoll 2011: 3), and indeed the majority of existing scholarship on 'teen movies' tend to deal with the American teen movies of the three decades since the 1980s. In her book *Teen Dreams*, Roz Kaveney goes so far as to suggest that the American teen film is such an enduring representation of adolescent experience that it has an impact on the way in which we recall our own adolescence, writing that 'through the teen genre of the last two decades, many of us are acquainted with an adolescence that has nothing in common with anything we actually experienced . . . yet sometimes it seems as real to us as our own lives' (Kaveney 2006: 1–2). Of course, the American high school is one of the archetypal features of teen movies, and as a motif is difficult to emulate in other national cinemas. In fact, in his book, *Teen!*, Olivier Davenas writes that there has never been a European equivalent of the American high school movie (Davenas 2013: 8). In France specifically, there is no real translation for 'teen movie': while the phrase *film d'ado* is used, both in academia and in popular culture, it does not have quite the same connotation as the term 'teen movie', signifying something closer to what Driscoll terms 'youth film', which she says is more 'subcultural' and less concerned with the 'institutional life of adolescents at home and school' than typical teen films (Driscoll 2011: 3). In general, there is a tendency to eschew the term *film d'ado* in favour of the italicised *teen movie*. If, then, teen movies are necessarily American, is it possible to have a non-Hollywood equivalent, and how would such a film be defined? Perhaps, in order to examine such a cinema, we must seek to use different terms. However, I would argue that the label 'teen movie' does not need to refer to only one specific type of film; indeed, the term encompasses so many different genres and styles already that there is no reason to limit the potential depth of the classification. In this essay, I aim to widen the somewhat narrow contextual frameworks in existing scholarship. Examining the teen film in a specifically French context, I explore how French teen films fit into the existing teen film corpus, and ask whether it is possible for these films to be classified in the teen movie genre.

Youth in French Cinema

French cinema provides a particularly interesting study for this enquiry, mainly due to the recent surge in films concerning the adolescent experience in France. Youth has long been a central concern of French cinema: since the time of the New Wave, filmmakers have been inspired by the lives and problems of young people (Reader 1996: 259). However, in recent years, there has been a major surge in films dealing with the youth experience, with an ever-growing number of filmmakers turning to youth as a main concern. Following the stark social realism of films in the 1990s that attempted to reveal the experience of young people living on the margins, some of most prominent filmmakers of the twenty-first century have also begun to focus on youth in their films. These new, youth-oriented films include those of Mia Hansen-Løve (*Tout est pardonné* (2007), *Le Père de mes enfants* (2010), *Un Amour de jeunesse* (2011), *Eden* (2014)); Céline Sciamma (*Naissance des pieuvres* (2007), *Tomboy* (2010), *Bande de filles* (2014)); Katell Quillévéré (*Un Poison violent* (2010), *Suzanne* (2013)); and Abdellatif Kechiche (*L'Esquive* (2003), *La Vie d'Adèle, chapitres 1 et 2* (2013)), among others. Consequently, this increase in youth film has inspired, somewhat predictably, a renewed interest in theoretical and analytical perspectives – such as those presented in the present volume – focusing on filmic representations of adolescence.[2] These works, like much of the existing work on youth cinema, often focus on the *representation* of youth, and the way in which the films portray particular aspects of the adolescent experience. However, what I am interested in, here, is the generic classification of these films, and whether these films can truly be considered 'teen movies'. There is no doubt that the examples mentioned above are *about* adolescents; however, they are not necessarily *for* adolescents: they are not marketed at a specifically 'teen' audience, and they are aesthetically very different from the American teen films that have become so recognisable. These films are also usually well-received by critics, a trait that Boutang and Sauvage suggest cannot be applied to most teen films, writing that teen movies 'ont longtemps suscité le mépris de la cinéphilie', and are judged to be 'superficiels, vulgaires, excessivement focalisés sur le corps et la sexualité, source de représentations dépourvues de profondeur, voire dégradantes' (Boutang and Sauvage 2011: 12). Some of the films mentioned above were (and remain) extremely highly regarded by critics, particularly by way of film festival selections and nominations. Nevertheless, there are some other recent film releases that are more traditionally 'teen' than others, attracting far less attention from critics and generally fulfilling common teen movie criteria more readily: notable examples of these films include Lisa Azuelos's *LOL* (2008), *Les Beaux gosses* (Riad Sattouf, 2009) and Ivan Calberac's *Une Semaine sur deux* (2009), among numerous others. Indeed, teen films in France can be convincingly split into two distinct categories, which I classify as follows:

- Type A films: these are films that can be defined more readily as 'teen'. These films are more *américanisés*, aimed specifically at a youth audience, do not attract much positive attention from academic or critical reviews, and fit much more readily into the aesthetic of a Hollywood teen movie.
- Type B films: these films are not so readily defined as 'teen movies'. These films are those usually chosen for inclusion in scholarly publications, definitely *about* teens, but not necessarily *for* them.[3]

In this chapter, it is my aim to examine these two subcategories, exploring how they differ from, or are similar to, Hollywood teen movies (and each other), in order to provide an introduction to both types of French youth film. Through this exploration, I examine the French teen genre as a whole, and aim to establish what it means to be a 'teen movie' *à la française*.

Type A: French Teen Movies *à l'américaine*

Firstly, I will deal with the films that are more readily defined as 'teen movies'. These films are much more like their American counterparts than the films I categorise into Type B, and fulfil many more of the generally accepted criteria for the teen movie genre: they are based, like the standard Hollywood 'high school' movie, predominantly at school or during the holidays, focusing on the relationships and friendships formed during this time, usually including some kind of generational or institutional conflict; they are aimed more specifically at a youth audience; and they do not attract particular attention from film critics. This lack of scholarly interest in the films stems, perhaps, from the French cultural establishment's efforts to reduce the *américanisation* of French culture, and the more general issues of difference between so-called 'high art' deemed worthy of scholarly study and 'low art' judged more suitable for popular culture but not 'serious' consideration. However, these films are not direct copies of the Hollywood teen genre – there are some notable differences as well as their similarities – and despite the reluctance of critics to include them in study, they still form an important part of the French teen genre, and should not be excluded from consideration.

Lisa Azuelos's *LOL (Laughing out Loud)* (2008) presents one of the most recognisable examples of a Type A film (indeed, Azuelos later directed an American remake of the film, starring Miley Cyrus, in 2012). Taking place over the course of one full school year, split into three sections corresponding with the school terms, the film follows protagonist Lola (Christa Théret) and her friends, as they navigate the trials and tribulations of everyday adolescence, including the making and breaking of relationships, and strong conflicts with parents. The film, as a coming-of-age narrative centred on a heterosexual romance plot involving generational conflict and the attempted control of adolescent characters by the older generation, conforms to many of Driscoll's teen film conventions. It also fits very well aesthetically into the 'teen' genre: with its bright colours, punchy pop soundtrack and general teen *feel*, there is no doubt that *LOL* is aimed specifically at a teenage audience. Despite Davenas's claims that there is no European equivalent of an American high school movie, if one does exist, then then *LOL* is definitely a strong candidate. In fact, 'American-style' teen films are not an entirely new development in French cinema: Claude Pinoteau's *La Boum* (1980) and its sequels are notable examples. However, while critics may disregard these films as mere Hollywood copies, there are in fact some notable differences between these films and their American teen movie counterparts. One of the most obvious differences is the position of adults in the films. Boutang and Sauvage suggest that, in American teen movies, adults are all but absent, writing that 'les teen movies à l'américaine construisent un territoire adolescent autonome, hermétique à la présence adulte' (Boutang and Sauvage 2011: 13). While the role of adults in these films is not quite so clear-cut as Boutang and Sauvage suggest, adults usually do play a marginal role in American teen movies, present in the narrative but not necessarily key figures in the plot. Consider, for example, *Mean Girls* (2004), in which the parents of the protagonists represent guides for their children, or in some cases are presented merely as more extreme versions of their offspring; or *10 Things I Hate About You* (1995), where father Walter (Larry Miller) exists as an extreme moral compass for his daughters Kat (Julia Stiles) and Bianca (Larisa Oleynik). In these Type A French films, however, parents tend to have a much bigger role. In *LOL*, for example, we are arguably as aligned with Lola's mother (Sophie Marceau) as we are with Lola herself: she has her own separate romantic subplot that, perhaps predictably, mirrors that of her daughter, and she undergoes significant character development throughout the film. That Marceau also featured in Pinoteau's *La Boum* adds some extratextual connotations here, as well as a nod to the teen movie tradition into which Azuelos is entering. This heightened role of adults in a narrative is not limited to *LOL*, but is a recurring feature in these Type A films. In *15 ans et demi* (Desagnat and Sorriaux, 2007), it is father Philippe (Daniel Auteuil) to whom we are introduced first, before being introduced to his daughter, Églantine (Juliette Lamboley). Similarly, in *Tel père telle fille* (Olivier De Plas, 2007), it is father Bruno (Vincent Elbaz) who introduces the plot and is equally aligned with the spectator once daughter Nancy (Daisy Broom) arrives on the scene. In both of these films, despite their definite 'teen movie' aesthetic and teen-based plot, it is the fathers, as well as their teen daughters, who overcome generational conflict to learn about themselves and their families. Continuing this trend, in Ivan Calberac's *Une Semaine sur deux*, while Léa (Bertille Chabert) is the main protagonist in the narrative, she also acts as a vehicle for the spectator to navigate the simultaneous stories of both of her parents. In all of these films, parents play a much bigger role than in Hollywood teen movies: indeed, one of the principal messages of these films seems to be that 'coming-of-age' narratives need not be limited to teenage characters. In these films, parents have just as much to learn about themselves as their children do, and their teenagers' own narratives often act as the catalyst for this discovery to take place. Overall, it seems, where in Hollywood teen films adolescents are shown to be starkly different from their parents, in these films teens are in fact more similar to their parents than is first suggested.

Further differences between these French films and their American counterparts can be observed in both the actors featured in the films, and the settings used. It is a well-known fact that in Hollywood teen movies, it is not uncommon for teen characters to be portrayed by distinctly non-adolescent actors. In *Clueless* (Amy Heckerling, 1995), for example,

Stacey Dash was twenty-eight when she starred as protagonist Cher's (Alicia Silverstone) best friend Dionne; more recently, in *Mean Girls*, sixteen-year-old Regina was portrayed by twenty-six-year-old Rachel McAdams. Indeed, this is a tradition dating back many years: Jennifer Grey was twenty-seven when she starred as Baby in *Dirty Dancing* (Emile Ardolino, 1987), and *Grease*'s (Randal Kleiser, 1978) Stockard Channing was thirty-seven when she played seventeen-year-old Rizzo. Conversely, in these Type A French films, the adolescent characters are much closer in age to their characters: *15 ans et demi* stars fifteen-year-old Juliette Lamboley; Bertille Chabert was fourteen in *Une semaine sur deux*; Daisy Broom was thirteen in *Tel père telle fille*, and Vincent Lacoste in *Les Beaux gosses* was fifteen at the time of release. While this difference may be attributed more to the casting practices of the US and French film industries, it nevertheless has a significant impact on the way the characters are received by audiences: younger actors present less of an idealised, 'fully formed' teen experience than adult actors, thus having the potential to make their films more relatable to their teen audiences, and adding a certain verisimilitude that increases spectator engagement.

The differences in settings that we see between US teen films and their French counterparts are largely due to the geographical differences between France and the US themselves. American teen films are mostly set in the suburbs outside urban centres, featuring predominantly white, middle-class families. While 'suburb' in the US denotes low-density areas, and conjures images of leafy avenues lined with single-family homes, however, the *banlieue* equivalent – at least in translation – in France is a place of marginalisation, characterised by grey tower blocks, low-cost housing and a lack of social mobility. Thus, while in Hollywood teen movies the characters usually reside in the suburban environment, the teens in French films inhabit affluent town and city locations, residing in Parisian apartments or town houses, rather than the large houses of the American middle classes. Consequently, while they are often similar in affluence and upbringing, the spaces these teens inhabit are vastly different from their American counterparts. This difference in space is most evident in the mobility of the characters in the films: in American teen films, the characters move little, often remaining in the same neighbourhood or occasionally travelling in cars; in French teen films, the characters move frequently, through the city landscape on predominantly public modes of transport such as buses, trains or the metro.

Nevertheless, despite their differences, these Type A films still very much *feel* like 'teen movies': we still recognise them as a distinctly 'teen' product. Indeed, I would argue that the concept of 'teen' is as much an emotional or affective response as a sociological concept:[4] we know how it 'feels' to be a teen, and the teen movie's aesthetic circulates this feeling. This goes some way to accounting for the fact that certain films can be identified as 'teen' even though they do not feature teenage characters, for example. This 'teen feeling' is heavily linked to nostalgia, as evidenced by Kaveney's suggestion that teen films affect our experience of remembering our own adolescence (Kaveney 2006: 2). When watching teen movies, spectators are invited to recall their own experiences of adolescence, thus aligning us to the characters on screen. Therefore, teen films are distinctly recognisable as both unrealistic and yet relatable: they do not speak so much to specific experiences as a generalist experience of 'teenagehood'. It is in this way that these French Type A films are still like their American counterparts, even despite their differences: above all, they still *feel* 'teen'. This unrealistic, idealistic and yet extremely relatable portrayal of adolescence may account for the lack of attention afforded to these films by academic studies: as Boutang and Sauvage suggest, they are regarded as overly simplistic and superficial. However, these films' similarities with Hollywood films should not mean that they are deemed less worthy of scholarly attention: they still form a major part of the French teen genre, and are still able to reveal certain aspects of French adolescence that must be considered in future study.

Type B: French Teen Movies *à la française*?

The second subcategory of French teen film encompasses those films that do not fit quite so readily into the teen genre. The intended audience demographic of these Type B films is much less clear-cut than the Type A films: while they feature teen actors, and are definitely *about* teens, it is less obvious that they are also *for* teens. These films also typically attract more critical attention than Type A films – they are selected for film festivals, they win awards and they receive favourable reviews, as well as appearing most frequently in scholarly works. Céline Sciamma's three films, for instance, are clear examples of Type B films: *Naissance des pieuvres* (2007) was selected for the Cannes Film Festival's *Un Certain Regard* section, was nominated for three Césars and won the *Prix de la jeunesse* at Cabourg; *Tomboy* (2010) was awarded various festival awards, including the Golden Duke at the Odessa International Film Festival; and her most recent film, *Bande de filles* (2014), was screened as part of the 'Directors' Fortnight' at Cannes, was nominated for four Césars and won various other awards, including the Special Jury Prize at the Lumières Awards. All three of Sciamma's films tell the stories of adolescent girls, in a largely teen-dominated space; however, they do not seem aimed solely at a teen audience. *Naissance des pieuvres*, for example, despite the fact that it had its own Myspace page for marketing purposes, does not, with its auteurist, arthouse-style feel, seem to be aimed specifically at a teen market. Indeed, *Bande de filles*, with its soundtrack, school setting and bright colours, is as close to a 'teen movie' as Sciamma's films allow, but the attempted realism and distinctly arthouse style, combined with the *banlieue* setting, inhibit its classification as such and do not evoke youth audiences to mind. Similar are Mia Hansen-Løve's films, particularly *Tout est pardonné* (2007), *Un Amour de jeunesse* (2011) and *Eden* (2014), which, despite their narrative focus on adolescent or teen experience, and distinctly nostalgic aesthetic, are not so obviously marketed towards a youth audience as the films in Type A. Rather, these films share the arthouse aesthetic of Sciamma's films, inviting much more readily the attention of film critics and scholars. Other examples of Type B films include Olivier Assayas's *Après Mai* (2012), Katell Quillévéré's *Un poison violent* (2010) and *Suzanne* (2013), and Rebecca Zlotowski's *Belle Épine* (2010) and *Grand Central* (2013). All of these films are aesthetically similar, featuring the pale, washed-out colours and sparse soundtrack that seem to have become synonymous with arthouse cinema. Despite the fact that these films are contemporaneous with the films in Type A, they are usually regarded separately; these films, and not those that feel more overtly 'teen', are the films usually cited as evidence of a rise in youth film in France, and they are more often discussed by both academic and journalistic film critics.

Are these films 'teen' movies? If we consider the argument in the previous section that there is a certain affective response or 'feel' to a teen film, then the answer would certainly be negative. These films are not only aesthetically very different from their Type A counterparts, they also *feel* different: these films are much less concerned with the brightly coloured, exaggerated teen lives that end happily ever after of both Type A and Hollywood teen movies, and are much more concerned with portraying the realistic struggles of adolescence. However, despite their differences, there do remain various similarities between these films and Hollywood teen films: firstly, the coming-of-age plot still forms the basis of the film's narrative: these characters all still have a journey that they must complete in order to learn about themselves and their place in the world; and secondly, they afford much the same status and position to adults as typical Hollywood teen movies. These films are generally, much more so than Type A films, set in an entirely adolescent space: adults are all but absent, and any adults that do feature are largely inconsequential. *Naissance des pieuvres*, for example, removes adults almost completely from the narrative.

The film is set during the school holidays, thus eliminating the need for school teachers, and also completely eliminates parents: Marie (Pauline Acquart) uses her own separate door to enter and leave her bedroom; we never meet Anne's (Louise Blachère) parents, and Floriane (Adèle Haenel) merely shouts goodbye to (presumably) her parents when she leaves the house. The only adults that do feature in the film are the swimming coaches who, while they attempt to regulate not only the swimmers' training and routines, but also their bodies, handing one girl a razor at the beginning of the film in order to improve her appearance, are both largely marginal to the film's main focus. *Bande de filles* affords a similar role to adults: while Marième's (Karidja Touré) mother does feature in the film, she is much less visible than the adolescent characters. In Hansen-Løve's *Un Amour de jeunesse*, we do meet Camille's (Lola Créton) mother and father, but their role in the narrative is limited: both tell Camille that she must learn to move on after her childhood sweetheart Sullivan leaves for South America but, overall, they play a minimal role in the film. Absent, too, are adults in *Belle Épine*, *Qui de nous deux* (Charles Belmont, 2005), and *Hell* (Bruno Chiche, 2006), all of which portray adolescents navigating their mid-to-late teens with little – if any at all – input from parents or other adult influences. In these films, it is the teens that control their environment; there is much less focus on adolescents finding their way in an adult world, and much more forging of an entirely adolescent universe. In this way, these films are much closer to Hollywood teen films than their Type A counterparts. Thus, even if there is a reluctance to define these films as 'teen movies', there remains a marked similarity between them, further inviting the question of why these particular films are chosen for analysis, and Type A films so determinedly avoided.

If these films are *not* 'teen' movies, then, how can they be defined? There is a tendency by scholars to avoid the label 'teen movie' completely for these films, instead using terms such as 'youth film'. Nevertheless, they still, as with Type A films, form part of the 'teen' genre in France, and can therefore not be judged as more or less useful to scholars of filmic representations of French youth. Is it possible, therefore, to examine these films alongside Type A films, or are their differences too marked? I argue that it is not only possible, but necessary, in order to fully explore the teen genre in France.

Making a *French* Teen Film

Is it possible for a true *teen movie français* to exist? If there is, how would it be classified? Would the genre comprise Type A films, with their more obviously 'teen' aesthetic but heavier focus on adolescent–adult relations, or would it also include Type B films, located in a purely 'adolescent universe' but lacking that teen 'feel'? While some of the films discussed here may be more overtly aimed towards a youth audience than others, and while both types have their differences, the representation of youth experience is what joins them together. Despite the reluctance from scholars to discuss 'low-brow' entertainment, including those films in Type A, the importance of considering both strands of adolescent cinema in France cannot be overstated. Both of these types of films reveal important aspects of the French youth experience, as well as current sociological ideals and expectations of adolescence, much like the Hollywood genre: where Type B films are more concerned with specific difficulties facing their characters – the death of a parent in *Belle Épine*, for example, or racial politics in *Bande de filles* and the challenges of getting over a first love in *Un Amour de jeunesse* – Type A films are much more concerned with the generic experiences of adolescence, complete with more 'universal' issues such as the conflict between generations and difficulties faced at school. Nevertheless, both types of film have much to offer the teen genre in France.

If, then, we were to attempt to define a specifically French youth film, what narrative conventions would feature, and how would they differ from those typically ascribed to Hollywood teen movies? It is in fact just as difficult to pin down such conventions for the French genre as it is for the teen movie genre in general, due to the variety of films on offer, and such a survey is beyond the scope of this chapter. Indeed, it could be suggested that, outside the town or city location, and the featuring of actors of a similar age to their characters, the French teen genre is in fact characterised with contradictions and oppositions: they centre on a narrative that *either* addresses adolescent issues as a whole *or* focuses on issues specific to its characters; and feature a plot that *either* privileges the visibility of adult characters such as parents *or* completely eschews them from the action. My aim here, however, has not been to attempt to force all French youth films into narrow confines, but rather to show the importance of considering the full breadth of films available to scholars of youth cinema.

Perhaps the term 'teen movie' is too entwined with the American experience to be applied to non-American cinema; and perhaps attempting to force French (or any other) youth cinema into the confines of the 'teen movie' genre in fact limits their usefulness. Nevertheless, it is important to acknowledge the youth film culture in French cinema, and not to limit analysis to one specific strand of youth film. In exploring French teen cinema in relation to the Hollywood genre, it is possible to identify the two different strands of youth cinema that exist in France, both just as important as the other in the representation of French youth experience and identity. As Henderson argues, youth film both portrays the lives of adolescents, and also provides options and examples for adolescents to form their own identities; this dual purpose of youth film is arguably impossible without both subcategories of film. Together, these groups help to define what it *is* to be a teen in France today, and therefore should not be examined in exclusion: these two types of film together make up the French teen genre, and can both reveal important social and cultural aspects of adolescence. Just as the Hollywood teen genre is difficult to define due to its breadth and variety of film genres, the French teen genre encompasses a wide range of perspectives. It is my hope that, in the future, scholars will begin to understand the importance of this genre as a whole, and we will see the examination of French youth cinema in its entirety, without a low-brow/ high-brow or arthouse/popular divide.

Appendix 1: Examples of Type A Films

Title	Director	Year
15 ans et demi	François Desagnat and Thomas Sorriaux	2007
Beaux Gosses	Riad Sattouf	2009
Et toi, t'es sur qui?	Lola Doillon	2007
La Boum	Claude Pinoteau	1980
La Boum 2	Claude Pinoteau	1982
LOL (Laughing Out Loud)	Lisa Azuelos	2008
Lou!	Julien Neel	2014
Neuilly sa mère!	Gabriel Julien-Laferrière	2009
Nos 18 ans	Frédéric Berthe	2008
Tel père telle fille	Olivier de Plas	2007
Une Semaine sur deux	Ivan Calberac	2009

Appendix 2: Examples of Type B Films

Title	Director	Year
Bande de filles	Céline Sciamma	2014
Belle Epine	Rebecca Zlotowski	2011
Eden	Mia Hansen-Løve	2014
Grand Central	Rebecca Zlotowski	2013
Hell	Bruno Chiche	2006

continued

Appendix 2 *Continued*

Title	Director	Year
L'Année Prochaine	Vania Leturcq	2014
La Vie d'Adèle, chapitres 1 et 2	Abdellatif Kechiche	2013
L'Esquive	Abdellatif Kechiche	2004
Naissance des pieuvres	Céline Sciamma	2007
Qui de nous deux?	Charles Belmont	2005
Respire	Mélanie Laurent	2014
Suzanne	Katell Quillévéré	2013
Tomboy	Céline Sciamma	2010
Tout est pardonné	Mia Hansen-Løve	2007
Un amour de jeunesse	Mia Hansen-Løve	2011
Un poison violent	Katell Quillévéré	2010

Notes

1. See, for example, Shary (2005, 2014) and Lewis (1992).
2. Major works in this area include Egloff (2007); Shary (2007); Dupont and Paris (2013).
3. A list of example films in each category can be found in the appendices to this chapter.
4. For more on the idea of adolescence as an affective experience, see Swindle (2011).

Works Cited

Boutang, Adrienne and Célia Sauvage (2011), *Les Teen Movies*, Paris: Vrin.
Davenas, Olivier (2013), *Teen! Cinéma de l'adolescence*, Montélimar: Les Moutons électriques.
Driscoll, Catherine (2011), *Teen Film: A Critical Introduction*, Oxford and New York: Berg.
Dupont, Sébastien and Hugues Paris (eds) (2013), *L'adolescente et le cinéma: De Lolita à Twilight*, Toulouse: Éditions Érès.
Egloff, Karin M. (2007), *Les adolescents dans le cinéma français: entre deux mondes*, Lewiston: Edwin Mellen.
Henderson, Scott (2006), 'Youth, Excess, and the Musical Moment', in Ian Conrich and Estella Tincknell (eds), *Film's Musical Moments*, Edinburgh: Edinburgh University Press, pp. 146–57.
Kaveney, Roz (2006), *Teen Dreams: Reading Teen Film and Television from Heathers to Veronica Mars*, London: I. B. Tauris.
Lewis, Jon (1992), *The Road to Romance and Ruin: Teen Films and Youth Culture*, London and New York: Routledge.

Reader, Keith (1996), '"Tous les garçons et les filles de leur âge": Representations of Youth and Adolescence in Pre-New-Wave French Cinema', *French Cultural Studies*, 7:3, pp. 259–70.

Shary, Timothy (2005), *Teen Movies: American Youth on Screen*, London and New York: Wallflower.

Shary, Timothy (2007), *Youth Culture in Global Cinema*, Austin: University of Texas Press.

Shary, Timothy (2014), *Generation Multiplex: The Image of Youth in American Cinema since 1980*, Austin: University of Texas Press.

Swindle, Monica (2011), 'Feeling Girl, Girling Feeling: An Examination of "Girl" as Affect', *Rhizomes* 22, <http://www.rhizomes.net/issue22/swindle.html> (last accessed 22 August 2018).

CHAPTER 3

Childhood and Gender Panic in *Ma Vie en rose* and *Tomboy*

Jeri English

In this chapter, I examine the intersections between childhood, family, gender identity formation and sexuality in Alain Berliner's *Ma Vie en rose* (1997) and Céline Sciamma's *Tomboy* (2011). In *Ma Vie en rose*, seven-year-old Ludovic firmly believes they were given a boy's body by mistake. In *Tomboy*, ten-year-old Laure identifies as a boy and is read as male by the children in their new neighbourhood; Laure inhabits this new identity as 'Mikaël' until forced to reveal their biological sex at the end of the film.[1] In both filmic universes, the children's affirmation of their non-biology-based gender identities provokes what Laurel Westbrook and Kristen Schilt term 'gender panics' (Westbrook and Schilt 2014: 34); both films show scenes in which Laure and Ludovic are tormented by adults and children 'frantically reasserting the naturalness of a male-female binary' (Westbrook and Schilt 2014: 34). Certainly, on-screen portrayals of disruptions to the sex–gender binary – and the gender panics these disruptions can provoke – have multiplied in the past thirty years, from 1990s films such as Neil Jordan's *The Crying Game* (1992), Stephan Elliott's *The Adventures of Priscilla, Queen of the Desert* (1994), Kimberly Peirce's *Boys Don't Cry* (1999) and Pedro Almodóvar's *Todo sobre mi madre* (1999), to more recent explorations that include Duncan Tucker's *Transamerica* (2005), Xavier Dolan's *Laurence Anyways* (2012), François Ozon's *Une nouvelle amie* (2014), Tom Hooper's *The Danish Girl* (2015) and Jill Soloway's Netflix series *Transparent* (2014–18).[2] One important element that distinguishes *Ma Vie en rose* and *Tomboy* from these other cinematic representations of gender nonconformity – as well as from Lucia Puenzo's *XXY* (2007), where fifteen-year-old intersex character Alex struggles with their gender identity in a pubescent body and while navigating their first sexual experience – is that Ludovic and Laure are not adults questioning their long-established gender identities or adolescents undergoing unwanted physical transformations, but rather prepubescent children whose certainty about their true gender identity disrupts the worldview of the adults around them.

Cinematographically, *Ma Vie en rose* and *Tomboy* employ wildly contrasting styles: Berliner uses a background of richly saturated colours and whimsical dream sequences to play on Ludovic's escapist fantasies and naïve ignorance of society's heteronormative gender constraints, whereas Sciamma uses an uncompromisingly realistic backdrop to examine Laure's quiet determination to embody a new gender identity. Throughout both films, Berliner and Sciamma anchor their young protagonists firmly in the realm of childhood and emphasise how their transgressive embodiments strongly code them as 'other' in their nuclear families. In *Ma Vie en rose*, Ludovic's long bob, ethereal dreaminess and fragility distinguish them from the virile physicality of their short-haired brothers. In *Tomboy*, Laure's decidedly 'unfeminine' clothes, love of 'boyish' pastimes and short hair are juxtaposed with their six-year-old sister's long curls, glittery barrettes and pink tutus, as well as with their mother's pregnant body. Both Ludovic and Laure refuse to embody what Chris Brickell names 'a socially acceptable maleness or femaleness' (Brickell 2006: 94).

As Westbrook and Schilt explain, the social exercise of 'determining gender' (Westbrook and Schilt 2014: 33) is a process whereby we automatically sort people into one gender category or another, 'authenticating' their identity according to the external cues they display. Given the very visual element of gender performance and embodiment, it is not surprising that *being looked at* – by the other characters, by the camera and by the spectator – plays a vital role in these two films. Ludovic is frequently the object of the gaze of the neighbourhood adults and children who, when confronted with the confusing gender performance of the self-proclaimed 'garçon–fille', react with varying degrees of shock and dismay. Laure, on the other hand, affirms their identity as Mikaël through the scrutiny of the other children, who validate this chosen gender until the final scenes of the film. While both characters endure the questioning gaze of others, Berliner and Sciamma also deploy the gaze of the young protagonists, as well as various scenes of gender rehearsal, as tools in the construction and enactment of Ludovic and Laure's new gender identities. These gender rehearsals are performed in the intimacy of the nuclear family, which functions both as a safe space in which Ludovic and Laure can explore new ways of being and, eventually, as a social enforcer of repressive sex and gender categories.

Being-looked-at

Since Ludovic and Laure are recent arrivals in their neighbourhoods, both children are initially read as their desired gender. When Ludovic first emerges from the house dressed in a pink princess dress, lipstick and heels at a barbecue the Fabre family is hosting to meet their new neighbours, the guests initially react with approving looks and noises, mistaking Ludovic for the family's daughter, Zoé. However, Ludovic's father, Pierre, instantly invalidates this recognition, dismissing Ludovic's first public appearance as a girl as 'une farce'. Immediately following this repudiation, we see Ludovic isolated in a shot and then, in a reverse shot, the neighbours grouped together in unity as their gazes transform from admiration to surprise and consternation once they register that this child is in fact the family's youngest son. Even before Ludovic becomes a spectacle to the neighbours of the family's satirically homogenous, candy-coloured suburb, they are fragmented and fetishised for our gaze: the first image we see of them is a shot of their hand reaching past a Pam doll for a hairbrush as they hum the theme song from the campy soap opera, *Le monde de Pam*. The camera then pans down to show a foot in a red high-heeled shoe sticking out from under a pink satin dress; there is then a cut to close-up of full red lips reflected in the mirror as Ludovic carefully applies their lipstick; and then another cut to a hand reaching past the tube of lipstick to pick up a dangly earring from a dressing-table. This scene, in which Ludovic carefully selects the frilly trappings of romanticised femininity for their first public performance in their new neighbourhood, is marked by the fragmentation of different body parts and feminine signifiers. Throughout the film, Berliner underscores Ludovic's strong association with *Le monde de Pam*, a show that represents 'as heterosexually normative a world as can be dreamt' (Ince 2002: 93), while at the same time queering the norms of heterosexual love 'by means of its excessive, coloured and kitschy aesthetic' (Ince 2002: 93). Since Ludovic's sense of femininity is at least partially constructed on that of a plastic doll and a fictional TV character, it is unsurprising that the first images we have of them are fragmenting shots of their individual body parts.

As the film progresses, various characters are confronted with Ludovic's quietly unrepentant conviction that they will become biologically female once they hit puberty, as well as with their romantic interest in Jérôme, a neighbour and classmate, and the son of their father's boss. Accordingly, we see Ludovic become the object of the questioning and increasingly hostile gaze of the neighbourhood adults. As the rigid and narrow-minded community unites against this ethereal, completely un-'masculine' child and their family, the gaze of the Other becomes less rooted in questioning and confusion, and more in mockery, anger and rejection. In one key scene, Ludovic attempts to literally perform as a girl in a school play, having locked Sophie, the girl who was cast as Sleeping Beauty, in the school bathroom. Dressed in her costume, Ludovic takes her place on stage to hopefully be kissed by Jérôme. When Ludovic's veil slides off, they are *seen* as a girl on stage by the horrified parents of the other children. Again, as in the film's first scene of public gender transgression, the reaction of the shocked parents in the audience is shown in a shot-reverse-shot sequence, where Ludovic-as-Sleeping-Beauty is physically divided from the staring adults, emphasising this child's difference from 'normal' society. The increasing isolation and ostracism that Ludovic faces are foreshadowed by the way in which the camera maintains a separation of this spectacle of gender disruption from its observers; a few scenes later, this performance results in Ludovic's expulsion from school.

As childhood studies scholar Emma Renold reminds us, for pre-adolescent children, school functions 'as a specific social and cultural arena for the production and reproduction of gender and sexual identities' (Renold 2005: 8). The context of *Tomboy* differs significantly, then, from that of *Ma Vie en rose*, since Laure's family arrives in their new neighbourhood during the summer and Laure's difference is therefore not performed within the institutional confines of school where gender norms are inscribed and reinforced. Darren Waldron observes that '*Tomboy* constantly places us at the height of a child's gaze' (Waldron 2013: 64); this technical emphasis on the point of view of the child is echoed thematically, as the adults are conspicuously absent from the outside world, existing mainly in domestic sphere of the family's apartment.[3] Laure's performance as Mikaël is in fact not even *seen* by adults for most of the film; with the children in the apartment complex, on the other hand, Laure is accepted unquestioningly as 'Mikaël'. Laure's success at enacting masculinity is ironically highlighted in one scene where Mikaël's body becomes the target of another boy's ridicule. Unable to urinate in front of the other boys after a soccer match in which they have successfully passed as Mikaël, Laure flees into the woods to find privacy. Sciamma's camera does not allow the spectator access to the image of Laure squatting to urinate: after showing the character standing with an anxious look on their face, the camera remains on the same plane as they drop out of view, showing only the trees as a backdrop as we hear the sound of urine against the ground. Once a boy's voice is heard, calling 'Mikaël', Laure stands quickly and pulls up their shorts to avoid being caught. Once this second boy finds Laure-as-Mikaël in the woods, the camera shows the main character framed from behind; the second boy faces us as he visually examines Laure's shorts and then calls out, 'Il s'est pissé dessus!' Although Laure's shame is clear afterwards – they run home and wash their shorts in the bathroom sink – the boy's use of the pronoun 'Il' confirms the success of their embodiment of Mikaël.

At home, as we will see further on, Laure's parents simply read this new gender identity as signs of tomboyishness and accept the difference in Laure's tastes and preferences from those of their younger daughter, Jeanne. It is, in fact, only once Laure's mother becomes aware of Laure's secret life as Mikaël – that is, once she understands that her daughter is not presenting to their new friends as a tomboy, but rather as an actual boy – and forces Laure to identify as a girl to their friends that we see the deleterious effects of the gaze of others on Laure's self construction. Warned by the mother of the impossibility of maintaining this chosen identity once the rapidly approaching school year arrives ('L'école est dans deux semaines, on n'a pas le choix, il faut le dire', she insists), Laure is physically forced out of their regular outfits of shorts and a T-shirt or tank top into a dress, and is paraded to two of their friends' apartments in order to be *shown* to be a girl to the children and their mothers. If wearing so-called 'boyish', sporty clothes, playing soccer, engaging in rough physical play and beginning a romantic relationship with Lisa – who, unlike Laure, has already started to develop breasts and who wears skirts – confirmed Laure as Mikaël in the children's eyes, the visual cue of the blue dress begins to undo this successful embodiment. Neither child speaks to Laure in these scenes; they simply stare at what to them looks like the boy they know as Mikaël in drag. Unlike in *Ma Vie en rose*, where Ludovic rarely shares a shot with the shocked viewers of their queer gender performances, Laure is framed with the other children, both while they accept Laure as Mikaël and once this new gender embodiment has failed. In both gender reversal scenes, Laure is left alone with their friend while their mother speaks to the other child's mother in another room. Both scenes show Laure standing silently *next* to the other children as they each visually evaluate the external signs of 'girlness'; we are therefore less spectators of Laure-as-object-of-curiosity, the way we often are with Ludovic, and more spectators of the *process* of gender determination. Once word gets out that 'Mikaël' is a girl, the children force Lisa to visually determine whether Laure is biologically male or female. The shot in which Lisa's gaze confirms the presence of a vulva and not of a penis shows a nearly immobile close-up of Laure and Lisa's faces in profile, with only Lisa's eyes flickering downwards to look at Laure's crotch. The juxtaposition between the framing of Laure and Lisa together as Laure's chosen gender is invalidated, and the reverse shot that shows the other children watching intently, serves as a *mise en scène* of the social process of determining gender.

Looking and Enacting

The gaze of the other characters – reflected in the framing of the protagonists – clearly has an important function in *Ma Vie en rose* and *Tomboy*. For Ludovic, the disapproving stares of the other neighbourhood adults and children – and the gentle yet clinical observation of the psychologist whose role is to 'fix' what is seen as Ludovic's gender dysphoria – are reproduced in the shots that establish the character as an object-to-be-looked-at. Berliner thereby highlights the way in which the normalising gaze of the adults alienates Ludovic and attempts to force them to be what they are not. Sciamma, on the other hand, contains Laure's embodiment of Mikaël to the unregulated arenas of childhood: the woods, the lake, the soccer pitch. Accordingly, the more important gaze in *Tomboy* is Laure's. There are many moments early in the film where we see Laure learning how to become Mikaël by watching the movements and interactions of the other neighbourhood boys. In one striking scene, there are multiple shot-reverse-shots between Laure's intently watchful face and the boys playing soccer.[4] As Laure observes the boys, standing next to Lisa who is barred from the game simply because she is a girl (one little boy emphasises her exclusion by suggesting ironically, 'tu n'as qu'à faire la pom-pom girl'), Laure learns which gestures they must master to become 'masculine', including spitting, removing their shirt and posturing. In the following scene, we see Laure reflected in the bathroom mirror in a medium shot, evaluating their capacity to perform as a boy as they remove their grey tank top, note the absence of developing breasts, feel their arms and chest for muscles and spit into the sink. Gazing at Laure as Laure evaluates their own body, we see them determine that they can indeed 'pass' as a boy; two scenes later, we witness the success of this rehearsal, as Mikaël integrates seamlessly with the other boys, re-enacting the same gestures they made previously. As Waldron aptly notes, Laure's triumphant embodiment of Mikaël serves to highlight the socially constructed nature of gender norms: 'By swaggering, spitting, playing football, and fighting, Laure implies that the outward signs of masculinity have no innate grounding in boys' (Waldron 2013: 67). This mirror-rehearsal scene is repeated later in the film as we watch Laure examine their reflection closely to see how convincing a phallus they have constructed out of play-dough looks stuffed into their modified swimsuit. Once Laure is satisfied with the image reflected back at them, this private gender practice again gets enacted in real life as they successfully embody Mikaël for an afternoon of swimming and roughhousing with the other children. As a seal of the validity of this gender performance, Mikaël receives a kiss from Lisa. The mirror scenes serve therefore not only as moments of rehearsal, but also as important moments where Laure can *recognise* themselves as Mikaël and can, therefore, truly embody a new gender identity.

Unlike Laure, Ludovic does not model their gender on the looks and actions of other little girls, but instead on the campy, over-the-top televised performances of Pam, a blonde, buxom, Barbie-doll-like character with merchandise and a television show. This highly idealised incarnation of girly femininity lives in a fabulously magical world called 'Le Monde de Pam', with her perfect boyfriend, Ben. Ludovic is shown throughout the film to associate strongly with the Pam character, bringing a Pam doll to school, singing and dancing to the theme song of her show, and imagining themselves as a character in her fantasy world. In one dream-like sequence, Pam rescues Ludovic from ostracism and punishment after Jérôme's mother witnesses Ludovic and Jérôme's pretend wedding, Ludovic dressed in Jérôme's deceased sister's dress. Pam swoops through the window into Jérôme's room to rescue Ludovic from Jérôme's mother's horror – again, represented in a shot-reverse-shot sequence to reflect the hyperconservative character's ideological distance from this disruptive child – and from Ludovic's mother's fury. Under a shower of fairy dust, Pam flies off with both children into her make-believe world where, later in the film, this alarming mock wedding becomes a socially validated celebration.

Ludovic's gaze is thus normally directed either inwards into daydreams, or to the television from which Ludovic learns Pam's version of romantic love. When Ludovic does stand in front of a mirror to gaze at their whole body, it is not to practice a queered gender enactment, like Laure does in *Tomboy*, but rather to practice *acting like a boy* – and, more specifically, like Ludovic's two brothers – in order to appease the family and society in general. In one sequence, we see Ludovic gazing out their bedroom window at their brothers who are playing cowboys in the yard; Ludovic is shot from behind and is framed by the window, which emphasises the character's isolation and separation from the world of the two rowdy brothers. There is then a cut to a medium close-up of one brother 'shooting' the other, and then a cut to Ludovic standing, reflected in the bedroom mirror, unconvincingly re-enacting the scene they have just observed and grabbing their crotch in a futile imitation of a boyish way. The open door that is also reflected in the mirror limits what Ludovic can see of themself (and what we can see of Ludovic); in order to view their whole body, they are forced to stand in the narrow space between the door and the frame of the mirror. The metaphor of this different and disturbing child trying to limit themselves to a narrow view of what is expected of 'boyish' behaviour is quite clear.

The very next shot is a subjective low-angle shot of a teenage boy and a girl kissing on a landing in the background while other teenagers cheer them on, as seen by Ludovic on the stairs of the school. The subjective shot allows the spectator of the film to merge with the character, 'adopting the latter's perceptive faculties, movements, and attitudes' (Casetti 1998: 61), and gives the spectator access to 'a lived, interior space, marked by the character's physical and psychological interaction' (Casetti 1998: 63). Once Berliner has sutured the spectator to Ludovic's experience of viewing heterosexual relations through queer eyes, he then shows how, in the following scene, Ludovic unsuccessfully tries to recreate this socially endorsed public display of heterosexuality by grabbing their crotch and attempting to kiss their classmate, Sophie, who laughs, pushes them away and scoffs, 'J'embrasse pas les filles', thereby ironically affirming Ludovic's chosen gender identity.[5] Unlike Laure, then, who successfully uses the mirror as a tool to rehearse their new identity as Mikaël, Ludovic makes awkward and fruitless attempts at rehearsing the gender that corresponds to their biological sex and at enacting heterosexual desire. These performances are experienced as a failure in the filmic universe by Ludovic and the other characters, and extra-diegetically by the film's spectator. This inability to embody the 'right' gender leads to Ludovic's ostracism from neighbours and classmates, homophobic graffiti on the family's garage, a violent bullying episode, a suicide attempt, Ludovic's father's dismissal from work and eventually the family's move to a new town.

Gender Panic and the Nuclear Family

In her analysis of the development of children's sexuality, Emma Renold examines how the family and the primary school function together as heteronormative institutions that reaffirm 'the intersection of gender essentialism (femininity is female), gender polarity (masculinity and femininity as binary opposites) and compulsory and gendered heterosexuality (heterofemininity and heteromasculinity)' (Renold 2005: 27). As Lori Girshick further notes, 'Parents, siblings, and other relatives are major influences on ideas of gender because family roles are strongly gendered. . . . Children observe and learn to model these binary roles. They learn what is expected and what is acceptable' (Girshick 2008: 52). These hegemonic gender ideals are then reproduced and naturalised through social interaction: 'As we do gender, we involve ourselves in the ongoing construction of distinctions between "male" and "female" and the accretion of social expectations onto those categories. These are then declared "natural", which in turn legitimates their ongoing existence' (Brickell 2006: 94). This process is what Judith Butler has named the *heterosexual matrix*, a binary model that assumes the existence of 'a stable gender (masculine expresses male, feminine expresses female)' and that imposes 'the compulsory practice of heterosexuality' (Butler 1990: 151). The roles that the family, the schools and daily social interactions play in the construction and reinforcement of conventional gender norms in children are reflected in the diegesis of both *Ma Vie en rose* and *Tomboy* where, despite their difference, Ludovic and Laure are both warily permitted to experiment with their identities within the confines of their nuclear families until their gender nonconformity becomes public, visible and therefore threatening to the social order. Their families then revert to the propagation of the heterosexual matrix and the suppression of the gender deviance shown by their children.

The staunch heteronormativity of the Fabre family's new community is made clear from the first sequence of *Ma Vie en rose*, which shows Sophie's parents, Jérôme's parents and finally Ludovic's parents getting ready for the Fabre family's barbecue. The sequence emphasises traditionally feminine primping: we see the women applying make-up, zipping their dresses (or being zipped into them by their husbands) and examining themselves in the mirror. Conventional masculine behaviours are also modelled in this sequence; when Jérôme complains to his father that he doesn't want to wear his bowtie because it feels too tight, his father agrees but insists they wear them anyway, because it is what is done ('Moi aussi, ça me serre! On sort, non? Allez'). But whereas Jérôme is brought into the realm of masculinity under the wing of his father, Berliner quickly establishes strong links between Ludovic and the maternal, juxtaposing the close-up shot that shows Ludovic's mother, Hanna, applying her lipstick and the mirror shot of Ludovic's own lipstick application before appearing in a pink dress at the party. The association between Ludovic and the realm of the maternal is later solidified when Ludovic is shown dancing in their mother and grandmother's embrace at the party. Not only is Ludovic safely protected in the loving arms of the two women, with lipstick marks still visible on their cheek from their mother's kiss, their orange T-shirt is simply a lighter hue of the grandmother, Elisabeth's, orange dress and Hanna's red one. In fact, Berliner employs similar colour-coding throughout the film to associate Ludovic not just with the warm pink, red, orange and purple of Pam's world, but also with the maternal elements of the nuclear family.

The vestimentary association of Ludovic with Hanna and Elisabeth reflects their close relationship and the two women's initial greater tolerance of Ludovic's gender variance. At the beginning of the film, Hanna respects her child's wishes for long hair, trimming off only the tiniest snippets and declaring 'J'aime bien ceux qui savent ce qu'ils veulent'. In this scene, Ludovic and Hanna are dressed in matching clothes, Ludovic in a red T-shirt with a blue towel over their shoulders and Hanna in a red flowered T-shirt with blue overalls over top. However, once the repressive views of others threaten the well-being of the family, Hanna succumbs to external pressures and forces Ludovic to comply with society's gender expectations. When Pierre is fired by Jérôme's ultraconservative, religious father, Hanna snaps and rages at Ludovic for bringing catastrophe to their family: 'Oui, c'est de ta faute, tout ce qui nous arrive c'est de ta faute!' After seeing a homophobic slur graffitied on their garage and comforting her weeping husband, she forces Ludovic to submit to a very short haircut. In this second haircut scene, shot in a flat grey light that contrasts starkly with Pam's brightly coloured fantasy world, Hanna and Ludovic are framed from the neck up in separate close-up shots that reinforce the growing emotional distance between them. The camera shows first Hanna's tear-streaked face then Ludovic's, and cuts to a shot of their feet on the floor as Ludovic's long hair falls to the ground. This spectacle of forced gender conformity, experienced as a violent act of betrayal by Ludovic, is witnessed by the other family members who stare, aghast, framed in the doorway to the kitchen. Hanna's symbolic violence to Ludovic's chosen gender identity devolves into physical violence after the family's move to a new town near the end of the film. When Ludovic again contravenes gender norms in the family's new neighbourhood – by wearing a princess costume forced upon them at a birthday party by Christine, a rough-and-tumble tomboy who initially presents as 'Chris' – Hanna chases Ludovic down, hits her child several times and has to be restrained by the other adults. The pursuit scene, shot with an unsteady hand-held camera, and showing, alternately, Ludovic's fleeing back and Hanna's enraged countenance as she charges forward, underscores Ludovic's fear of this unrecognisably furious mother as the physical manifestation of society's intolerance of their gender deviance.

Ludovic's grandmother, Elisabeth, is the one character who remains steadfast in her attempts to shield her grandchild from the gender panic that nearly destroys them. With her blonde hair, orange dress and unconventional lifestyle – she lives alone, drives a yellow sports car, decorates her home with contemporary art and brightly coloured modern furniture and tells Ludovic stories about her former lover – 'Granny' is represented as a real-life, aging incarnation of Pam. In one early scene, she enters her living room to see Ludovic dancing to the music from *Pam et Ben*; as she also begins to dance, we see their complicity reflected not only in their mirrored gestures, but also in the matching shades of blue and brown they are both wearing. Elisabeth is the only character who seems to predict the extent to which Ludovic's gender nonconformity will upset the heterosexual matrix of the filmic universe; while holding a jewellery box that was a present from her lover – in which a tiny, Pam-like ballerina spins – she advises Ludovic to follow her example and to escape into a fantasy world once the real world becomes too difficult: 'Je ferme les yeux et le monde devient celui que je veux.'

Whereas Ludovic begins *Ma Vie en rose* under the protective mantle of the feminine and the maternal, Laure enters *Tomboy* in the realm of the paternal; the first shot of the film is a close-up of the back of Laure's head and we gradually understand, as the camera cuts between Laure's face and shots of trees passing by overhead, that Laure is riding standing up in a car, with their father holding onto their leg as he drives. He then allows Laure to sit in his lap and steer the car, a clear nod to the freedom and adventure that Laure will seek by leaving the family's apartment and roaming the neighbourhood with their new friends. Laure's mother encourages this love of movement and freedom, giving Laure the keys to the apartment so they may come and go as they wish. The contrast between the physical freedom and movement associated with the masculine, and the confined, limited gestures of the feminine, are emphasised through several characters: Jeanne who, too small to roam around on her own, often stays at home to colour, draw and play with dolls; Lisa who, having physically matured, is not allowed to join the boys in some of their games; and Laure's mother, who is pregnant and confined to bed rest. Most scenes involving Laure's mother show her engaging with her children and occasionally her husband on one of their three beds. Although these scenes are touching and demonstrate the closeness between all members of the nuclear family, Laure chafes when stuck indoors and escapes outside at first chance.

Laure's mother, like Ludovic's mother, initially supports private displays of her child's difference; she lovingly caresses Laure's short hair and has painted Laure's new room blue, especially to please her tomboy child. However, as in *Ma Vie en rose*, the correction of Laure's gender nonconformity occurs once the mother realises her non-binary child's transgressive performance might threaten the nuclear family. Confronted at her apartment door by a boy and his mother after Laure has beaten the boy in a fight, Laure's mother learns that it was in fact her *son*, Mikaël, who was the culprit. The framing of this scene emphasises the extent to which the true menace to Laure's identity comes from outside. The boy, Rayan, and his mother are initially shot from inside the apartment and are framed by the door as they stand in the hallway; when Rayan insists 'Si, c'est lui, Mikaël', we see neither the accuser nor the object of the accusation, but rather Laure's mother's face in profile. As the truth she learns from the two strangers washes over her, she looks to Laure in shock. The reverse shot shows Laure staring at the ground; in a moment of affirmation, they raise their eyes to their accuser and declare, 'Oui, c'est vrai, c'était moi.' Once Rayan and his mother have left, Laure's mother becomes violent, slapping her child; the close-up of her horrified expression and her tearful face bring to mind Hanna's reaction to her own verbal and physical attacks on Ludovic. Sciamma's use of the shot-reverse-shot technique reinforces the sudden emotional break between mother and daughter.

Certainly, the trauma that Ludovic's gender transgression provokes in their nuclear family is much greater than the effects that Laure's secret life as Mikaël have on theirs. This is partly because, as we have seen, *Tomboy* occurs in the summertime, and Laure's public embodiment of Mikaël takes place mostly out of doors in natural settings and entirely in unsupervised contexts. But it is also because, as Girshick observes, in childhood '[t]omboys (girls "trying to be boys") are acceptable, but sissy boys (boys "trying to be girls") are not' (Girshick 2008: 47). As Robbie Duschinsky aptly notes, Laure's tomboy qualities are tolerated up until the point that Laure is supposed to conform to the heteronormative imperative placed on young girls, namely that they become 'à la fois présexuelles et hétérosexuelles' (Duschinsky 2014: 197). Once Laure nears puberty, it is necessary for the gender identity they present at school to correspond to the heteronormative model.

Seemingly, both *Ma Vie en rose* and *Tomboy* end on somewhat optimistic notes: Ludovic is embraced by their repentant mother and is integrated into a new group of children that includes the tomboy Chris, and Laure reunites with Lisa under their given name after losing their identity as Mikaël. But it is unclear whether these films present truly hopeful endings for their young protagonists. When Laure pronounces their given name to Lisa with a hint of a smile at the end of *Tomboy*, does this indicate that they are entering the realm of conventional girlhood in defeat, overcome by the power of institutional norms? Or will Laure continue to enact a masculine identity under their given name? Do the final seconds of *Ma Vie en rose*, which show an overhead shot of the children dancing hand in hand at Chris's birthday party and then, as the camera pans up, Pam flying through the sky, hint at Ludovic's ability to queer the sex–gender binary and overthrow the heterosexual matrix, or rather at the sad possibility that the idea of the acceptance of genderfluid children by their peers is a beautiful fantasy? I would argue that the lack of easy conclusions to draw from these films is intentional and that Berliner and Sciamma highlight both the indeterminacy of gender and society's reluctance to accept nonconforming gender identities.

Notes

1. In order to avoid enforcing Ludovic and Laure's biologically based gender and to prevent potentially confusing transitions between masculine and feminine pronouns, I will use 'they', 'their' and 'them' to refer to both characters throughout this chapter.
2. Actor Jeffrey Tambor, who played the transgender matriarch Maura Pfefferman on *Transparent*, was fired from the show in early 2018 after an investigation into sexual harassment claims made against him by two transgender women. Tambor will not appear in the fifth and final season of *Transparent*.
3. Laure's mother and father do not even have names in the film.
4. Renold points to soccer as 'the most commonly cited activity of the monopolization of outdoor space' (Renold 2005: 68) in terms of enacting and maintaining a hegemonic masculinity in childhood.
5. This blending of a moment of humiliation – being mocked and rejected by Sophie – with the corroboration of Ludovic's identification as a girl echoes the scene in *Tomboy* in which Laure is humiliated by the boy in the woods for having urine on their shorts, while simultaneously having their identity as Mikaël confirmed.

Works Cited

Brickell, Chris (2006), 'The Sociological Construction of Gender and Sexuality', *The Sociological Review*, 54:1, 87–113.

Butler, Judith (1990), *Gender Trouble: Feminism and the Subversion of Identity*, New York: Routledge.

Casetti, Francesco (1998), *Inside the Gaze: The Fiction Film and its Spectator*, Bloomington: Indiana University Press.

Duschinsky, Robbie (2014), 'Féminités schizoïdes et espaces interstitiels. Enfance et genre dans *Tomboy* de Céline Sciamma et *Peter Pan* de P. J. Hogan', *Diogène*, 245, pp. 196–214.

Girshick, Lori (2008), *Transgender Voices: Beyond Women and Men*, Hanover: University Press of New England.

Ince, Kate (2002), 'Queering the Family? Fantasy and the Performance of Sexuality and Gay Relations in French Cinema 1995–2000', *Studies in French Cinema*, 2:2, pp. 90–7.

Renold, Emma (2005), *Girls, Boys and Junior Sexualities*, London and New York: Routledge/Falmer.

Waldron, Darren (2013), 'Embodying Gender Nonconformity in "Girls": Céline Sciamma's *Tomboy*', *L'Esprit créateur*, 53:1, pp. 60–73.

Westbrook, Laurel and Kristen Schilt (2014), 'Doing Gender, Determining Gender: Transgender People, Gender Panics and the Maintenance of the Sex/Gender/Sexuality System', *Gender and Society*, 28:1, pp. 32–57.

Films and Television Series

Boys Don't Cry, film, directed by Kimberly Peirce. USA: Fox Searchlight Pictures/IFC Films/Killer Films, 1999.

Laurence Anyways, film, directed by Xavier Dolan. Canada: Lyla Films/MK2, 2012.

Ma Vie en rose, film, directed by Alain Berliner. France/Belgium/UK: Canal+/Eurimages/CNC/ TF1 Film Productions, 1997.

The Adventures of Priscilla, Queen of the Desert, film, directed by Stephan Elliott. Australia: Polygram Filmed Entertainment/AFCC, 1994.

The Crying Game, film, directed by Neil Jordan. Ireland/UK/Japan: Palace Pictures/Channel Four Films, 1992.

The Danish Girl, film, directed by Tom Hooper. UK/USA/Belgium: Working Title Films/Pretty Pictures, 2015.

Todo sobre mi madre, film, directed by Pedro Almodóvar. Spain: El Deseo/Renn Productions/France 2 Cinéma, 1999.

Tomboy, film, directed by Céline Sciamma. France: Hold Up Films/Arte France Cinéma/Canal+, 2011.

Transamerica, film, directed by Duncan Tucker. USA: Belladonna Productions, 2005.

Transparent, television series, created by Jill Solloway. USA: Amazon Studios, 2014–18.

Une nouvelle amie, film, directed by François Ozon. France: Mandarin Cinéma, 2014.

XXY, film, directed by Lucia Puenzo. Argentina/Spain/France: Cinéfondation, 2007.

CHAPTER 4

Bargaining the Body: Love, Death and Rites of Passage in Three Films by François Ozon

Ericka Knudson

'On n'est pas sérieux quand on a 17 ans . . .'

Citing Rimbaud in his 2013 film, *Jeune et jolie*, François Ozon suggests a possible answer to the enigma his films seek to explore: the mystery behind his adolescent characters' reckless behaviour and their willingness to transgress moral codes. Ozon's directorial style, like that of Gaspard Noé, Catherine Breillat and the 'New French Extremity' movement, is often noted for 'shock tactics' (Quandt 2011: 18). Looking beyond this categorisation, however, we find in his films portraits of youth and rites of passage that seek what lies beneath the surface, exploring characters in moments of transition and in search of identity.

Asked why he chooses to film adolescents so frequently, Ozon replies, 'What is very beautiful are all the first times, first emotions . . . and filming, for the first time, a face that is not aware of what it is' (Baumann and Tobin 2013: 24).[1] Stories of adolescence, with their rich opportunity for narratives of first times, are not new to French cinema or literature – we remember Françoise Sagan's *Bonjour tristesse* (1958), and films by Eric Rohmer or Maurice Pialat. Echoing his predecessors, authors and directors who drew upon their own experiences to make their films authentic, Ozon says of his own work: 'it recalls, of course, something from my own adolescence' (Baumann and Tobin 2013: 24).[2]

Besides these autobiographical implications, Ozon's films, with their box-office success, trace certain social trends, as well as audiences' appetites for fresh takes on cinematic clichés. Combining portraits of adolescent girls with figures such as the *femme fatale* or the prostitute allows for aesthetic experimentation with variations on a theme inside his narratives. Placing young women in ambiguous leading roles is not a new choice in French cinema either: from Jean-Luc Godard's Nana in *Vivre sa vie* (1962) to Eric Rohmer's Haydée in *La Collectionneuse* (1967), idealised heroines are shown using their bodies to gain power over male protagonists, either for money or as a game. At the same time, the directors of these films have sought to harness the enigmatic and elusive qualities of their female characters through close examination by their cameras. Although Ozon may not have the same intimate relationship with his actresses that New Wave directors (who often cast their wives or lovers in leading roles) experienced, similar dynamics of voyeuristic scrutiny arise in Ozon's films over half a century later. Ozon places his young female characters in stories of rites of passage that lead them into adulthood with a new freedom that reflects an evolution in female representation in French cinema.

Through films spanning over a decade and marking the transition from the twentieth to the twenty-first century, I will examine how Ozon's representations of – and relationships to – his characters fit into the broader historical landscape of French cinema and, at the same time, reflect changes marking the 'rite of passage' in contemporary French cinema. Concentrating on three particular films – *Jeune et jolie* (2013), *Swimming Pool* (2003) and *Les Amants criminels* (1999) – I examine Ozon's aesthetic representations of the young female protagonist, the 'use' of her body in negotiating power, and the rites of passage into adulthood that lead to acceptance, connection and greater agency.

In Transition: Double Identities in *Jeune et jolie*

The behaviour of teenagers experimenting with identity escapes adult understanding, yet fascinates the adult world. Over the course of *Jeune et jolie*, the main character, Isabelle, having turned seventeen, experiments with first love and at the same time, inexplicably, with prostitution. What drives her to this choice? She is from a wealthy family, does not need the money and is not being forced into the role. Here, as in so many of his films, Ozon seeks to unlock the mystery of adolescence, asking the question: Why?

Using Ozon's heroine as a case study, the authors of a recent article in *L'Évolution psychiatrique* explain that during adolescence, 'identity quest and reactivation of infantile conflicts confront the young with feelings of loss and bereavement', and that 'this distress often manifests itself by symptoms of acting out' (Benarous and Munch 2015: 425). Additionally, Ahovi and Moro's article on adolescence and psychology discusses the structuring function of rites of passage, explaining that these experiences give meaning to life, death and the world, but also have a constraining function that is internalised and can be a source of psychological identity issues (2010: 862).³ The most intense rites of passage, according to the authors, are those that celebrate 'first times': through these experiences, adolescents confront and overcome their fear of the unknown.

First times are central to Ozon's *Jeune et jolie*, punctuating the narrative that traces the heroine's rite of passage from adolescence to adulthood. Divided into four seasons (echoing Eric Rohmer's *Contes des quatre saisons*: *Conte de printemps* (1990), *Conte d'hiver* (1992), *Conte d'été* (1996) and *Conte d'automne* (1998)), the film is framed by four songs by Françoise Hardy that announce in stages the concerns of Ozon's heroine, Isabelle, and of adolescent girls in general: *L'Amour d'un garçon* (first love), *À quoi ça sert* (disappointment), *Première rencontre* (questioning) and *Je suis moi* (finding identity). The film opens during the summer months, with Isabelle's experiments in first love. Vacationing in the south of France with her family, Isabelle meets a young German boy who will become her first lover. Though apparently attracted to him physically, she remains ambivalent, refusing to invite him to dinner with her family because, in her words: 'he is too stupid'.⁴ She decides, however, to lose her virginity to him anyway, using him on her path to adulthood. Ozon films the 'love' scene as an out-of-body experience for Isabelle, creating a double who looks on, watching herself endure it, without pleasure, deriving nothing from the experience except the alleviation of the weight of her virginity. When she comes home, sneaking back into her room, her little brother is waiting for her: 'So?' he asks. 'It's done', Isabelle replies. 'You slept with him?' he insists. 'Yes . . . I don't feel like talking about that with you',⁵ Isabelle answers, ending the discussion.

As she blows out the seventeen candles on her birthday cake the next day, in the next scene, we witness the 'conventional' rite of passage juxtaposed against the previous night's private ritual. As her mother encourages her to blow out her candles and not to cry,⁶ the music of Françoise Hardy ironically echoes Isabelle's transformation: 'The love of a boy, can change everything . . . I am no longer what I was, the little girl that you knew, no, I am no longer.'⁷ Now in autumn, we follow Isabelle up an escalator into the unknown. Her outer appearance is that of an elegant woman, wearing make-up, 'dressed up' in a suit and silk blouse that she took from her mother's closet. When a much older man, Georges, answers the door and asks her name, Isabelle responds 'Léa.' We discover that Georges is her first client. Assuming a new identity, 'Léa' says that she is twenty and a student at the Sorbonne. Interestingly, this sex/love scene (with Léa in the role of prostitute) takes place off screen, in ellipses. When she comes out of the bathroom at the end of the scene, she is dressed as Isabelle again.

Stripping off her new identity along with her new clothes, she slips the 300 euros into her jeans pocket and takes the escalator back down to go home.

In the next scene, Ozon offers an implicit commentary on his own relationship with his actresses. Léa's next client directs her, much like a filmmaker would direct an actress: 'Be natural, don't look!'[8] Deciding her services do not equal the agreed price, however, Léa's client fires her, adding: 'Sorry, you are not worth it.'[9] After this initial fumble, Isabelle/Léa continues to test her value, slowly learning the ropes and how to stand up for herself: asking for her money in advance, and negotiating a price for various services. Parallel to this evolution, as she continues to see Georges, she begins to experience shared intimacy: they kiss affectionately, implying shared feelings, but he also gives her extra money. He confides in her, expressing disappointment in not having been a good father, and in turn, she offers stories about her own absent(ee) father. Suddenly, though, in an abrupt shift, the *jeune fille/confidante* transforms into a true *femme fatale*: as they move to the bed, transitioning from confidantes to lovers, Georges suffers a heart attack. Léa panics, tries CPR, but cannot revive him. After some hesitation, she takes the money she has 'earned' and leaves Georges as her victim. The moral dilemma surrounding George's death causes personal trauma for Isabelle that will ultimately help her realise her feelings and bring her a step closer to subjectivity, connection and adulthood.

During the winter chapter, the police track down Isabelle, find the large stash of money hidden in her closet and force her to confess her double identity to her mother. Isabelle goes into counselling, describing to the therapist how she thought of prostitution like a game. She explains that she did not feel anything until George's death: 'With him, it was more tender. He didn't want very much, just to caress me, to look at me . . . except the last time.'[10] Here, Isabelle seems to imply that it was sleeping with her that killed him. She confides in her therapist that she now feels dirty and guilty, a remorseful *femme fatale*.

With the arrival of spring, we anticipate Isabelle's renaissance. Back at her high school, she starts to study again, and meets a boy at a party who awkwardly asks if he can kiss her. Although we cannot help but calculate the value of her kiss, we are now back in the adolescent world of innocent first loves. Isabelle kisses him (for free) and starts a new romance. In a conventional Hollywood narrative, the story might end here, a *parcours initiatique* in which the hero makes mistakes on a path leading to redemption. But in Ozon's film, our heroine soon becomes bored, and as Isabelle puts her old SIM card back in her phone, Léa, too, comes back to life as the numerous messages waiting for her secret self arrive, sounding in her phone like a slot machine jackpot. 'What am I worth?', Isabelle asks throughout the film: the number of text messages, the rate per trick, the money she stashes in her closet but does not spend. According to Benarous and Munch, all of these eliminate what is lacking in her inner-world – desire, in other words – and protect her from the irruption of anxiety (2015: 427).[11]

In the final sequence, she returns to the hotel where she first encountered Georges, taking the elevator up, but this time dressed as Isabelle, in jeans and a baggy jacket. As the camera follows her inside, an older woman's voice says, 'You are young, very beautiful . . . too beautiful.'[12] Charlotte Rampling appears in the counter-shot as Georges' wife. When she asks Isabelle's age, this time, she answers 'Seventeen.' 'Beautiful age',[13] the woman replies. Georges' wife confesses to having fantasised about having men pay to make love to her too when she was young, but adds with regret: 'Now, I am too old; I'm the one who would have to pay.'[14] Rampling's character, a surrogate maternal figure, helps Isabelle through the traumatic event, marking one of the last steps in her rite of passage into adulthood. George's wife has reserved the same hotel room in which Isabelle first met Georges, and offers Isabelle the same price, 300 euros, adding: '[W]e loved each other until the end, always with the same tenderness.'[15] Isabelle asks if she should take her clothes off, but George's wife motions her instead to come to the bed next to her. They lie down side by side and she caresses Isabelle's face, reassuring her with acceptance and love, a sign of a human connection. Isabelle awakens alone. The final song signals a resolution in her search for identity: 'I am me, I have heaven at the tips of my fingers . . . the world below me as if for the first time.'[16] In their case study on Ozon's film, Benarous and Munch show that the meeting with Charlotte Rampling's character allows Isabelle to stop repeating the ritual and to experience a unique encounter where we see the normally cold and distant Isabelle finally in touch with her emotions (2015: 428).[17] In representing this story of adolescence, here we can see how Ozon's camera traces the evolution of his character through the moments of her life marked by heavy transformation while the film records the physical and psychological evolution of both the heroine and the actress.

Ahovi and Moro explain that, 'with the physical transformation during puberty, adolescents are forced to "modify themselves", accepting the differences that separate them from their "child-I"' (2010: 868–9).[18] Alongside psychological transformations, explored in the narrative, the film also traces the physical transformation of the actress over time, through the sheer documentary aspect of the medium. Commenting on a possible ending of the film that was not used, Ozon recalls,

> the summer after, the heroine was with her boyfriend again. But, I had filmed this scene on the second day of shooting, so it wouldn't work: Marine Vacth's face is not the same as at the end of the film. I really think that I shot, in a very documentary way, the face of a young actress who matured after this very strong experience of filming ... If I had respected the original order of editing, it would have seemed like a flash-back. (Baumann and Tobin 2013: 26)[19]

By the end of shooting, Ozon tells us, the actress had acquired a certain maturity and also trusted him with the more delicate scenes (Baumann and Tobin 2013: 25).[20] The evolution Ozon describes here, their own rite of passage building trust, underscores how the close relationship between artist and model/director and actress influences the aesthetics of the film itself – echoing a common theme of French New Wave cinema as well.

Traces of New Wave Heroines: Prostitutes and Confidantes

Examining Ozon's female protagonists in the context of French cinema, we notice a strong connection between these characters and some of the modern heroines of the New Wave. In the 'neo-romantic' cinema of this era, the New Wave filmmakers make a clear effort to avoid representing the female body, even in these fantasised figures: prostitutes become confidantes, like Ozon's Isabelle, or remain as sublimated images, objects invested with an iconic power.

The character of Isabelle is particularly reminiscent of Buñuel's *Belle de jour* (1967),[21] whose heroine also assumes a double life: prostitute by day, proper wife by night. Both directors focus on their heroine's transformation out of prostitution and into agency through a process that leaves the male character crippled or dead. In the case of Buñuel's heroine, after disabling her husband, Belle de jour finally assumes her role as wife, simultaneously re-establishing the social order and inverting it through the power she gains over her husband. Ozon's heroine likewise gains autonomy when she leaves Georges dead; her future is now open. It becomes clear over the course of the film that Isabelle has truly undergone a transformation. Her rite of passage, we can assume, will help her to strengthen her identity, reinforcing her 'I am me',[22] while also teaching her empathy through the lessons in love she receives from Georges and his wife.

More human than Belle de jour, Isabelle is also less romantic than Godard's Nana in *Vivre sa vie*, although again we see a similar attempt to gain autonomy through financial negotiations and power plays. In Godard's film, Nana accepts her first experience of prostitution with disgust, refusing the client's kiss ('pas sur la bouche'), and then enters a period of uncertainty before settling into the profession, gaining confidence and learning to negotiate her self-worth through the price she sets for her services. Like Nana, Isabelle is negotiating her independence through her acts of prostitution, distancing herself from the 'child-I'. Intriguingly, Isabelle does not spend any of her earnings (except to pay a therapist later), choosing instead to hide the money away in her own secret 'account' in her closet. Contrasting these motivations with those of other girls in her class who prostitute themselves for pocket money to buy luxury items, Ozon's film echoes Godard's documentary-type social commentary, evoking practices described in interviews at the time. In Ozon's case (and in his own words), this contrast reveals the deeper motivations of Isabelle: 'money allows her to protect her feelings and to take control' (Baumann and Tobin 2013: 23).[23] Similarly, Godard uses Nana as a metaphor for society in decline while simultaneously playing on the literary portrait that describes the 'natural tendency' of women to be corrupted by desire (Hollier and Bloc 1994: 783).[24] In both cases, however, Godard and Ozon portray a melancholy, pensive heroine. Indeed, Ozon specifically explains that he chose his actress because she was 'there and not there' at the same time.

Both heroines are therefore romanticised by their directors' representations, even in the role of prostitute. Godard displays a certain modesty (*pudeur*) in filming his actress Anna Karina's body in the role of Nana, and it is surprising to learn that, in France, viewers found this trait in Ozon's representation of Isabelle as well. According to *Écran Total*, 88 per cent of French moviegoers interviewed reacted positively to *Jeune et jolie* but found the director's portrayal of prostitution 'modest', describing it as 'a good French film on desire that portrays prostitution in a rather modest way' (Gauthier 2013).[25] Comparing this reception to that of a critic in the United States, we find a stark cultural difference as the American review described *Jeune et jolie* as a 'horror film or a nightmarish Exorcist-like tale of possession' (Alexander 2014). Shocking or modest, we can safely say that Ozon pushes the envelope, displaying his heroine's body in explicit scenes, moments of pure erotic contemplation, while at the same time granting her autonomy. And unlike Nana, whose ultimate fate is death, Isabelle is granted freedom and agency by the end of the film.

Jeunes Filles, Femmes Fatales and Fetishism

Under Ozon's lens, traces of the *jeune fille* and *femme fatale* figures consistently appear in his young female protagonists – echoing, again, the efforts of male directors of the New Wave to unlock women's mystery. Just as Roger Vadim showed a new type of woman in 1957 with Brigitte Bardot in

Et Dieu créa la femme – free in her movements, speech, clothing, hairstyle, attitude – Ozon's films present avatars of heroines that renew cinematic codes, 'short circuiting reassuring explanations and blowing up clichés' (De Bruyn 2013: 89).[26]

Although Isabelle enjoys more freedom than Bardot's character during much of the film, both women incarnate a paradox. Describing Bardot in the 1950s, Ginette Vincendeau proposes that she is a sexual object dreamed of by men but fascinating to feminists: both *vamp* and *gamine*, with the threatening *savoir-faire* of the *femme fatale* (1993: 143). In the case of Isabelle, the innocence of the *gamine* is reinforced further by her young age. The structure of Ozon's film follows that of Vadim closely as well: 'opposing the narrative that gives [the heroine] status as subject and the spectacle that makes her an object' (Vincendeau 1993: 143–4).[27] Though the action in *Jeune et jolie* takes place from Isabelle's point of view, the narrative is sometimes suspended by moments of erotic contemplation, objectifying and distancing her. In an interview, Ozon admits, 'the aim of the film was to examine this young girl with binoculars, then to try to approach her. To break through her mystery' (Baumann and Tobin 2013: 24).[28]

In the opening scene, for example, Isabelle is at the beach, framed by binoculars in a subjective shot, emphasising the audience's place as voyeur – a position we take alongside Isabelle's little brother, who is holding the binoculars. The director's camera scrutinises Isabelle's body in much the same way that Eric Rohmer examines and dissects Haydée, one of the freest heroines of the New Wave, in *La Collectionneuse*. As Ozon presents Isabelle in *Jeune et jolie*, Rohmer introduces us to his heroine in the natural setting of a beach in the south of France. In an opening scene without dialogue, Haydée emerges from the water, assuming the posture of Venus, associating her with nature. A series of shots of her body in movement focus on its details, in pursuit of the director's quest to reveal her beauty by capturing it with his camera. Representing the elusive, unattainable woman, Haydée serves to exorcise the intimate conflicts surrounding the *femme insaisissable*, as does Isabelle. T. Jefferson Kline suggests that 'the narrator in Rohmer's film finds himself "incapable of controlling the destabilizing role of desire"' (1992: 130). Haydée, the origin of his anxiety, frustrates the narrator with her instability; she brings home multiple conquests, yet does not seem interested in romantic love. Because Haydée escapes the male protagonists' control, they try to devalorise her with humiliating remarks. But Rohmer presents a truly modern and strong heroine who continues to escape their control. As the theoretician Sylvie Robic states, Haydée 'responds with impassibility and her blinding smile, pure enigma that pretends not to mean anything, and reinforces the narrator's trouble and his rage' (2002: 91).[29] Ozon reflects a similar desire when discussing his casting choice: 'I wanted a girl who escapes us' (Baumann and Tobin 2013: 24), both 'there and not there'.[30] Instead of frustrating her male protagonists, however, Isabelle offers herself in exchange for money; the romantic male character from the New Wave films who longs for control no longer exists, as the male characters in Ozon's film are reduced to 'clients'.

Variations on the *jeune fille* and the themes of youth and beauty also mark Ozon's *Swimming Pool*, incarnated by the character Julie (played by Ludivine Sagnier). Traces of Brigitte Bardot's freedom and sex appeal mix with Haydée's elusiveness and power over men in Ozon's protagonist, and Charlotte Rampling again plays an older maternal substitute in the role of Sarah Morton, a famous British crime novelist who is at a loss for inspiration. Accepting her publisher's offer to stay at his home in the south of France, Sarah begins work on her next novel. All is going well until, unexpectedly, the publisher's daughter Julie arrives. Like Haydée, who annoys Rohmer's male protagonists who are trying to enjoy their vacation, Julie, with her impulsive, free-spirited lifestyle, disrupts Sarah's work and need for control. As in *La Collectionneuse*, Julie also brings home multiple lovers, who reflect her lack of standards or desire for romantic love and characterise her as reckless. Nevertheless, Sarah is fascinated by Julie (as Rohmer's characters are with Haydée), and the novelist starts to use her as the source of inspiration for her new thriller.

As in *Jeune et jolie*, Ozon presents his young heroine to the audience voyeuristically, with a focus on her body. Now we approach the heroine through the eyes of the older female protagonist, who gazes secretly at Julie, lying by the pool in her bikini, from the balcony. Anticipating Charlotte Rampling's character in *Jeune et jolie*, Sarah sees in Julie what she once had: the freedom and power that come from youth and beauty. When Sarah and Julie's rivalry over a waiter in the local restaurant leads to his murder, the two women work together to hide the body. The bond created between them by this crime allows Julie to gain a reassuring maternal confidante whom she can trust. Thus, we see again how the death of the shared male love interest enables both characters' rites of passage: into adulthood for Julie with an authentic relationship to another, and into an author with her own voice for Sarah, as she escapes her publisher's desire for a plot based on blood, sex and money and chooses instead to write a love story inspired by Julie.[31] Instead of banishing the free-spirited Haydée character from the narrative, as Rohmer does, Ozon allows Julie to be integrated in Sarah's world, marking a rite of passage for the author and allowing her to express her voice and her story.

Role Reversals and Gender in *Les Amants criminels*

Similar voyeuristic representations had already appeared in one of Ozon's earlier works, *Les Amants criminels*, but here our gaze is focused on an adolescent boy in the context of a 'splatter film' (Quandt 2011: 18). Echoing the publisher's desire for blood and sex in *Swimming Pool*, Ozon states: 'What I am interested in is violence and sex because there is a real challenge in rendering the strong and powerful, as opposed to the weak and trivial', adding, 'I like something that asks moral questions' (Quandt 2011: 19). It is interesting to note, however, that this film was practically disowned by Ozon later (and, indeed, the inner conflict over the author's creation around sex and violence shows up in Sarah's quandary in *Swimming Pool*, as we have just seen).

Les Amants criminels opens with a love scene, in which two adolescents are playing a dangerous game, testing the bounds of trust and intimacy. The inexperienced boy is the object of the veteran girl's menacing gaze. Alice (Natacha Régnier) incarnates simultaneously both the *jeune fille* and the *femme fatale*, threatening Luc (Jérémie Rénier) with humiliation through her powerful gaze. She pretends to take photos of his naked body, directing Luc as he lies blindfolded and powerless on the bed. Explicitly violent, this film offers a variation on the extremes of power dynamics that Ozon will explore in a more muted way in his later films. Juxtaposing this morally violent sex scene with an explicit and gory murder scene, Ozon explicitly equates the two events, underscoring the danger of the adolescent girl associated with desire and death, a true *femme fatale*.

In flashback, we learn that Alice had convinced Luc to murder their classmate Saïd, for having raped her, she claimed. She asks for this as proof of his love, citing Rimbaud, as in *Jeune et jolie*. Alice calls for 'Un crime, vite!' and we see her recite the poem by heart in her literature class. Like Julie in *Swimming Pool*, Alice keeps a diary and writes the murder scene where Luc kills Saïd. But she also describes her attraction to Saïd, objectifying him as well in her secret narrative. After the murder, Alice and Luc flee to the country, lovers on the run in the tradition of Bonnie and Clyde or *Pierrot le fou*, robbing a jewellery store, and disposing of Saïd's body in the woods. After they are captured by a mysterious older man in a 'Hansel and Gretel'-type fable, a series of obstacles tests their love: the man locks Alice in a basement with Saïd's dead body, which he then forces Luc to eat. Luc becomes the old man's love slave while Alice looks on from the trapdoor of the basement. After they escape, Alice initiates Luc into adulthood through their final love scene in the forest, where Luc loses his virginity – his first rite of passage. Immediately afterward, however, Alice is shot by the police, who have discovered their trail. As Luc is being taken away in a police van, begging them not to punish the man who enslaved him, we witness a sort of second rite of passage, similar to that of the female protagonists in *Jeune et jolie* and *Swimmng Pool* who bond with the older female character: a rite of passage through compassion in which Luc silently assumes his own homosexuality through an exchange of glances with the older man, followed by an open-ended *regard-caméra*.

In his article, 'Flesh and Blood: Sex and Violence in Recent French Cinema', James Quandt notes the 'growing vogue for shock tactics' in contemporary French cinema: 'this recent tendency to the willfully transgressive' by directors 'determined to break every taboo . . . Images once the provenance of splatter films and porn . . . proliferate in the high-art environs of a national cinema whose provocations have historically been formal, political, or philosophical (Godard, Debord) . . .' (Quandt 2011: 18). He posits a possible cultural crisis that forces French filmmakers to respond to the death of French identity, language, ideology and aesthetic forms with desperate measures.

In the 1960s, conflicts between romantic love (internalised by New Wave directors through their own literary models) and a newfound sexual freedom required a reconfiguration of men's and women's roles. This conflict surfaces throughout the New Wave directors' films, reflected in the birth of new, freer, modern female characters who nevertheless remained trapped in a *mise en scène* that portrayed them as threatening and dangerous, characters who were often punished at the end without gaining full subjectivity. Sixty years later, these dualities are still present in Ozon's films, but the heroines (with the exception of Alice in *Les Amants criminels*) are no longer punished for their freedom. In *Jeune et jolie* and *Swimming Pool*, Isabelle and Julie each undergo an awakening, a rite of passage into the adult world through a shared connection with a mature female character that allows them to trust and gain subjectivity. The same trend is reflected, albeit in a darker form, in Ozon's earlier work, in which the objectified boy (in a feminised role) undergoes a rite of passage through sex with Alice and a perverse relationship of masculine complicity with the older male character. Here, though, the *femme fatale* is still punished by death.

Following the chronological evolution of his work, and the representation of his heroines, we may speculate that Ozon himself has undergone his own transformation. In his earlier work, Ozon's heroine is punished, while his (objectified, feminised) male protagonist gains self-awareness as well as a more solid identity but ends up imprisoned; in his later films, however, this New Wave trope is broken, and his female characters are no longer prisoners of a male protagonist's desire for control. The question of gender is blurred in these films: the focus of all three works is on the rites of passage of his adolescent characters – be they female or male – through a reconciliatory scene with an older character of the same sex[32] who ushers them into a state of agency, solidifying their identity and allowing them to connect with another person. In *Jeune et jolie* and *Swimming Pool*, the narrative evolves along with the characters, taking place through the eyes of heroines who are close to becoming autonomous, gaining complexity and subjectivity. The inexplicable decisions and recklessness of adolescence, echoed in the opening quote by Rimbaud, are thus the perfect mystery for Ozon's camera. As Julie explains to Sarah in *Swimming Pool*, 'it's blood, sex and money that sells' – but for Ozon, this pretext offers the perfect medium through which to explore what lies beneath the surface: the search for love, connection, and independence . . . a rite of passage perhaps also accomplished in contemporary French cinema.

Notes

1. 'Ce qui est très beau, ce sont toutes les premières fois, les premières émotions . . . et filmer, pour la première fois, un visage qui n'a pas conscience de ce qu'il est' (my translation).
2. 'Mais ça rejoue, bien sûr, quelque chose de ma propre adolescence' (my translation).
3. 'La connaissance de la fonction des rites nous aide à comprendre et à soigner des souffrances des adolescents . . . en quête de sens car le processus de séparation-agrégation nous semble constitutive de toute adolescence.'
   '. . . les rites de passage . . . ont, en plus des fonctions sociologiques et psychologiques, une fonction élaboratrice et structurante en ce qu'ils donnent un sens à la vie, à la mort, au monde. Ces rites de passage ont un côté contraignant qui est intériorisé par les individus. Cette contrainte peut être source de difficultés psychiques identitaires . . .'
4. 'Il est trop con!' (my translation).
5. 'Alors?', 'C'est fait', 'Tu as couché avec?' 'Oui . . . j'ai pas envie de parler de ça avec toi' (my translation).
6. 'Allez souffle, tu vas pas pleurer!' (my translation).
7. 'L'amour d'un garçon, peut tout changer . . . Je ne suis plus ce que j'étais, la petite fille que tu as connue, non, je ne suis plus' (my translation).
8. 'Sois naturelle, regarde pas!' (my translation).
9. 'Désolé, tu les vaux pas' (my translation).

10. 'Avec lui, c'était plus tendre. Il voulait pas grand chose, juste me caresser, me regarder . . . sauf la dernière fois' (my translation).
11. 'Est-ce le nombre de texto reçus, le tarif demandé pour une passe (et dont la cote grimpe régulièrement) ou bien ces billets froissés accumulés dans son placard ? Cet argent, dont finalement elle ne fait rien et qui remplit sa fonction fétiche, élimine la dimension de manque – donc de désir –, et protège de l'irruption de l'angoisse' (my translation).
12. 'Vous êtes jeune, très belle . . . trop belle' (my translation).
13. 'Bel âge' (my translation).
14. 'Maintenant, je suis trop vieille, c'est moi qui devrais payer' (my translation).
15. 'On s'est aimés jusqu'au bout, toujours la même tendresse' (my translation).
16. 'Je suis moi, j'ai le ciel au bout des doigts . . . le monde au-dessous de moi comme pour la première fois' (my translation).
17. Noting that Isabelle's familial environment is marked by promiscuity and generational confusion, an atmosphere that makes it even more difficult to develop intra-familial conflict, which is essential to build individual identity, they show how temporary mechanisms of perversion can appear during adolescence and that Isabelle's acting out also carries a message for the parents, in order both to test the familial law and to internalise the familial values.
18. 'La transformation pubertaire physique place l'adolescent face à une obligation: . . . L'ado est alors contraint à un travail psychique considérable dans la mesure où il doit "se modifier", accepter les differences qui le séparent de son "Je-enfant"' (my translation).
19. 'On se retrouvait l'été d'après, l'héroïne était de nouveau avec son petit ami. Mais, comme j'avais filmé cette scène dès le deuxième jour du tournage, elle était ratée: le visage de Marine Vacth n'est pas le même qu'à la fin du film. Je pense vraiment que j'ai filmé, de manière documentaire, le visage d'une jeune actrice qui a mûri, après cette expérience de tournage très forte. Si je respectais le montage d'origine, on croyait du coup à un flash-back' (my translation).
20. 'Elle avait acquis une certaine maturité, elle était en confiance' (my translation).
21. Deneuve is a 'blank page on which we can project our fantasies' ['une page blanche sur laquelle on peut projeter ses fantasmes'] (Baumann and Tobin 2013: 24; my translation).
22. 'Je suis moi' (my translation).
23. 'L'argent lui sert à se protéger des sentiments, à contrôler' (my translation).
24. Hollier and Bloc argue that 'Sexual desire, the generative force of life, is conceived by Zola as potentially the most destructive of deviations from life's wholesome balance. He implies that, once perverted by desire, any woman, whatever her class background, will embrace prostitution as her natural mode' (1994: 783).
25. '[U]n bon film français sur le désir et qui montre la prostitution de manière assez pudique' (my translation).
26. '. . . qui court-circuite les explications rassurantes et dynamite les clichés' (my translation).

27. 'Mais c'est au niveau de la structure de ses films que l'aspect contradictoire de BB prend toute sa valeur, opposant le récit – qui lui donne la place de sujet – et le spectacle – qui en fait un objet. Elle est – ce qui est exceptionnel pour un personnage féminin – l'agent qui déclenche le récit, par son désir, à la fois sexuel et existentiel: pour sa "liberté" . . .' (my translation).
28. 'Le principe du film, c'était de scruter cette jeune fille avec des jumelles, puis d'essayer de s'en approcher. Pour percer son mystère' (my translation).
29. '. . . répondent l'impassibilité de Haydée, . . . et son éblouissant sourire, pure énigme qui prétend ne rien signifier et renforce . . . l'aveuglement du jeune homme, son trouble et sa rage' (my translation). As Sylvie Robic writes, 'Haydée never eludes men and spectators as much as when she seems to offer them – us – her smile. Haydée's smile is the emblem of a deep ontological ambiguity of Rohmer's cinema . . .' '[j]amais Haydée n'échappe autant aux hommes et aux spectateurs que quand elle semble leur – nous – faire l'offrande de son sourire. Le sourire d'Haydée est l'emblème de la profonde ambiguïté ontologique du cinéma de Rohmer . . .' (my translation).
30. 'Je voulais une fille qui nous échappe' (my translation).
31. Struggling to craft her story, Sarah finds inspiration in Julie's diary. Sarah's act of encountering the *journal intime* brings to mind de Certeau's description of reading as 'an activated space', a secret scene, '. . . a place one can enter and leave when one wishes; to create dark corners into which no one can see'. Thus, Julie's diary inspires Sarah's own fantasy in revealing her own story while pointing to her mystery: 'Reading is an activated space, a "secret scene" – to read is to be elsewhere, where they are not, in another world, it is to constitute a secret scene, a place one can enter and leave when one wishes; to create dark corners into which no one can see' (quoted in McNamee 2000: 489).
32. These types of narratives, alluding to an Oedipal struggle, call for a psychoanalytic reading as well that is not in the scope of this paper.

Works Cited

Ahovi, Jonathan and Marie-Rose Moro (2010), 'Rites de passage et adolescence', *Adolescence*, 4:74, pp. 861–71.

Alexander, Andrew (2014), 'Young and Beautiful's "nightmarish" sexploration fails to arouse', *Creative Loafing*, vol. 43, no. 4, <http://www.clatl.com/news/article/13078418/young-and-beautifuls-nightmarish-sexploration-fails-to-arouse> (last accessed 6 October 2016).

Baumann, Fabien and Yann Tobin (2013), 'Je voulais une fille qui nous échappe', *Positif*, September, pp. 22–6.

Benarous, Xavier and Guillaume Munch (2015), 'Perverse Temptation in Adolescence: A Case Report from the Movie *Jeune et Jolie*', *L'évolution psychiatrique*, 80, pp. 424–32.

De Bruyn, Olivier (2013), 'Jeune et Jolie', *Positif*, July, pp. 88–9.

Gauthier, David (2013), '"Jeune et Jolie" de François Ozon: demi-échec ou demi succès?', *Destination Ciné*, 14 September, <http://destinationcine.com/box-office/jeune-et-jolie-ozon-demi-echec-ou-demi-succes/> (last accessed 6 October 2016).
Hollier, Denis and R. Howard Bloc (1994), *A New History of French Literature*, Cambridge: Harvard University Press.
Kline, T. Jefferson (1992), *Screening the Text*, Baltimore: Johns Hopkins University Press.
McNamee, Sara (2000), 'Foucault's Heterotopia and Children's Everyday Lives', *Childhood*, 7:4, pp. 479–92.
Quandt, James (2011), 'Flesh and Blood: Sex and Violence in Recent French Cinema', in T. C. Horeck and Tina Kendall (eds), *The New Extremism in Cinema: From France to Europe*, Edinburgh: Edinburgh University Press, 2011, pp. 18–25.
Robic, Sylvie (2002), 'La Vraie beauté et son fantôme: *Six Contes moraux* d'Eric Rohmer', *Cinéma 03*, Spring, pp. 82–92.
Vincendeau, Ginette (1993), 'L'Ancien et le nouveau: Brigitte Bardot dans les années 50', *20 ans de théories féministes sur le cinéma*, CinémAction 67, pp. 141–6.

Films

Belle de jour, film, directed by Luis Buñuel. France: Carlotta Films, 1967.
Et Dieu . . . créa la femme, film, directed by Roger Vadim. France: Cocinor, 1957.
Jeune et jolie, film, directed by François Ozon. France: Mars, 2013.
La Collectionneuse, film, directed by Éric Rohmer. France: Les Films du Losange, 1967.
Les Amants criminels, film, directed by François Ozon. France: Mars, 1999.
Swimming Pool, film, directed by François Ozon. France: Mars, 2003.
Vivre sa vie, film, directed by Jean-Luc Godard. France: Solaris Distribution, 1962.

CHAPTER 5

Repetition and Difference: The Representation of Youth in the Films of Céline Sciamma

Karine Chevalier

Céline Sciamma (1978–), a graduate of La Fémis (the prestigious French state film school) finds her inspiration as much in the *cinéma d'auteur* as in more commercial cinema and TV. Her work can be situated somewhere between the twilight of the New Wave and the coming of the *cinéma du milieu*,[1] a new genre that sought to counter 'the bipolarity of today's films'[2] (Prédal 2013: 359). A new generation of filmmakers emerged, who played with the format of auteur films on the one hand and the established format of big-budget TV production on the other.[3] The resulting style, central to Sciamma's cinematic approach, is a melange of both aesthetics. The purpose of this article is to analyse how Sciamma renews the representation of youth in her triptych (*Naissance des pieuvres*, 2007, *Tomboy*, 2011 and *Bande de filles*, 2014). What is her position in regard to the highly codified American teen movie? How does she see herself in relation to the tradition of French auteur cinema in which teenagers are confronted with social reality and its laws? These are some of the questions that will inform my discussion. Firstly, I will analyse how Sciamma's debut *Naissance des pieuvres* revolves around two strategies: to repeat the conventions of American teen movies and to reposition the representation of youth in French cinema. Secondly, I will show how Sciamma's *mise en scène* aims more specifically to portray the birth of hidden desires in young female characters. From her first movie, Sciamma has sought to represent youth as a time when one is free to experiment with gender and sexual identities and in which cultural norms are both reproduced and subverted, resulting in a tension that deliberately creates confusion in the audience. Thirdly, I will discuss *Tomboy*, with particular attention to the ways Sciamma questions the standard representation of the tomboy figure, focusing on pre-adolescent identity games within the framework of documentary realism. Finally, in the third film of the triptych, *Bande de filles*, I will examine her treatment of the character of a teenage girl from the inner city and her evolving identity. In this too, her attention focuses on redefining the cinematic image of youth in *banlieue* filmmaking. I will conclude by showing how Sciamma's narrative and aesthetic concerns connect her to the *cinéma du milieu*, which allows her to reassure the audience with familiar formats, on the one hand, while driving it progressively to question the generic norms of gender identity, social cliché and film genre, on the other.

Individuation through Repetition

In *Naissance des pieuvres*, her first feature film, Sciamma draws inspiration from American teen movies. From *American Graffiti* (George Lucas, 1973) to *The Breakfast Club* (John Hughes, 1985), Hollywood transformed the teenage movie (teen pic) into a successful standardised subgenre. Sciamma's tribute to the teen pic seems strange, even deliberately provocative in the context of French cinema, which traditionally supports independent auteurs and does not target the adolescent audience the way teen movies usually do (Boutang and Sauvage 2011: 25). Sciamma admits to having played with the teen pic's conventions in order to prise her audience from their comfort zone and 'to further explore these starting points and offer the audience another journey' (Jousse 1994). This comment prompts the question as to how the film articulates the conventions of the teen pic in the context of French film production and for what purposes.

The codes of the adolescent film are clearly visible throughout the three stock characters. Floriane (Adèle Haenel), a blond girl with sensual curves, is the captain of the synchronised swimming team. She seems cold and haughty and yet has the reputation of being promiscuous. She embodies the smouldering *femme fatale* who attracts everyone's attention. Marie (Pauline Acquart), the intellectual, is the thoughtful one in the trio. Skinny, with an undeveloped body, she is fascinated by Floriane. Anne (Louise Blachère), her best friend, plays the role of the oddball. She is self-conscious about being fat but nevertheless indulges in mythomaniac fantasies. Sciamma explained: 'I wanted the physique of my actors to fit that *American Pie* template. The beautiful girl had to be very beautiful and blond, and the fat one quite uninhibited and awkward' (Jenkins n.d.). Too beautiful, too skinny, too big, these characters all have to manage a body image that determines their relationship to others, and Sciamma exaggerates these templates to the point of caricature.

Sciamma's codified *mise en scène* relies mainly on a play of opposites, pushing psychological concerns into the background. For example, in the locker rooms of the swimming pool Marie chastely removes her cotton bra without lifting her T-shirt while, in the same frame, Floriane shows off her silk bra and her developed breasts. Anne waits until the locker room is empty to get fully naked, her arms in the form of the Cross, symbolically offering her body to the absent François (Warren Jacquin), the boy she madly desires. Similarly, in the dance scenes, Marie, motionless, watches the inaccessible Floriane who dances seductively though completely immersed in her own world. In contrast, Anne, sweaty from the dance, is constantly on the lookout for François. These plays on opposites allow Sciamma to make her characters either sublime or grotesque. She faithfully relies on one of teen pic's conventions, which posits that empathy toward the adolescent body can only be based 'on the body of a god or that of a monster' (Davenas 2013: 26; my translation). The way Anne presses her lips onto the glass door of Marie's room is thus the monstrous version of Floriane's sensual kiss.

The characters' feelings are first and foremost conveyed by their bodies and actions, rather than through dialogue. Marie's fascination for Floriane extends to her sitting in the bathtub wearing a swimsuit and pointing her toes like an aquatic dancer in a pathetic imitation of the other girl's style. Meanwhile, Floriane's superficiality and solipsism are confirmed through the repetition of the make-up scenes. The film's sparse use of dialogue often echoes some of the clichés of American 'chick flick' movies, as is illustrated in the scene where Floriane eats a banana and is rebuked by another swimmer for acting indecently: 'Boys are all eyes when a girl eats a banana in the canteen. Everybody knows that. You don't care. You've gone to the other side' (my translation).[4] Playing up to her reputation, Floriane tongues her banana erotically and the audience can appreciate the joke as the scene takes place in a very dull and cold locker room away from any male gaze. Certainly, the film *American Pie* (Paul and Chris Weitz, 1999) 'reflects a major shift in contemporary teen culture that the girls ... are as hip to sex as the boy' (Shary 2005: 105), but Sciamma takes it a step further, adding her own brand of caricature and humour to the emancipation of the female voice on the subject of sex. Still a virgin, Anne longs to be deflowered: 'I'm really late. You see countries where girls are married at 14; I think it's cool. If I lived there, I wouldn't be in the situation I'm in' (my translation).[5] These outrageous comments, based on cultural differences, are deliberately subversive in the context of chick flicks.

The highly codified stylisation of the characters also applies to the setting. The Parisian suburb of Cergy-Pontoise is frequently depicted by the media as a violent area. Sciamma chooses to represent it as an uneventful and dull place. Her locations are defined by their anonymity, with red brick houses lining up quiet streets that resemble the American suburbs of the teen pic. 'It's a modern place where one can consider the present and the future ... The particular town in which *Water Lilies* is set doesn't have a French feel to it' (Jenkins n.d.). These *villes nouvelles* or new towns are the result of political planning and development designed to ease the pressure on a densely populated Paris. According to Sciamma, nobody has ever really filmed these towns and the stories they tell about the people who moved there: today's French lower-middle class (Jousse 1994). In the past, French cinema has often portrayed teenagers and their conflicts with authority figures (parents, school, police) against the iconic backdrop of Paris. With Sciamma's depiction of the suburb, the French audience thus discovers a part of the national space that had remained absent from the big screen until now. Following the 1995 riots, when French *banlieues* erupted in an unprecedented wave of violence after police *bavures* (slip-ups), some filmmakers had begun to bring into view on-screen the stigmatisation of young people living in deprived suburbs, their failure at school and violent conflict with the police. *Banlieue* filmmaking, whose aesthetic and themes are more firmly rooted in social realism, traditionally places parents in the background, stressing their ineffective authority. By erasing all adult presence, Sciamma adopts a radically different position regarding figures of authority. While adults often play a minor part in American teen pics, or are even totally absent, they retain their importance in France. Teen pics are aimed at a teenage audience whereas adults are French films' primary focus. Only popular French comedies targeting families, such as *La Boum* (Claude Pinoteau, 1980), establish a clear parallel between adult and adolescent characters, as they are seen undergoing similar sentimental crises. Sciamma, through her use of teen pic codes, manages to erase all adult presence without exclusively addressing an adolescent audience.

The originality of Sciamma's cinema lies for the main part in its ability to arouse the interest of film critics all the while using some of the tropes of a 'discredited' commercial genre. Indeed, French teen films are usually characterised by a dichotomy between adolescent and adult space to show the confrontation of the adolescent with the law and the reality (Egloff 2007: 179). These films reveal the nostalgia of the adult gaze onto a lost age and depict an existential crisis from an adult point of view. French films about adolescence seem devoid of structure, which reflects the uncompromising desire for freedom characteristically associated with youth. Conversely, Sciamma's highly constructed cinema offers to portray adolescence without the memes of the French neo-realism found in *À nos amours* (Maurice Pialat, 1983). She focuses solely on the teenager's perspective, shot 'epidermically, as inside a bubble' (Jousse 1994). The repetition of the conventions of the teen pic allows Sciamma to invite an adult audience to gradually venture into an unfamiliar space. The highly codified American teen movie powerfully shows how adolescence, based on a game of repetition and difference, is a spectacle, a parody of itself. The audience is left pondering what lies behind this adolescent masquerade.

Birth of a Hidden World

While American teen movies reveal an adolescent universe in which coming of age is the central issue, French filmmakers address the topic while generally focusing on emphasising the psychological development of the characters (Scatton-Tessier 2009: 235). In *Naissance des pieuvres*, Sciamma abandons the linear evolution of the traditional coming-of-age story and creates a stagnant time–space. Her main artistic concern is the depiction of the emergence of hidden female desire, the latter falling into three categories: frigidity, physical attraction and love. Floriane is frigid and remains so during the entire film. Her appearance is reminiscent of the typical blond characters of Gus Van Sant's movies. The American filmmaker is known for having renewed the representation of adolescents by combining the tradition of the European auteur film with the codes of the teen pic. Van Sant's mechanical dolls, as opposed to rebel girls, are conformist, speak robotically and seem lacking in emotion. Unlike these dolls, Floriane is able to confide to Marie that she is suffering from still being a virgin. This crucial task of losing her virginity is performed clinically, but Floriane continues to be a lonely *bimbo* in search of desire. The traditional pattern of the coming-of-age narrative has failed here. One can conclude that Floriane is in fact as marginal as Marie or Anne. The character of Anne strikes the audience with her infantile eccentricities, as in the scene where she buries her bra as an offering in front of François' house. In a scene mentioned previously, she stands naked, with her arms shaped like a cross, in front of the men's locker room, hoping that the young man, who usually ignores her, will emerge and be forced to look at her body. Religion is commonly used in cinema to impede the awakening of youth's physical pleasure (Davenas 2013: 72), such as in *Hadewijch* (Bruno Dumont, 2009). However, Anne's mystical tendencies attest to both her physical desire for François and her need for love, as she offers her body to the young man. Once she realises that she is only a sexual substitute, she spits on his face. Meanwhile, Marie's admiration for Floriane is limitless. She eats out of her friend's dustbin, and even manages to kiss Floriane at the swimming pool, at the end of the film. Floriane remains her usual cold and distant self, whereas Marie starts crying. Floriane, a narcissus type in love with her own image, reapplies her lipstick while Marie, through her tears, looks at herself in the mirror, as though confronting the image of a girl filled with desire for another girl for the first time.

In *Naissance des pieuvres*, feminine subjectivity finds its visual translation in the many representations of bodily fluids (tears, kisses, spittle, blood, sweating). Fluids are used as metaphors for feminine sexual desire, which Sciamma likens to a monster, or an octopus releasing its ink (Lalanne 2007). She films the three teenage girls as one female body with three hearts rather than as individuals. In the swimming pool, the girls are seen spreading their tentacle-like arms in offering. They open and close their legs hatching a tentacular desire. In their bedroom, they squash their lips against the windows like suckers. Despite centring her plot on the birth of homosexual desire, Sciamma's film cannot be considered as a *slasher*, a subgenre of the American horror film that evokes fear of deviant sexualities, but instead falls within the category of European auteur film. According to Shary, 'European films dealt with the issue of adolescent homosexuality more often and more confidently' (Shary 2005: 94). Sciamma frees her film from drama and passes no judgement on the discovery of homosexual desire. 'For me, homosexuality is not a subject, it is a journey. Overall, the film stops where most of the films that deal with this issue begin' (Jousse 1994). While coming-out narratives usually show the character developing from adolescence into adulthood, Sciamma freezes space and time in an aquatic universe, using blue filters to participate in the creation of an underwater world and focusing mainly on closed spaces. *Naissance des pieuvres* thus gradually moves away from realism to become a metaphor for the elusiveness of female desire. The latter finds its visual translation at the end of the film, when Floriane is seen dancing alone, her eyes closed, lost in her inner world. The *mise en scène* sets her apart from the other teens, who constitute a static and blurry background. In the final scene, Anne and Marie float on their backs in the swimming pool, their eyes closed. A high-angle shot reveals how the two bodies take the shape of a floating star, or octopus. In the last shot of the film, Marie opens her eyes and stares at the ceiling. The audience can associate the image of the ceiling with Marie's prior confession to Floriane:

> When you think about it, the ceiling is probably the last thing most people see. At least 90 per cent of the people who die, don't you think? I'm sure of it. And another thing, when you die the last thing you see stays printed in your eye, a bit like a photo. (My translation)[6]

This last shot of Marie may also refer to *la petite mort* (whether orgasmic for Marie, melancholic for Floriane or spiritual for Anne), which brings the viewers to reflect on their own mortality and desire. The 'death' of the film ends with this subjective teenage vision that transforms both the inner and outer world into one space of hidden desire.

In the teen pic, 'places symbolising submission to adult authority are opposed to places symbolising emancipation and that enable teenagers to elude the adult world' (Boutang and Sauvage 2011: 25; my translation). Sciamma avoids this binary opposition to focus instead on space as a metaphor of feminine sexuality, defined by a symbolic *fissure*. This is exemplified by the breach in Marie's fence, through which the girls slip in and out, or the long, hollowed-out line which divides the monumental architectural space leading to the columns of 'l'Axe Majeur' at Cergy-Pontoise, under which Floriane talks about the excessive presence of male desire in her daily life. Moving past the mundane American version of the suburb, Sciamma films the architecture of this utopian French suburb to highlight its sexual symbolism. In the same way, she films the pool as a seeping place, evoking the moist windings of desire. Filming the synchronised swimming, an exclusively female sport, allows Sciamma to evoke the feminine experience and society's pressure to conform to ideals of beauty. Teenage girls face the simultaneous birth of desire lived as an internal monster and the pressure of gender normativity imposed by society on the female body. The long tracking shot during the inspection of the swimmers to check that they are perfectly shaved reveals this insistence on uniformity and the need to discipline the body. 'For me, the film shows what a hard job it is to be a girl. It is therefore from the female's internal point of view' (Jousse 1994). These 'little soldiers made up like dolls' (Jousse 1994) are obedient to the dual imperatives of seduction and combat. At first glance, their bodies are harmonious and feminine, hiding their physical efforts behind smiles. By watching Floriane's training, both Marie and the audience discover the other side of this masquerade, as the military aspect inherent to this discipline is revealed to us once the music stops. We can then hear the laboured breathing interspersed with the rhythm counted out loud by the swimmers. Opening her eyes underwater, Marie sees a surreal spectacle of bodies, with limbs that open and close like octopuses. Filming the synchronised dance allows Sciamma to evoke the simultaneous birth of desire lived as an internal monster and the pressure of gender normativity imposed by society on the female body.

In a complete departure from the teen pic, which prioritises types over groups, Sciamma concentrates on the identity of the group. Like the synchronised swimmers, the boys, who all play water polo, form a homogeneous entity. At a party, they are all seen wearing panties over their faces. Only François, a typically successful sportsman without any psychological depth, emerges from the group, only to be quickly replaced by another boy. In *Douches froides* (Antony Cordier, 2005), released two years before *Naissance des pieuvres*, Antony Cordier refers to the construction of men's virility using sporting discipline as a backdrop. Whether it is combat sport or synchronised swimming, these activities work as a magnifying glass for the performances imposed on young people based on their gender. Both films attempt to show that a person is not born, but rather becomes a man or a woman. Cordier evokes the conflict of generation and social differences within a neo-realistic aesthetic framework, while Sciamma is interested only in the construction of femininity. While Cordier does not question social norms, Sciamma challenges them, following Judith Butler's ideas that:

> This 'being a man' and this 'being a woman' are internally unstable affairs. They are always beset by ambivalence precisely because there is a cost in every identification, the loss of some other set of identifications, the forcible approximation of a norm over one never chooses . . . but which we occupy, reverse, resignify to the extent that the norm fails to determine us completely. (Butler 1990: 339)

On the surface we see the swimmers' performance of femininity but the underwater scenes reveal a monstrous, allegorical body. Through a highly stylised *mise en scène* (the luminous scenery of pink waves embellishing the swimmers, and the subterranean and surreal atmosphere transforming them into an aquatic monster), Sciamma challenges the audience to understand youth in a new way in terms of cinematic standards. Sciamma reuses the codes of the teen pic to better distance herself from the realism of French auteur cinema. These auteur filmmakers have usually failed to explore the female inner world in the same way they have failed to throw any light on the coded nature of teenagers' performance and desire. In that sense, Sciamma's cinema echoes that of Catherine Breillat, who is known for questioning the traditional idea of the female adolescent as an object of male desire and instead chooses to depict female desire and its fantasies, including sadomasochism and rape, like she does in *À ma sœur!* (2001). Sciamma nevertheless avoids Breillat's propensity for abrasiveness and aggressiveness, so that, compared to Breillat's pornographic and morbid approach, Sciamma's feminism seems much more moderate. This does not prevent Sciamma from referring to the incestuous trends of French cinema: 'The adolescent girl, a frequent trope of mainstream French cinema, is most frequently represented as a Lolita-like-child-woman, an object of sexual desire designed to titillate the male voyeur and circumvent the challenge and threat of adult female sexuality' (Tarr and Rollet 2001: 37).

When Floriane is about to be deflowered by an older man as she initially wished, Marie comes to rescue her by hitting the window of the car parked outside the nightclub. 'She has to hurry because her father is waiting for her . . . He accompanied us because he was afraid that we would be approached by old perverts. Bye pop!' (my translation).[7] The girls laugh at the man's attraction towards young girls, and this laugh de-dramatises the scene. This stands in stark contrast with the final rape scene in Breillat's *À ma sœur!* that serves to underline the girl's incestuous fantasy. Sciamma only wants to depict the birth of desire without confining the characters to a sociological and sexual framework. Instead of adopting the male gaze, the audience identifies with a girl who happens to be attracted to someone of the same sex.

> I wanted everyone in the room to be gay for just ten seconds and, if not gay, to feel the love. Even as far away as that may be from the viewers' taste, they experience it. It becomes a journey that's not theirs, but it's familiar. (Oumano 2010: 214)

The spectator is thus free to decide about Marie's sexual identity and whether or not she has idealised the object of her passion. In so doing, Sciamma claims a political approach to filmmaking: 'It enables you to live experiences you would never otherwise undergo, and it opens your mind and body to other people's feelings' (Oumano 2010: 214).

With this first film, Sciamma positions herself between the conventions of the teen pic and independent cinema. Both types of filmmaking have evolved over time to offer a more accurate account of female subjectivity and to extricate the feminine figure from a male-centred gaze. Using the tropes of the teen pic to represent adolescence, Sciamma takes the spectator through familiar territory in order to better establish her view on the gendered representation of identity. This theme is central to her work as she addresses it throughout her trilogy.

Sexual Determinism: Between Repetition and Difference

Tomboy tells the story of Laure (Zoé Héran), a pre-adolescent girl who has just moved to a new town. She meets Lisa (Jeanne Disson) who initially mistakes her for a boy. Unbeknownst to her parents, and with the complicity of her younger sister Jeanne (Malonn Lévana), she pretends to be Michael, to all the other children's belief. Built on a Hitchcockian model, the suspense throughout the film consists in wondering when and how Laure's lie will be exposed. From the beginning, the spectator sees an individual with masculine attributes (short hair, blue sports clothes) and behaviour. Laure is seen driving the car with her father (Mathieu Demy), taking sips of beer, playing football and enjoying fights with boys. She is in every way opposed to Jeanne's display of femininity (she wears long hair, likes pink dresses, dances in a tutu and wants to be a hairdresser). In this film Sciamma lays out the dual signifiers of gender that have come to shape the representation – as well as our understanding – of childhood. There is an unmistakable critique of the commercial world that divides games, songs, television programmes or the colour of clothes by gender: pink and blue, girly and boyish, and so on. Such is the power of these signifiers that it is only when Laure is seen naked in the bath that her sexual identity is finally revealed to us. Puzzled at first, the audience gradually becomes an accomplice of Laure's performance and her pretending to be a boy. Gender performance, as defined by Butler, depends on the use of simulacra. In *Tomboy*, these simulacra are specifically associated with the world of childhood and the idea of play. Laure makes a phallus for herself out of Plasticine. She creates a boy's swimsuit by cutting up a girl's bathing suit. Michael's character is based on the principles of imitation and repetition of boys' gestures. The football scene, where only boys are playing, is very effective in this respect. While Lisa is relegated to the role of cheerleader, Laure/Michael carefully observes the boys before she runs on to the pitch. Her subjective point of view sheds light on the signifiers of masculinity on display during the scene (spitting, taking off your shirt, victory's shout). She imitates them and her success at doing it is confirmed by Lisa – who still has not realised she is not a boy – when she tells Laure/Michael 'You play well!' Gender is defined not only by acts, but also by social and linguistic norms, as is confirmed during Laure and Lisa's first encounter, when Lisa addresses Laure using a masculine pronoun. Laure subsequently assumes her new social identity successfully: she is stronger than boys when she fights and Lisa falls in love with her. Unfortunately, at the end, Laure has to reveal her sexual identity and dress as a girl to conform to social norms. Within her family, Laure is given greater leeway from her parents when it comes to her display of 'masculine' behaviours. However, when her mother (Sophie Cattani) discovers that she goes by the name Michael, she asks Laure to dress as a girl to be able to blend in with the other kids when term starts. 'I do not mind you playing "the boy". It doesn't even make me sad. But this can't go on' (my translation).[8] Beyond punishment, Laure's mother exerts her parental duty over her to protect her against possible discrimination.

The tomboy is a strong cultural figure that offers an alternative to the dominant feminine code of conduct, even if it runs the risk of perpetuating masculine gender stereotypes (Thorne 1993). However, this state of affairs is evolving, with the growing involvement of girls in traditionally male sports. Sciamma uses the figure of the tomboy to question and complicate gendered performances. According to Butler, these performances, based on gender stereotypes, have no ontological status. It is only the representation of various acts that constitutes a possible reality. Sciamma shows how her characters' identity is defined by a succession of female and male performances via a strange game of *mise en abyme*. When Lisa invites Michael to her room to put on make-up, the spectator witnesses a performance within a performance: Laure, a girl, is playing being a boy who is playing being a girl. Laure/Michael is a single entity made up of imitations and multiple identities superimposed throughout the film. 'Gender is a kind of imitation for which there is no original; in fact, it is a kind of imitation that produces the very notion of the original as an effect and consequence of the imitation itself' (Butler 1991: 19). Sciamma depicts identity as something fluid that cannot be defined by the binary male/female opposition. Laure dresses as a girl, yet she is also defined by some of the masculine attributes and behaviour developed throughout the film. Zoé Héran, who was specifically casted for her androgyny, successfully conveys this gender indeterminacy through her performance.

Sciamma's film techniques when directing child actors play a significant part in the director's naturalistic tendencies. She only uses two cameras so that the young actors are not disturbed by the presence of the crew (Frois 2011). She avoids rehearsals and favours long shots to capture the spontaneity of her young actors, but does not favour improvisation. Sciamma's work relies on a precise choreography of the bodies, usually shot in large static takes to allow freedom of movement. Sciamma prefers silences to monologues. She trusts the immediacy of children's games (football games, dancing, drawing, playing cards, water fights). The children forget that they are acting, caught up in the intensity of the game. Sciamma's aesthetic choices also challenge the spectator, as the audience is used to films with the opposite scenario, and boys exploring gender nonconformity. However, these portrayals often rely on caricature, as is the case in *Ma Vie en rose* (Alain Berliner, 1997). According to Waldron:

> [o]n a similar theme, Sciamma adapts a naturalistic approach and sets her nonconformist protagonist firmly within the material reality of her lived existence. As such, *Tomboy* removes the cushion of camp parody that Berliner offered his audience to soften the blow of the sub-urban intolerance he depicted. (Waldron 2013: 61)

While the two filmmakers show the dichotomy between sex and gender, Sciamma avoids any hyperbole thanks to her documentary-like approach that merges authenticity and social realism. Yet, the audience is called to distance themselves from the characters in order to better appreciate the *mise en scène* of gender performance and the double entendre of the dialogues. When the children discover the truth, they attack Lisa by stating that 'If Michael is a girl, then you kissed a girl; it is disgusting!' (my translation).[9]

Lisa is not angry but sad. Her reply is ambiguous. 'It is disgusting' can be understood as condemning Laure's lie more than the same-sex kiss. The public will be able to read her love and her homo-heterosexual attraction for Laure/Michael beyond gender borders. Sciamma intends to reinforce the ambivalence of the signified so the audience understands the inconsistency and the lack of definition with regard to gender identity. She is also stating that attraction for a person does not depend on what sex they are, as can be seen in the girl's reconciliation at the end.

According to Gilles Deleuze in *Différence et répétition*, simulacra reveal 'a world of *impersonal individuations* and *pre-individual singularities*; a world which cannot be assimilated to everyday banality but one in which . . . resonates the true nature of that profound and that groundlessness which surrounds representation' (Deleuze 1968: 347). The character of Laure/Michael is presented as experimenting with a series of possible individuations: at this age, gender identity has not yet been influenced by sexual identity. Children's games allow a more fluid identity. As the psychologist and psychoanalyst Serge Tisseron notes in his preface to *L'Adolescente et le cinéma* (Tisseron 2014), adolescence used to be synonymous with existential crisis. Today, it corresponds to the entry into the world of multiple identities, as is most notably evidenced with video games and their avatars. From a sociological and psychoanalytical point of view, the process of individuation is the result of the internalisation of multiple patterns of interaction under the effect of intersubjective and external communication. Maturity is measured by the ability of individuals to integrate different facets of their personality. Multiple identities are 'floating identifications'. Psycho-rigidity is avoided, provided that 'its identities do not escape the subject and that it is capable of differentiating the inside from the outside, the interiority from exteriority' (Tisseron 2014: 11). After the Second World War, the figure of the female adolescent evolved from the image of the girl–woman into an emancipated character. Dupont and Paris conclude that with the rise of economic liberalism and its corollaries (exclusion, unemployment, precariousness and insecurity) it is necessary to analyse 'the scope of the possibilities offered by the different ways of being a woman or a man in the housing projects' (Dupont and Paris 2014: 62). The pressure of the social and racial determinism specific to French political reality associated with the *banlieue* is to be added to the sexual determinism.

Social Determinism: Between Repetition and Difference

In the third film of her 'youth trilogy', *Bande de filles*, Sciamma locates her narrative in the fraught climate of the Parisian *banlieue*, as the story focuses on a young Black teenager named Marième (Karidja Touré) and the development of her character in relation to a group of girlfriends. Sciamma rejects the stereotype of the *crapuleuses* or 'bad girls', a social group who has been the subject of recent studies (see Rubi 2005). Sciamma plays with the aesthetic and thematic codes of *banlieue* films by avoiding the subgenre's predilection for male characters, ethnic mixing and physical violence captured with a hand-held camera. *Banlieue* filmmaking has shown the marginalisation of young people from immigrant backgrounds (see Tarr 2005). It has also changed the approach of the female character, moving from misogyny to feminism and from passivity to violence (see Milleliri 2011). As I have written previously (see Chevalier 2016), Sciamma internalises violence, minimising it thematically and aesthetically. This coming-of-age narrative, divided into acts, evokes the structure of the classical novel. Separated by fades to black, these acts can be perceived as Marième's different persona: her exclusion from school, her initiation into a gang, her association with a drug lord and her escape from the *banlieue*. Marième must transform herself to play the various roles that will enable her to advance as a *banlieue* girl. Whereas with *Tomboy*, Sciamma played with the conventions of gender, with this film she explores the conventions associated with the *banlieue* film (theft, racketeering, drugs, vengeance for honour, dance battles, sex). Marième is aware of the power of these rituals and accepts them to preserve her independence (a room of her own, a chosen lover). Despite her physical transformations (hair style, clothing), she remains the same caring girl, looking after her younger sisters. She first emulates Lady (Assa Sylla), the leader of the gang, only to gradually supplant her. In order to survive in the world of dealers and to avoid becoming a prostitute, she opts for a more masculine look (breasts bandaged, loose clothing, short hair). To fulfil the stereotype of the *kebla* ('black' in *verlan*) and go unnoticed in the Parisian parties, she wears a blonde wig and heavy make-up. These constant makeovers do not erase her strong determination to free herself from social and ethnic determinism. Yet, this possible freedom is only hinted at towards the end of the movie. Marieme lives each transformation with a Deleuzian intensity: 'do not add a second and a third time to the first, but carry the first time to the "nth" power' (Deleuze 1968: 2). Individuation, according to Deleuze, is experienced through a string of accidental relationships. Marième, like any other girl, is under the various pressures associated with the construction of femininity. Lady, the head of the girl gang, Abu (Djibril Gueye), the drug dealer, and Ismaël (Idrissa Diabaté), her boyfriend all incite the performances necessary to Marième's freedom. Filming teenagers allows Sciamma to represent human transformations and their confrontation with their surrounding world. This confrontation often starts within a group, which then allows for the individuation process to take place, as it does in the opening scene of *Bandes de filles*. The way Sciamma films female American football evidently echoes the *Friday Night Lights* series (Peter Berg, 2004–6). This opening scene offers a powerful metaphor for existence: from mud comes life. Masked figures emerge in succession from a blurred image of amorphous matter and proceed to grapple with each other. The gendered identity of the girls is revealed gradually, as their mutual emulation and solidarity beyond the formless and anonymous group. Back home, away from the brightly lit stadium, the group cowers under the pressure of the male gaze and the law of silence that prevail in the *banlieue*. The group is dismantled, the girls parting in different directions until disappearing in the dark. The camera eventually focuses on the main character of the film, Marième. Sciamma films the girl's loving gaze towards Ismaël, the first spark that will give her strength throughout her various masquerades and confrontations. From the group to the gang, and under her many disguises, Marième remains unchanged, ready to take on new identities and blend into a new group. Rather than try to fit in (back in the family home, getting married, having children with Driss), Marième, in the last scene of the movie, symbolically comes out of the frame, then goes in again as if she were willing to take possession of it, filmed in profile, determined, ready for all the new metamorphoses which will help her advance in life.

Sciamma intentionally casted mainly Black actors to erase differences and focus on Marième's will to escape her destiny, regardless of her skin colour, ethnic and social identity. However, Sciamma tends to reduce the sociological reality to superficial sitcom images. She leaves aside the conventional low-angle shots of the greyish and oppressive council flats. She focuses instead on the fluidity of space (bridges, arches) using blue filters to mirror Marième's stable personality. As in Sciamma's previous films, the female vision predominates, counteracting cinema's sexist tendencies to please a voyeuristic male gaze with images of naked female bodies. During the scene where Marième loses her virginity, Sciamma shows Marième's subjective view on Driss's body. Marième takes the initiative for sexual intercourse by starting to undress Driss, but the scene ends here. A feminist, Sciamma does not resort to the avant-garde aesthetic advocated by Laura Mulvey (*Visual and Other Pleasures*, 1989) to fight the sexist viewpoint. Sciamma's feminist discourse is elaborated within cinematic conventional forms. Claire Johnston argues that playing with stereotypes from commercial cinema allows filmmakers not only to reveal and provoke female desire but to break away from stereotypes. 'In order to counter our objectification in the cinema, our collective fantasies must be released: women's cinema must embody the working through of desire: such an objective demands the use of the entertainment film' (Johnston 1973: 31).

A clear example of this strategy is given in Sciamma's first film, *Naissance des pieuvres*. We see Marie hidden behind a column in the changing rooms of the pool, watching Floriane being caressed by a boy. This *mise en abyme* of voyeurism in a film about female sexuality gives way to a multilayered depiction of the act of looking, both at the diegetic and extra-diegetic level, as the characters' voyeuristic gaze echoes that of the viewer in the fictional world. This heterogeneity of desire activates a dialogue with patriarchal traditions and clichés. Playing with social, sexual and cinematographic forms thus appears to be the foundation on which Sciamma's trilogy is based.

Each of Sciamma's films questions conventions in a game of repetition and individuation. Shot in Cinemascope, *Bande de filles* clearly shows Sciamma moving away from TV aesthetics, and gives a cinematographic presence to young Black women, who are generally ignored by the big screen. Sciamma plays with depth of field and blurry images to erase any geographical references, which allows her to focus on characters' subjectivity and physicality. The dance battle scene in the Parisian business district of la Défense is a perfect example of what Sciamma is trying to achieve through her *mise en scène*. She opts for a lateral travelling shot introducing the smiling girls and their accomplices one by one, revealing their individuality and their power as a group. Dance scenes in movies traditionally conjure up femininity and serve as a mating ritual, while sports assert masculine virility (Dupont and Paris 2014: 283). Here, the dance battle is spontaneous and friendly. The female dancers are represented as sexual beings who are in control of their lives. They are not subject to the male gaze. Physical activities such as the synchronised dance in *Naissance des pieuvres*, the football in *Tomboy* or the street-dance in *Bande de filles* are the result of gender differences. For Sciamma, dance and sport are symbolic of intense energy, releasing the body of male–female polarity and representing it as free from voyeurism. This is exemplified in the scene where Marieme dances with her friends in a hotel room. In a similar fashion to Laure's dance in Lisa's bedroom, as portrayed in *Tomboy*, the scene in the hotel room operates in a vacuum, without any outside onlookers witnessing it. The sequential structure of her films as well as her frequent use of tracking shots serve to heighten the feeling of immediacy and the multiplicity that make up the present time. Sciamma's cinema endeavours to reveal true human nature as an assemblage of progressive, moving and multiple individuations. According to this view, nothing is ever identical and individuation is ontological to the world.

Conclusion

Sciamma's cinema depicts the process of individuation over a lifetime. The experience is more intense during adolescence, a time when young people gain agency over their own lives. Adolescence is thus neither defined by confrontation with authority nor by a nostalgic projection filtered through the adult gaze, but instead by a perpetual existential becoming. Sciamma's feminist approach demonstrates the pressures of gender, and social and ethnic norms by playing with cinematographic codes. In a French national context, her work corresponds to the *cinéma du milieu*. This style of cinema can be conceived of as a commercial product designed by an auteur who chooses to play with the narrative and/or aesthetic codes pertaining to a specific film genre. Sciamma subverts these codes by infusing them with a feminist discourse. She does not wish to become the spokesperson for same-sex relationships, but instead for the desire for love in general. One desires a human being before a gendered being. I have shown that her cinema should not be viewed in opposition to the codes of the teen pic or of *banlieue* filmmaking. Sciamma's films are the sum of the repetitions of the signifiers that interact with these conventions with humour, sublimation and deterritorialisation. Finally, while recent studies on adolescence have mentioned the play-acting nature of teenagers,[10] Sciamma shows how the repetitive nature of these performances allows for the transgression of norms *through* repetition. According to Deleuze, repetition is philosophically transgressive. In films, repetition encourages a cathartic distance. Beyond the familiar depiction of youth, the audience is introduced to various issues specific to French society, such as the marginalisation of the young people living in the *banlieue*, the under-representation of Black people in the media or the lack of acceptance for same-sex marriage. Cinema for Sciamma is a political art form that uses the simulacrum to reveal the truth. 'Cinema is a total intervention on reality. Even a documentary that is edited is a lie that tells the truth, as Jean Cocteau said. And Picasso said it's a lie that tells the truth about lies' (Oumano 2010: 168). The Cartesian rationalist tradition wants to believe in the reality of things in terms of their stability and permanence. For Sciamma, as for Deleuze, the opposite is true: everything is becoming and the figure of youth has the power to embody this becoming in cinema.

Notes

1. The expression *cinéma du milieu* refers to 4 to 7 million euro budget films perceived as art films targeting a mainstream audience. It is associated with *Le club des 13* (a group of filmmakers led by Pascale Ferran) who reported on the dysfunctional bipolar nature of French film production (auteur versus mainstream film, art versus industries, small versus big budget) that endangers the quality and diversity of French cinema.
2. '[c]ontre la bipolarité du cinéma actuel (art et industrie, mini et maxi budgets, indépendants et formatage TV, film d'auteur et bandes commerciales . . .)' (Prédal 2013: 359).
3. Such as François Ozon or Christophe Honoré.
4. 'Tous les mecs regardent quand une fille mange une banane à la cantine. Je t'assure, c'est connu. Remarque, toi, tu t'en fous, t'es passée de l'autre côté'.
5. 'Je suis vraiment en retard. Tu vois les pays où on marie les filles à 14 ans, moi je trouve ça cool. Si j'habitais là-bas je n'en serais pas là.'
6. 'Quand on y pense, le plafond, c'est sûrement le dernier truc que voient plein de gens. Au moins 90% des gens qui meurent, tu crois pas? C'est sûr! En plus quand tu meurs, la dernière chose que tu vois elle reste imprimée dans ton œil. Un peu comme une photo.'
7. 'C'est pour dire à ma copine qu'il faut qu'elle se dépêche, parce qu'il y a son papa qui l'attend! Il nous a accompagné parce qu'il avait peur qu'on se fasse aborder par des vieux porcs! Salut papa!'
8. 'Ça me dérange pas que tu joues au garçon, ça me fait même pas de la peine, mais ça peut pas continuer.'
9. 'Si c'est une fille, tu l'as embrassée! C'est dégueulasse!
10. See for example recent feminist research challenging Deleuze's concept of becoming with bodies as in Rebecca Coleman (2008) 'The Becoming of Bodies'.

Works Cited

Boutang, Adrienne and Célia Sauvage (2011), *Les 'teen movies'*, Paris: Librairie philosophique J. Vrin.

Butler, Judith (1990), *Gender Trouble: Feminism and the Subversion of Identity*, New York: Routledge.

Butler, Judith (1991), 'Imitation and Gender Insubordination', in Diana Fuss (ed.), *Inside/Out: Lesbian Theories, Gay Theories*, New York: Routledge, pp. 13–31.

Chevalier, Karine (2016), 'Le cinéma français face à la violence: du *New French Extremism* à une violence intériorisée', *Modern & Contemporary France*, 24:4, pp. 411–25.
Coleman, Rebecca (2008), 'The Becoming of Bodies', *Feminist Media Studies*, 8:2, pp. 163–79.
Davenas, Olivier (2013), *Teen! Cinéma de l'adolescence*, Montélimar: Les Moutons électriques.
Deleuze, Gilles (1968), *Différence et répétition*, Paris: Presses Universitaire de France.
Dupont, Sébastien and Hugues Paris (2014), *L'Adolescente et le cinéma. De Lolita à Twilight*, Toulouse: ERES.
Egloff, Karin M. (2007), *Les Adolescents dans le cinéma français: Entre deux mondes*, Lewiston, NY: Edwin Mellen Press.
Frois, Emmanuelle (2011), 'Filmer à hauteur d'enfant. Propos recueillis par Emmanuelle Frois', *Le Figaro*, 20 April, <http://www.lefigaro.fr/cinema/2011/04/19/03002-20110419ARTFIG00607-filmer-a-hauteur-d-enfant.php> (last accessed 7 December 2017).
Jenkins, David (n.d.), 'Céline Sciamma: interview', <http://www.timeout.com/london/film/caline-sciamma-interview> (last accessed 7 December 2017).
Johnston, Claire (1973), *Notes on Women's Cinema*, London: Society for Education in Film and Television.
Jousse, Thierry (1994), 'Entretien avec Céline Sciamma, réalisatrice de *Naissance des pieuvres*', <http://www.cinemotions.com/interview/10573#6kPsTPHUeXuOlorY.99> (last accessed 7 December 2017).
Lalanne, Jean-Marc (2007), 'Entretien Céline Sciamma – "A cet âge-là, tous les désirs sont invivables"', *Les Inrockuptibles*, 31 July, <http://www.lesinrocks.com/2007/08/30/cinema/actualite-cinema/entretien-celine-sciamma-a-cet-age-la-tous-les-desirs-sont-invivables-1165339/> (last accessed 7 December 2017).
Milleliri, Carole (2011), 'Le cinéma de banlieue: un genre instable', *Mise au point*, 8 August, <http://map.revues.org/1003> (last accessed 7 December 2017).
Oumano, Elena (2010), *Cinema Today: A Conversation with Thirty-Nine Filmmakers from Around the World*, Piscataway, NJ: Rutgers University Press.
Prédal, René (2013), *Histoire du cinéma français: Des origines à nos jours*, Paris: Nouveau Monde éditions.
Rubi, Stéphanie (2005), *Les Crapuleuses, ces adolescentes déviantes*, Paris: Presses Universitaires de France.
Scatton-Tessier, Michelle (2009), 'Filmer l'adolescence au féminin: *Les filles ne savent pas nager* d'Anne-Sophie Birot', in Danieka Di Cecco (ed.), *Portraits de jeunes filles: L'adolescence féminine dans les littératures et les cinémas français et francophones*, Paris: L'Harmattan, pp. 231–46.
Shary, Timothy (2005), *Teen Movies. American Youth on Screen*, London: Wallflower Press.

Tarr, Carrie (2005), *Reframing Difference: 'Beur' and 'Banlieue' Filmmaking in France*, Manchester: Manchester University Press.
Tarr, Carrie and Brigitte Rollet (2001), *Cinema and the Second Sex: Women's Filmmaking in France in the 1980s and 1990s*, New York: Continuum.
Thorne, Barrie (1993), *Gender Play: Girls and Boys in School*, New Brunswick, NJ: Rutgers University Press.
Tisseron, Serge (2014), 'Préface', in Sébastien Dupont and Hugues Paris (eds), *L'Adolescente et le cinéma. De Lolita à Twilight*, Toulouse: ERES, pp. 8–12.
Waldron, Darren (2013), 'Embodying Gender Nonconformity in *Girls*: Céline Sciamma's *Tomboy*', *L'Esprit Créateur*, 53:1, pp. 60–73.

Films

À ma sœur, film, directed by Catherine Breillat. France: Rezo Films, 2001.
American Graffiti, film, directed by George Lucas. USA: Universal Pictures, 1973.
À nos amours, film, directed by Maurice Pialat. France: Gaumont, 1983.
Bande de filles, film, directed by Céline Sciamma. France: Pyramide Production, 2014.
Douches froides, film, directed by Antony Cordier. France: Bac Films, 2005.
Hadewijch, film, directed by Bruno Dumont. France: Tadrart Films, 2009.
La Boum, film, directed by Claude Pinoteau. France: Gaumont 1980.
Ma Vie en rose, film, directed by Alain Berliner. France: Haut et Court, 1997.
Naissance des pieuvres, film, directed by Céline Sciamma. France: Haut et Court, 2007.
The Breakfast Club, film, directed by John Hughes. USA: Universal Pictures, 1985.
Tomboy, film, directed by Céline Sciamma. France: Pyramide Distribution, 2011.

CHAPTER 6

Mia Hansen-Løve, Postfeminism in France and the Melancholic Girl

Fiona Handyside

Father: So, Clémence, what's going on?
Clémence: OK, I'm coming! I was just finishing this chapter.
Father: Are you sulking?
Clémence: No, but I'm not in a great mood.
Father: Why?
Clémence: Because.[1] (Mia Hansen-Løve, *Le Père de mes enfants/Father of My Children*)

Mother: Come on, get up. Don't lie around like that. Honestly, it's not working out for you.
Camille: What?
Mother: Your relationship.
Camille: I'm happy. I mean, I can be depressed from time to time if I like.
Mother: Camille, since you started going out with Sullivan, you haven't stopped crying.
Camille: I'm crying for joy. I cry because I'm melancholic, that's why.[2] (Mia Hansen-Løve, *Un amour de jeunesse/Goodbye First Love*)

Introduction

In these two pieces of dialogue taken from the second and third of Mia Hansen-Løve's films, a parent and a daughter argue about the daughter's state of mind. While the parent attempts to chivvy their child into action, the daughter responds that her emotional state is part of her way of being, not open to alteration, and furthermore, beyond a rational explanation. She has the right to feel sad, to cry, to be depressed, to be in a bad mood. Notably, both these girls will suffer loss, but these conversations take place early on in each film, before any major dramatic occurrence, and thus signal not so much a reaction to events as an emotional disposition. Hansen-Løve herself identifies her first three films as a trilogy of sorts. While they don't share characters, settings or narrative, what they do share, Hansen-Løve explains, is an interest in exploring girlhood through a melancholic perspective:

> [t]o me it's very obvious that they make a trilogy . . . they are so much connected – three portraits of young girls, about the passing of time, about the power of filming – about melancholy, in a way. They come from the same parts of me. But I have a hard time finding a title for this trilogy. It would be easy to make a title with 'fathers and daughters,' but that's not exactly what I want to say. (Wilner 2012: n. p.)

My interest in this chapter is in how these three films – *Tout est pardonné/ All is Forgiven*, *Father of my Children* and *Goodbye First Love* – offer us stories of girlhood infused with a melancholic sensibility, and what the feminist politics of this might be. These are films invested with the cultural prestige and specificity of contemporary French auteur film while partaking of a transnational and cross-cultural interest in female adolescence and its cinematic expression. They respond to changing social, cultural and political norms for adolescent girls, who have grown up from the 1990s onwards in an era labelled as postfeminist, and offer us a specifically French representation of contemporary cinematic girlhood and its attempts to grapple with the rapidly shifting gender norms which frame adolescence and its relation to social expectations. They present us with girls who live in comfortable if slightly bohemian middle-class worlds, whose parents or partners operate in artistic milieu as poets, museum curators, film producers or architects. The girls are slim, dark-haired, white, heterosexual and attractive, impeccably and beautifully dressed; we see them studying, playing with younger children, going to the cinema, visiting the countryside, walking in parks. These are girls who would seem on the surface then to be able to take advantage of the opportunities for travel, education and employment that feminism has offered for young women, and certainly they operate in worlds which take for granted girls' access to legal and social equality. Yet all three films finish ambiguously, leaving the lone girl's fate uncertain. In the first film, Pamela/Constance Rousseau gets up from a table and walks away into the dark woods, away from her family. In the second, Clémence/Alice de Lencquesaing cries in the back of a taxicab, being driven away from Paris. Her mother tells her they have no time to go and visit the cemetery where her father is buried, and the song 'Que sera, sera' plays over the images of the car driving through the streets. At the end of *Goodbye First Love*, Camille/Lola Créton swims in a river by herself, as Johnny Flynn and Laura Marling's neo-folk anthem 'The River' plays.

Music and images work together to offer us the sense of girls' grappling alone with uncertain futures, when surely they should be in a position to conquer the world? Catherine Driscoll illustrates that a focus on white, affluent, middle-class teens such as those of Mia Hansen-Løve's trilogy usually belongs to the 'clean teen' genre; a light-hearted depiction of carefree adolescence, as opposed to films that depict youth as a problem (Driscoll 2011: 29–38). Samantha Colling argues that, similarly, millennial girl teen films maintain a white, middle-class perspective and promote the same carefree version of youth. Girls from this environment become associated with the feeling of fun, and films communicate ideals and images of girls as perfectly poised between innocence and experience (Colling 2017: 1–20). In contrast, Mia Hansen-Løve's white, middle-class girls suffer traumatic losses and are associated with feelings of sadness and melancholy. Rather as Colling demonstrates these girl teen films' aesthetic investment in key moments of fun (via for example fashion, makeovers, sports and dance performances), so Hansen-Løve's films offer an investment in moments of solitude, quiet contemplation, journeys and walks that prompt thought, nostalgia and melancholy. A repeated shot from all three films is of the girl alone, lying on a bed, curled in on herself (see Figures 6.1, 6.2 and 6.3).

As Hansen-Løve's comment quoted above indicates, it is especially in their approach towards time that these films carve out a different approach to girlhood. They eschew mapping out a suitable life cycle for their female heroines and promoting the narrative closure of the heterosexual happy ending that frequently marks 'clean teen' films. The films spend time with their girl protagonists as they variously, depending on their ages, play with

Figure 6.1 Clémence in *Father of My Children*.

Figure 6.2 Camille in *Goodbye First Love.*

dolls, travel on the métro, walk in Parisian parks, paddle in lakes, swim in rivers, go to parties, put on theatre shows, attend classes, visit old ruined churches, go to the cinema. They offer us a series of images with little dialogue, often accompanied by music, to compress the action. While more classically this technique is used to speed up time, here it is used

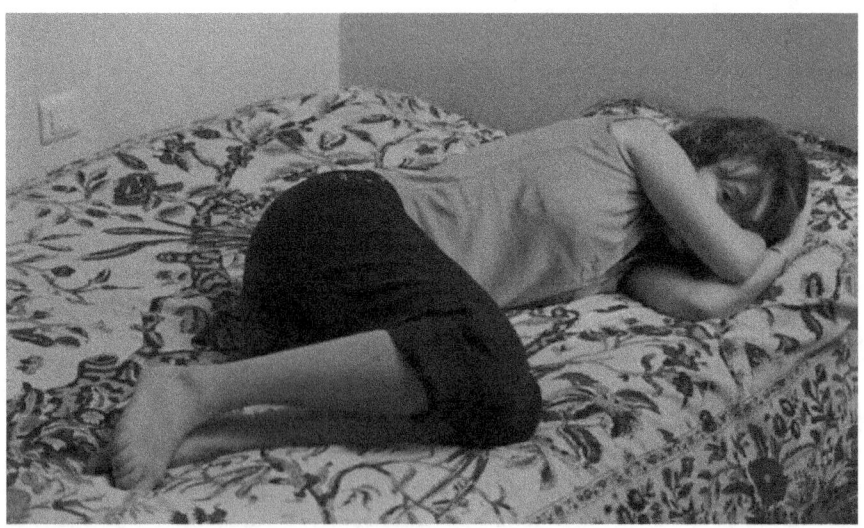

Figure 6.3 Pamela in *All is Forgiven.*

to slow down and dilate time. Time weighs on us in its materiality and depth, answering indeed Laura Mulvey's call for a feminist cinema that would 'free the look of the camera into its materiality in time and space' (1975: 18), making us aware of the passing of time and the losses that mount up.

French Models and Transnational Girlhoods

While Mia Hansen-Løve's take on the teen film owes something to the French, New Wave tradition, rather than the American teen genre, in its promotion of a singular aesthetic and auteur-based trilogy alongside its pro-youth stance, in other ways it updates and twists it through its sympathetic engagement with the figure of the girl rather than the boy. Geneviève Sellier has demonstrated how, despite its innovation and youthful zeal, the New Wave was dominated by masculine subjectivity and concerns, with *Cléo from 5 to 7/Cléo de 5 à 7* (Varda, 1962) and *Hiroshima Mon Amour* (Resnais, 1959) 'the sole films from this period to attempt to position a female character as a focal consciousness with whom the subject might identify' (Sellier 2001: 126). The male buddy tendency in French cinema persists to the present day, with films such as *Welcome to the Sticks/Bienvenue chez les Ch'tis* (Boon, 2008) and *Brice de Nice* (Huth, 2005) proving extremely popular at the box office. Nevertheless, commentators such as Emma Wilson (2005), Tim Palmer (2011) and Mary Harrod (2015) have noted a relatively equal allotment of narrative subjectivity to women in some films, especially romantic comedies; a growth in the number and success of female filmmakers; and a concomitant attention to female perspectives and experiences in French film. While René Prédal rejects the notion of the 'women's film',[3] he nevertheless observes that films by women offer 'studies of women, conceived by women, whose gaze gives us personal works with a tone that is sometimes far removed from that of masculine filmmakers'[4] (2002: 141). As Wilson notes, Prédal's emphasis on individuality is significant in a film culture which greatly values auteur status. Within this focus on individual style and tone, Prédal does note a recurrent theme of the 'runaway girl',[5] which Wilson (2005: 218) explains shows how auteurist approaches need to take into account questions of gender and genre. Furthermore, as Palmer (2011) demonstrates, given French cinema's long-standing institutional support for the debutant and youthful filmmaker, this increased representation of female experience and emotion has been especially marked by an intense interest in girlhood. Palmer discusses the five 2008 nominations for the Best First Film César to illustrate his point; all directed or co-directed by female filmmakers

(Lola Doillon, Céline Sciamma, Mia Hansen-Løve, Anne le Ny and Marjane Satrapi) and four of the five specifically focused on a girl's coming of age. Such an interest in girls and girlhood in French cinema echoes an increasing visibility of girls within the global mediascape, to the extent that Sarah Projansky (2014) has labelled girls hypervisible. While the ability of girls to secure attention and articulate sociocultural anxieties is not unique to contemporary life, girlhood is currently constructed in the media as a lightning rod for questions of social progress, as girls are objects of either adoration or derision. Girl culture circulates through international media texts that cross national borders with ease. For example the Disney behemoth *Frozen* (Buck and Lee, 2013), with its sweet story of sisterly love and captivating landscape of icy sparkle,[6] was released in France as *La Reine des neiges*, where it was in first place at the French box office for 2013, with over 5 million tickets sold; this was part of a global success, with the film translated into forty-one languages and earning a worldwide box office gross of over $1.2 billion.

This complex accommodation between French specificity and the transnational nature of contemporary cinematic representations of girlhood marks Hansen-Løve's films as they perform a conscious modelling on the New Wave but incorporate multiple European cities (Vienna, Paris, Copenhagen) and various languages (German, Italian, English), gesturing toward the porous nature of identity, filmic or otherwise. As Catherine Driscoll explains, Hollywood films about youth tend to be analysed from a sociological and discursive perspective, rather than for any formal or aesthetic innovations (Driscoll 2011: 6). They are assumed to be aimed at an idealised teen audience who wishes to see their lives reflected on the screen, so that genre studies of what gets labelled 'teen film' tend to concentrate on the films of, for example John Hughes, rather than those of François Truffaut. This creates a circular effect, when only films produced within Hollywood are seen as 'teen' films, with other cinemas' interest in narratives of growing up placed into the more amorphous category of 'youth' cinema. Yet, argues Driscoll, it is more productive to ask whether the idea of adolescence we find in the Hollywood teen film is intrinsically an American one exported to other contexts, or if we can find cross-cultural patterns and motifs in films that place teen experiences fore and centre. Driscoll emphasises how teen film across national borders shares a discourse on adolescence. Some films emphasise the institutionally framed world of adolescent dependence, others the refusal of or struggle against that framing, and many the interdependence between the two (Driscoll 2011: 18). Hansen-Løve's recurrent exploration of the domestic lives of her characters and the inchoate emotion of both loving and resenting parents fits her films into this broad category, even if the emphasis on her auteur status seems to make them not entirely or 'just' teen films in the usually accepted terms of the genre.

Furthermore, while Hansen-Løve's characters share with American teen film protagonists the struggle between a desire for autonomy and the need to belong to networks of love and obligation, the emotional quality of the films is very different. The teen film tends towards either romantic comedy, from *Sixteen Candles* (Hughes, 1984) to *Clueless* (Heckerling, 1995) and *Easy A* (Gluck, 2010), or horror, from *Hallowe'en* (Carpenter, 1978) to *Scream* (Craven, 1996) and *It Follows* (Mitchell, 2014), so that its emotional range is open to relatively easy verbal communication (either laughter or screams) and neat narrative resolution (sex or death). In contrast, Hansen-Løve develops an understated realism, with elliptical narratives, lack of resolution, and dramatic events (such as the suicide of a father) occurring off-screen. Her main focus is on a girl learning to live with the pain of loss. Her characters do not so much work through their loss, as incorporate it into their way of being, so that the loss accompanies them and perhaps even sustains them. This revisiting of, and dwelling within, loss, makes Hansen-Løve's girls melancholic. Rather than embracing the fun and sparkle that mainstream girl culture promotes as the most appropriate behaviour and style for girls, her girls are quiet, nostalgic, alone, often in tears. Camille's mother's exasperated response to Camille's distress upon her second rupture from Sullivan, 'when you are finally going to mourn this love?',[7] could stand as an epigraph for all Hansen-Løve's girls, stuck as they are in a state of melancholia and in rebellion against their mothers whose decisions and attitudes they chafe against. Meanwhile, fathers, while loved, abandon their children, leaving them stuck. In the first two films, the fathers commit suicide. In the final film of the trilogy, Camille's father divorces her mother during an ellipsis in the narrative and simply disappears from the story. This positioning of the mother and father in relation to the girl echoes perfectly Angela McRobbie's argument that

> [t]he young woman in contemporary political and popular culture is asked to reconcile autonomy and possibility of achievement with compliancy with a patriarchal authority which is dissolved, de-centralised and nowhere to be seen. She must do this also in a context where feminism and feminist theory have also in effect and for good reason dismantled themselves. (McRobbie 2009: 122)

While the young woman is promised a new world of possibility, she is required to reach this destination on her own, with no resource, and has only herself to blame if she fails.

Melancholic Scenes

It is helpful at this point to draw this discussion out by exploring scenes and situations that exemplify this melancholic girl, before going on to consider how we might understand Mia Hansen-Løve's films' broader relations to postfeminist cultural production through their articulation of this emotion. There is a peaceful interlude in *Father of my Children*, where the family take a holiday in Italy, a sequence discussed in detail by Wilson, whose thoughts inform my own reading. Clémence, the oldest daughter, has stayed at home in Paris, allowing the film to focus on the middle child, Valentine/Alice Gautier. The sequence allows her to rehearse the loss of her father, Grégoire/Louis-Do de Lencquesaing, making its focus the question of her autonomy. The family arrive at a small church and the framing closes in on an image of Valentine and her younger sister Billie/Manelle Driss sitting on a pew and Grégoire moving in behind them. From this vantage point, looking over their shoulders, he shows them the mosaics in the church dome, pointing out palm trees, olives, white lilies, birds and squirrels. He then asks the children if they have noticed the hand at the top of the dome; Valentine asks who it is, and Grégoire, himself pointing upwards, replies that is the hand of God. As Wilson explains,

> the visual rhyme of the mosaic and Grégoire's hand seems lavish. Yet the film is so understated, there is such simplicity, naturalness and candour in the editing and in the rhythm of the conversation, that the symbolism does not disrupt the sure, smooth, realist surface. (Wilson 2012: 280–1)

The film subsequently cuts to the children playing by a pool in the grotto. At first, we watch Grégoire and Valentine playing, but the gentle, unobtrusive camera moves into close-up on Valentine as she wonders off by herself, tracing her features as she submerges herself into the milky waters of the pool. Wilson comments that 'the image of her face amidst the opacity of the water is at once vivid, dimensional, and other worldy . . . Valentine is always moving, slipping in and out of the field of vision' (Wilson 2012: 281). The scene ends with her mother's hand reaching out for her to help her from the pool. In its gentle substitution of hands (from God, to father, to mother), the film suggests the inevitability of shifting relations, of loss. Valentine floats in a pool, cut off from the world. The scene expresses the very strangeness and mystery of human existence and its meaning as it recalls the foetus in amniotic fluid and looks toward the non-existence of death, in a world in which God's presence is at best uncertain.

Similarly, Camille in *Goodbye First Love* exists in a world in which social relations are tentative and febrile and God is absent. As an architecture student, she studies a series of modernist buildings, including the Bauhaus building in Dessau-Rosslau, the Kastrup sea baths in Copenhagen and the Sanatorium d'Aincourt. This final building contains within it the history of the twentieth century, having served as, in turn, a sanatorium, concentration camp, children's medical centre and finally a rehab clinic.[8] Buildings operate in this world less as functional objects than as symbols of loss and pain. Furthermore, her own building designs serve as an index of her melancholic state. Early in her student training, Camille submits an architectural maquette for a student hall of residence. A tutor comments on its qualities and defects, admiring its austere nature but commenting on the cramped nature of the rooms and the impracticality of separating dining and studying facilities with a large lake. He concludes that 'this hall of residence is more suitable for a solitary retreat than a student community. You've designed a monastery.'[9] This final comment draws a slight smile of recognition from Camille who has remained silent throughout his discussion, shrugging when he asks her opinion. The film cuts to Camille in a classroom listening to another student reading aloud from Adolf Loos' treatise on architecture, containing his philosophy that the house is judged from different criteria to the work of art, but must please everyone. The camera moves from the student reading to focus on Camille, slowly approaching her face so that the sequence finishes in a close-up on her profile. We watch Camille listening, but the impact of the words, and their emphasis on architecture as a social act, is left ambiguous, the contrast with Camille's own aesthetic left implicit. We see Camille, still dressed in the same outfit, sitting at a different desk, reading her diary. Focusing in on the girlish handwriting, we too can read Camille's recording of her loneliness and estrangement as she records how long it has been since she split up from her boyfriend Sullivan/Sebastien Urzendowsky. We cut from this to a scene of girls in a dressing room, its concrete walls lit through a bluish filter that enhances their coldness. A pair of red shoes is passed to Camille, who we seeing dressing herself into a uniform of blue vest top, red sparkly shorts, stiff red net tutu and bright blonde wig. As she puts on the wig, fast disco music plays, and Camille steps out into a club, her face more animated than in the entire previous sequence. This scene, far more typical of the fun aesthetic described by Colling, is here marked as entirely performative and artificial, as Camille fakes happy girlhood for money.

Hansen-Løve's films are structured so that audiences too can have the affective experience of melancholia, as we revisit certain moments that trigger memories for us as well as for the characters in the film. For example, *All is Forgiven* opens with shots of Vienna at sunrise. We begin with an image of the airport at night, the runway and traffic control tower lights twinkling; cut to an image of a park and then a courtyard, progressively lighter; and finish with the image of a tram interchange, the sky crisscrossed with overhanging electric wires. A tram glides into the frame on a circular track before the image fades to black and we learn we are in Vienna. Over these establishing images, Matt McGinty's miner's lullaby, 'Corrie Doon', plays. The deceptively simple lullaby, with its hypnotic tune, compares a baby snuggling in its cot to a father working in the mine. The contrast between the song – in English – and the images of Vienna, and between the intent of the song – to lull a child to sleep – and the time of day, dawn, is curious. Eleven years later in terms of the story, and seventy minutes later in terms of screen time, in a different city, Paris, we see a young woman, Pamela, travelling on the metro with her friend, having just spent the day with her father from whom she has been estranged. The camera moves from close-ups on Pamela's face to images of the city shot through the window of the moving carriage, the buildings cropped by the frame of the window or obscured by the graffiti tagged on it; we see the orange glow of the sun, telling us it is sunset. Over these images, 'Corrie Doon' plays. In both sequences, the music is extra-diegetic. The resonances between the sets of images – of trams and metros, of sunrise and sunset, of Vienna and Paris – are reinforced through their accompaniment by the same music. The lyrics, talking of father and child relations, take on a new emotional power, while the repetition of the music takes the spectator back to the start of the film, echoing the intense nostalgia and regret Pamela feels for time lost. The sequence concludes with an image of Pamela lying alone on her bed, curled into the foetal position.

Postfeminism and Melancholia

Such an interest in and deployment of melancholia, and its attachment to adolescent girls bears a significant relationship to Angela McRobbie's account of contemporary girlhood, in which she argues that gender melancholia has become tied into the very definition of what it means to be a young woman. Hansen-Løve's films then offer us a strikingly different perspective from which to analyse postfeminist culture and its impact on girls, outside Hollywood teen genre representational and affective norms but with an intense interest in the figure of the girl that is relatively new to the French cinematic landscape.

For McRobbie, the melancholic girl is the normative product of postfeminist culture. One of McRobbie's main claims about contemporary society is that it develops a particularly pernicious attitude towards feminism, in what she calls a double entanglement. In political and popular culture, feminism is both taken into account as a kind of common sense ('of course women should have the vote!') but also dismissed as irrelevant, angry and old-fashioned. More broadly, this double entanglement involves invoking social and liberal progress, in the areas of, for example, sexual rights, which leads to the subtle undoing of more radical agendas associated with the more combative politics of anti-racist, anti-heterosexist thinking. What need lesbian, gay, bisexual and transgender (LGBT) activism now that equal marriage is available? Where this invokes the end of the need for such radical politics, this very discussion of ending invokes its own failure, that is the failure to truly bring about an equal society, and as such, civil society is haunted by what it repudiates, and this re-emerges as melancholia and loss. For middle-class young women, who have been exposed since birth, through their education and within their families, to feminist 'common sense', this haunting takes the form of disavowed longing for what feminism might have achieved. Feminist thought has questioned, rather than overturned, traditional gender roles. Women are addressed as if they are equal to men, and girls as if they are equal to boys, but in reality there has been no radical overhaul of gender hierarchies. This sense of loss then is perhaps not so much for the revival of a historically accurate version of feminism, but a utopian feminism which is an object-to-be-desired, but for which the longing must be repressed. Girls are exhorted to manage themselves as an index of their agency and control, so that popular culture borrows a language of feminism with none of its structural critique. It is girls and women, rather than society, who are encouraged to change.

In particular, McRobbie focuses her attention on the fashion photograph, which she explains produces 'heterosexual melancholia'. She argues that the fashion photograph operates at a distance from heterosexuality which puts it at a distance from the magazine's other content. Images produced by the fashion photograph conjures up a sphere of female homosexuality, a same-sex eroticism that gives the genre a pleasurable mystique but that means it must also be very carefully controlled. She suggests that in order to hold up the prohibition against female homosexuality, culture invokes this desire among women, only to eliminate it. However, this illicit desire leaves a trace, becoming a kind of haunting around the edges of the fashion image. McRobbie uses Diana Fuss's argument that the fashion image locks its viewers into a kind of rerun of the mirror phase through the endless looking from certain angles at faces so beautiful they are brimming with maternal *jouissance* and plenitude. This produces an interplay of pleasure and panic, as the viewer is reminded of a time of unbounded love, but also total dependence. Finally, this genre is dominated by a tendency to cut the body up into parts, showing legs, arms or parts of the face, echoing the young girl's experience in the early post-mirror phase development, when she is asking 'Is what I see me?' 'Do my parts make up a whole?' 'What have I lost?' The fashion image is therefore a psychically overloaded genre, and the fascinated looking it invokes bears a relation to the girl's always shaky passage to adulthood and acquisition of mature female sexual identity. Fashion photographs play over and over the distance from heterosexuality, the model gazes are distracted, turned away from the camera, sullen, refusing the male gaze. The images frequently invoke a drug-induced hallucinatory experience, and the models look depressed, unstable and neurotic. McRobbie argues that the fashion photograph therefore performs an important role in female psychic life, as it provides a distance, or reprieve, from the demands of the heterosexual matrix at the level of fantasy. It also activates a nostalgic longing for a time lost, pregnant with impossible and undirected desire. It visualises the disturbance that comes from the interplay of desire with constraint, with models hemmed in by the frame, held within the fashion asylum. These settings then become the site for the playing out of heterosexual melancholy, that is to say the mourning for the same-sex object which was once loved but which must be abandoned in order for gender to become intelligible within the heterosexual matrix. The fashion image both contains and compensates for the loss. Containment also works metaphorically, for with the loss of feminism (and the love between women it promised), women come to have no alternative than to recognise themselves with the 'feminine pathologies' of popular culture. Their sense of loss transforms into self-berating for not being perfect enough to compensate. McRobbie explains that it is important to engage with the fashion photograph's psychic underpinnings because this

> [e]nables us to engage with why the source of pain remains so nebulous and opaque. There is endless displacement in relation to precisely where subordination and subservience 'kick-in'. What does it mean for young women to live out a situation which tells them they are now equal, and that for sure there is no longer any need for sexual politics, and yet also suggests this equality has been mysteriously arrived at, without requiring adjustment or serious change on the part of patriarchal authority? (McRobbie 2009: 105)

McRobbie concludes that feminism itself becomes an 'unavowable loss' for young women; it exists only as a ghost of itself. The State, media and popular culture work together to produce female melancholia and its associated 'illegible rage'; girls and women punish themselves for their failure to perfect themselves. This pre-empts the reinvention of feminist politics and instead sends female energy into constant self-surveillance and encourages the speaking of female pathologies as a way of regaining control (McRobbie mentions artwork by Tracey Emin or the songs of Amy Winehouse as typical cultural products working through these issues). Over time, these practices become normalised as part of modern femininity itself. Young women then find themselves constituted as melancholic subjects three times over: first, through the abandonment of same-sex love object; second, through the losses sustained in approaching a feminine identity within a patriarchal world; third, through the unavowed loss of feminism and its promise of sexual equality. What emerges is both an attachment to this loss as constitutive of the self (so that the young women berates the older feminist) and a rage at the forced powerlessness of the abandonment of the feminist ideal.

How then might we understand Mia Hansen-Løve's distinct study of melancholia and girlhood to resonate with McRobbie's discussion of melancholia's importance to understanding feminism's role in contemporary social life and popular culture? In similar terms to the fashion photograph discussed by McRobbie, the male gaze is frozen out of the frame in her films, both in narrative terms, as the films document men leaving, and metaphorically, through a dynamic, moving, often hand-held camera which observes alongside the girl in an attitude of sympathetic encouragement rather than sexual objectification. Furthermore, the films underline the self-sufficiency and privacy of their girl subjects, whose thoughts and needs are not entirely evident, and whose future trajectory extends beyond the narrative reach of the film. Emma Wilson argues that, in their close and careful attention to the embodied nature of human experience, and the particularly fraught passage of the female adolescent toward womanhood, Mia Hansen-Løve's films show us how our identities are not fixed, but rather shifting, precarious and ultimately unknowable, even fully to ourselves. She goes on to suggest that 'despite their melancholy subject matter – . . . the fathers commit suicide – these films are about an affirmation of an ongoing, precarious, shifting subject position and identity' (Wilson 2012: 278). Bearing in mind McRobbie's comments that I discuss above, we can in fact link together the films' interest in the girls' opacity and melancholia. The interest in the girls' becoming, their changing subjectivity on screen, is intimately connected in these films to the loss of patriarchal influence. Rather than understanding this as a chance to embrace new futures, as the more extreme postfeminist notions of the girl subject might encourage, Hansen-Løve shows us how girls are compelled to move forward, to develop, but that to do so means living with pain. Hansen-Løve's girls come then to crystallise a particularly vicious aspect of postfeminist culture, which demands that girls view themselves as projects to perfect while diffusing patriarchal authority into some distant but still powerful memory to be lived with. While clearly these stories of rupture and loss are not just metaphors for changing patriarchal power structures, they powerfully call up the strong emotions of melancholia and attachment to lost objects, showing how these permeate the privileged and pampered worlds the films describe. An early exchange between Clémence and her father seems exemplary here, and I cited it at the start of the chapter. Clémence is unhappy simply 'because'; she does not need to (or cannot) name the source of her dissatisfaction. Her father tells her she should be grateful for the material opportunities she has, and their big house. On this occasion, what snaps her out of her unhappiness is not this reminder of her privilege, however, but watching her two younger sisters Valentine and Billie performing a show, as if a retreat to an earlier stage of girlhood, one less marked by the pressures of gender and sexual identity, and where there is a joy in trying on different ways of being, eases the weight of her angst.

The postfeminist injunction to be an agentic and active woman as a sign of one's liberation, while still conforming to rigid gender norms, is given a particular twist in contemporary France, where a certain version of feminism has become instrumentalised as the Republican way of life in service of a heavily racialised agenda. In one of his presidential campaign videos, Sarkozy explains that controlling immigration is in line with Republican values, through exhorting a vision of French Republicanism as intimately linked to female emancipation which is itself symbolised through legal abortion. 'Women, in France, are free, like men; free to circulate, free to marry, free to divorce. The right to abortion, equality between men and women, is part of our identity'[10] (quoted in Fassin 2012: 167). The French girl/woman is one who has embraced equality as common sense, and has embraced her professional and sexual autonomy, and therefore gender equality has become mainstreamed. In this context, however, any failure to achieve on the part of girls is construed as an individual failure within an egalitarian framework, and in particular any perspective which takes into account class or race difference is dismissed, thus perpetuating once again a neo-colonial perspective in which white middle-class French society and especially the French State offer opportunities to girls and women they lack elsewhere. Hansen-Løve's films show us the toll on girls of this model of French citizenship, as any failure to progress is due to individual flaws rather than any institutional structures. It is worth remembering this in the context of a government that has banned the veil in schools and in which French ministers proclaim the naked female body as a symbol of the Republic and freedom.[11] The French government endorses a form of liberation which expects women to be attractive to men on the street and to show their bodies, to act as sexual free agents, as a sign of the nation's well-being and good health. This fusion of the national and the universal results in a narrative of citizenship that suggests that the choice of universalism is one that can be made only by those who have been historically formed to be capable of making it. The suppression of difference slips into Hansen-Løve's films almost despite themselves, as when Clémence's father recounts the story of the Templars to his daughters, or when in a fit of rage Victor calls his wife a German bitch. Furthermore, a discourse of French exceptionalism, from the mid-1990s onwards, associated with commentators such as Mona Ozouf, renders feminism itself an American object and anathema to a French Republican tradition of *galanterie* and celebration of sexual difference. As sociologist Eric Fassin makes clear, the 2000s has seen the enthusiastic reception of the 2005 translation of Butler's *Gender Trouble*; the flourishing of Master of Arts (MA) programmes in gender studies in French universities, such as at the *École des Hautes Études en Sciences Sociales*; the introduction of civil partnerships, known as PACS (Pacte civil de solidarité); Ségolène Royal as the first woman to reach the second round while representing a major party; and finally supporting gay marriage and adoption, and controversies surrounding pornography and prostitution (Fassin 2011: 143–58). Sexuality and gender are clearly very much part of the French political landscape rather than foreign to it. However, as Mona Chollet explains, following the strength of the exceptionalism discourse, played out as recently as the Dominic Strauss-Kahn affair, which in some quarters condemned 'American puritanical attitudes' more than rape culture, there has been a lack of any kind of critique of beauty culture in France compared to the US. On the contrary, beauty culture is increasingly ingrained. In particular, the skirt has been mobilised as a symbol of a liberated Republican femininity. In November 2010, the organisation *Ni Putes, Ni Soumises* organised an auction of celebrity skirts at the Palais de Tokyo in Paris, in aid of female victims of violence. In spring 2011, the TV channel ARTE organised a themed evening around skirts, culminating in the appearance of Loubna Méliane, contrasting herself to oppressed veil wearing women and claiming her place as a daughter of the Enlightenment in her denim skirt and fishnet tights. French femininity is enshrined as a national treasure, almost a brand mark. Luxury brands such as Louis Vuitton Moët Hennessy and Pinault Printemps Redoute (owner notably of Saint Laurent and Gucci) promote a glamorous French beauty culture, frequently incarnated by French female film stars and models such as Catherine Deneuve, Audrey Tautou, Inès de la Fressange, and communicated to the mass market through such bestsellers as Mireille Guiliano's *French Women Don't Get Fat* (2005) (Guiliano works for LVMH) (Chollet 2012). The melancholia McRobbie describes finds a particularly harsh twist in French culture where beauty culture itself, and repressive feminine norms, become tied into Republican discourses of citizenship which ironically claim to be entirely gender-blind. French postfeminism promotes a rhetoric of Republican equality while constantly reminding girls that performance of that very liberated femininity depends on a narrow conception of beauty culture. Hanson-Løve's slender, white, heterosexual, Francophile girls are afflicted by melancholia in a culture which places such performances of femininity into an impossible double bind. In such a context, the films' endings, with their emphasis on uncertainty, ambivalence and hesitancy, provide the only solution, which is to keep going even while the pain remains. Hansen-Løve's girls' defiance is that they insist on their right to sadness, and to feel pain, rather than attempting to mask or overcome it.

Notes

1. 'P: Eh, Clémence, alors?
   C: Ça va, j'arrive! Je terminais juste mon chapitre.
   P: Tu fais la tête?
   C: Non, mais je ne suis pas de très bonne humeur.
   P: Et pourquoi non?
   C: Parce-que.' (All translations my own unless otherwise stated.)
2. 'M: Allez. Remets-toi. Reste pas prostrée comme ça. Vraiment, ça te réussit pas.
   C: Quoi?
   M: Le couple.
   C: Je te dis que je suis heureuse. J'ai bien le droit de me déprimer un peu des fois.
   M: Camille, depuis que tu sors avec Sullivan tu n'arrêtes pas de pleurer.
   C: Je pleure de joie. Je pleure parce que je suis mélancolique, voilà.
3. 'Film de femmes'.
4. 'des études de femmes conçues par des femmes dont le regard donne des oeuvres personnelles au ton parfois éloigné de celui des cinéastes masculins'.
5. 'Fille en fuite'.
6. I thank Clara Goulart for first drawing this film to my attention.
7. 'Quand est-ce que tu feras enfin le deuil de cet amour?'
8. This discussion of Hansen-Løve's buildings is indebted to Catherine Wheatley, who kindly sent me an as yet unpublished paper (2017).
9. 'cette résidence est plus adaptée à la retraite solitaire qu'à la vie collective. Ce que tu as imaginé, c'est un monastère'.
10. 'Les femmes, en France, sont libres, comme les hommes, libres de circuler, libres de se marier, libres de divorcer. Le droit à l'avortement, l'égalité entre les hommes et les femmes, ça fait partie aussi de notre identité.'

11. I am thinking here especially of Manuel Valls' claim in August 2016 that 'Marianne elle a le sein nu parce qu'elle nourrit le peuple, elle n'est pas voilée parce qu'elle est libre ! C'est ça la République!' ('Marianne has a bare breast because she feeds the people, she's not veiled because she's free! That's the Republic!').

Works Cited

Chollet, Mona (2012), *Beauté fatale: Les Nouveaux Visages d'une aliénation féminine*, Paris: La Découverte.
Colling, Samantha (2017), *The Aesthetic Pleasures of Teen Girl Film*, New York: Bloomsbury.
Driscoll, Catherine (2011), *Teen Film: A Critical Introduction*, New York: Bloomsbury.
Fassin, Eric (2011), 'A Double-Edged Sword: Sexual Democracy, Gender Norms, and Racialized Rhetoric', in J. Butler and Elizabeth Weed (eds), *The Question of Gender: Joan W Scott's Critical Feminism*, Bloomington: Indiana University Press, pp. 143–58.
Fassin, Éric (2012), *Démocratie précaire. Chroniques de la déraison de l'État*, Paris: La Découverte.
Harrod, Mary (2015), *From France with Love: Gender and Identity in French Romantic Comedy*, London and New York: I. B. Tauris.
McRobbie, Angela (2009), *The Aftermath of Feminism: Gender, Culture and Social Change*, Thousand Oaks, CA: Sage.
Mulvey, Laura (1975), 'Visual Pleasure and Narrative Cinema', *Screen*, 16:3, pp. 6–18.
Palmer, Tim (2011), *Brutal Intimacy: Analysing Contemporary French Cinema*, Middletown, CT: Wesleyan University Press.
Prédal, René (2002), *Le Jeune cinéma français*, Paris: Nathan.
Projansky, Sarah (2014), *Spectacular Girls: Media Fascination and Celebrity Culture*, New York: New York University Press.
Sellier, Geneviève (2001), 'Gender, Modernism and Mass Culture in the New Wave', in J. S. Williams and Alex Hughes (eds), *Gender and French Cinema*, Oxford: Berg, pp. 125–37.
Wheatley, Catherine (2017), 'Vocation and the Quest for God in the Films of Mia Hansen-Løve', unpublished paper given at *Film and Philosophy* conference, Lancaster University 4–6 July 2017.
Wilner, Norman (2012), 'Interview with Mia Hansen-Løve', *Now*, 23 August, <https://nowtoronto.com/movies/features/interview-with-mia-hansen-landoslashve> (last accessed 1 August 2018).
Wilson, Emma (2005), 'État Présent: Contemporary French Women Filmmakers', *French Studies*, 59:2, pp. 217–23.
Wilson, Emma (2012), 'Precarious Lives: On Girls in Mia Hansen-Løve and Others', *Studies in French Cinema*, 12:3, pp. 273–84.

Films

Le Père de mes enfants, film, directed by Mia Hansen-Løve. France: Les Films du Losange, 2009.

Tout est pardonné, film, directed by Mia Hansen-Løve. France: Pyramide Distribution, 2007.

Un Amour de jeunesse, film, directed by Mia Hansen-Løve. France: Les Films du Losange, 2010.

CHAPTER 7

Frames of Desire and Otherness: Queer Bodies Caught *in-between* France and the Maghreb

Walter S. Temple

Youth populations in France occupy a unique position in the economy of transnational relations. Maghrebi adolescents and young adults throughout the *hexagone* are often relegated to peripheral or in-between spaces of Franco-Arabité, giving way to problematic constructs of identity and trans-belonging. In a similar way, but from the *inside looking out*, 'French' youth who challenge cultural norms of expected social behaviours also find themselves at the margins of 'mainstream' society. Further complicating this scenario, and of particular interest to this study, many young lesbian, gay, bisexual, transgender and queer (LGBTQ) North Africans are under intense pressure to adopt a heteronormative lifestyle. As Abdelwahab Bouhdiba reminds us in his landmark study *Sexualité en Islam*, 'the entire Arabo-Muslim cultural system is centered on the need to identify, analyze and understand Tradition' (Bouhdiba 2014: 4). In such context, and as the data that follows suggests, 'tradition' often becomes linked to various modes of heteronormativity as the adolescent embarks on a sobering journey toward self and being in the context of queer-inclined scenarios and situations.

Taking cue from Bouhdiba's understanding of tradition, I argue that France, certainly prior to a revision of anti-LGBTQ legislation in 1980,[1] continues to be qualified as a nation redolent with deeply rooted hetero-norms. As such, LGBTQ 'French' youth, much like the Maghrebi adolescent, are equally subjected to forms of gross marginalisation, a condition that is further exacerbated when relationships blend race and national origin. Such cross-pollination gives way to queer subjects who are caught in-between two highly distinguishable spaces of desire and belonging. This article examines the relationship between film and contemporary culture – and how the camera's lens aptly captures the realistic fault line that is the north/south divide. Jacques Martineau and Olivier Ducastel's *Le Drôle de Félix* (2000) and Abdellah Taïa's *L'Armée du salut* (2013) will be placed into dialogue with a case study that was conducted in Paris, France, during the summer of 2016. The questions that inform the anthropological inquiry are closely related to the films examined in that they help us to further delineate the interwoven topoi of race, sexuality and migration that qualify Ducastel and Martineau's, and Taïa's work.

In addition to the inherent psychosocial difficulties associated with being homosexual in both Western and Arab cultures, a number of studies[2] have shown that unemployment rates among young adults in France remain high, a thematic we will return to momentarily when considering *Le Drôle de Félix*. In this vein, LGBTQ youth, particularly those who identify as belonging to migrant populations, are too often ostracised, thereby widening the gap that separates them from the northerner – who is often empowered by his race and/or national origin in both professional and social milieus. The films that I consider here underscore such thematics and respond, either implicitly or explicitly, to questions of trans-identity and immigration as they relate to queer desire and belonging among French and Maghrebi youth. Power constructs will be revisited as the French and Maghrebi youth character is visualised in the films under consideration – and quite literally embodied by the real-life subjects interviewed. This study also places into question how visual representations of same-sex desire challenge, and in some instances reverse, the divide between north and south.[3] Field research will be compared to (and juxtaposed against) the visual narratives examined.

Dennis Altman argues that questions of identity become linked to 'finding the right balance between tradition and modernity, while recognizing that these terms are vague, problematic, and politically contested' (Altman 1996: 79). In what is perhaps a foreshadowing of an argument Joseph Massad underscores in *Desiring Arabs* (2007),[4] Altman appears to evoke what is here the fragility of blending North African and French identities as they relate to the pillars that define and delineate the cultures of the two regions.

As revealed in a series of interviews I conducted in markedly diverse neighbourhoods[5] in Paris, LGBTQ youth appear to be divided on whether transnational and bicultural relationships[6] are socially acceptable. Subjects who identified as having North African origins expressed at least some concern in regards to how they are perceived and consequently negatively labelled by the 'French', particularly when navigating 'spaces dominated by French attitudes'. Participants who self-identified as being 'Français de souche',[7] on the contrary, overwhelming agreed that France is moving toward more expansive inclusion measures, and argued that within the last ten years in particular, the country has moved beyond the problematic discourse associated with colonial-era racism. This is perhaps due in part to limited recognition of colonial power structures, as well as the 'French' youth's inability to personally relate to the trauma of migration. Yet despite recent and often-widely publicised conversations on immigration and inclusion, France's migrant and minority communities continue to reside at the margins of contemporary French society. As such, the various ways in which the northern subject perceives and interacts with the southern body begs renewed consideration of how power structures are evolving somewhat, yet remain stagnant in certain settings.

The medium of film allows us to more closely examine the in-between space of otherness by responding to visual representations of alterity as spoken by French and Arab voices at the north/south divide. In order to elucidate the problematics of the transnational encounter at stake here, I consider two films that underscore, through a diversity of modalities, the inherent difficulties of navigating modes of queer desire that are synonymous with implied 'forbidden liaisons'. What is particularly interesting to examine is the at times contrastingly different ways these encounters are framed – and how they underscore the motif of otherness by drawing our attention to the filmmakers' visualisation of such desire.

Before commenting more specifically on these films and how they relate to contemporary French and Francophone youth subjects, it is helpful to consider how the film industry engages with what some critics understand as the changing dynamics of the north/south encounter. Speaking of Morocco's film industry following *les années de plomb*,[8] Valerie Orlando suggests, 'Since 1999, [Morocco] has turned many pages of its dark past . . . in order to move forward to embrace the global age, all the while wrestling to keep its cultural uniqueness intact' (Orlando 2011: 1). In reflecting on the significance of a so-called global age, one must acknowledge not only the larger opus of human rights, but how, specifically, the 'opening up' of these cultures impacts minority groups who are now presumably better positioned to express their desire for a lifestyle that may go against the grain of 'tradition'. In a similar manner, a number of French filmmakers, including Ducastel and Martineau, draw attention to the tensions that continue to be observed in metropolitan France vis-à-vis discriminatory behaviours.[9] In viewing Ducastel's and Martineau's films, we are confronted by such egregious acts and are thereby propelled to more closely consider the intersection of these cultures. In so doing, the filmmakers confront a number of questions that are central to understanding the present-day lived experiences of LGBTQ youth, revealing an uncomfortable reality as dually noted by the participants in this study.

In order to map recent and emerging cartographies of queer desire and trans-belonging among French and Maghrebi gay youth, I begin my investigation at the turn of the twenty-first century by considering *Le Drôle de Félix*, a film that places into question constructs of what I understand as queer transnationalism. This film is a platform from which we can more closely examine the stigma associated with being both gay and Muslim in contemporary France as we transition into an epoch in which the notion of a society *en pleine mutation* merits critical analysis. Ducastel and Martineau's work underscores on a number of occasions instances of racial and ethnic discrimination, as well as the sociocultural implications associated with de-marginalising the queer Arab body. Yet, and perhaps in an ironical way, this film also captures numerous moments of unexpected *jouissance* as the main character negotiates his desire to identify a locus of belonging in a society of contradictions. One must consider, however, that the film precedes what we may understand today as the postmodern 'gay rights liberation' movement. Let us recall that at the turn of the century, the Arab Spring uprisings had not yet occurred, nor were Arab writers and filmmakers embracing queer scenarios quite as avidly or openly as they do today.[10] One could argue, however, that the turn of the twentieth century ushered in a new era of queer cinema, thereby permitting LGBTQ youth to more easily negotiate their sexuality through the visual text.[11]

As part of the field component of the research that informs this study, randomly selected participants[12] were asked if they had seen *Le Drôle de Félix*. Out of twenty-one youth interviewed, seven participants indicated that they were familiar with the character of Félix, played by Sami Bouajila. Five of the respondents out of this subgroup who had seen the film, and who identified as having North African origins, felt as if any suggestion of a positive outcome for the protagonist was 'pure fantasy'. Furthermore, these participants each expressed unanimously that the possibility of establishing a long-term relationship with a European lover was often highly problematic, and not likely to endure due to societal pressures linked to both their native and adopted cultures.[13] We will return to the notion of the transnational encounter when examining a primordial scene in the film that involves an elderly French woman who becomes enamoured with the Arab traveller.

Interestingly, these interviewees, all of whom rose to adolescence and young adulthood in a post-Arab Spring era, appear to harbour colonial-driven sentiments of earlier generations. This suggests that while we are now increasingly engaged in more global conversations on queer identities in France and North Africa, the trauma of heteronormativity, or the burden of tradition to recall Bouhdiba's argument, remains problematic – certainly in regards to blending Western and Arabo-Oriental cultures. As we will see shortly, the queer voices in *Le Drôle de Félix* become qualified by an emboldened tonality as we transition beyond the first decade of the twenty-first century. In order to underscore such transition, let us consider Taïa's work as it relates to the present-day youth subject caught in-between France and the Maghreb.

Abdellah Taïa's *L'Armée du salut* also underscores many of the issues at stake in *Le Drôle de Félix*, including the Arab youth character's ability to navigate his redefined and emergent transnational identity in European spaces of otherness. In comparing and juxtaposing these two films, however, we note a number of critical differences related to the gay youth's ability to be seen – and to be heard. The first decade of the twenty-first century, then, can be qualified in part by a change in the power dynamics that inform the youth character's worldview. As such, Félix's voice resurfaces in Taïa's film, thus giving way to renewed constructs of transnationalism as the main character, Abdellah, travels north. Contrary to Félix's status as having pre-existing 'roots' in France, Abdellah's perception of the north is based on a phantasmal vision of Europe, which plays outs in slightly different, yet comparable ways. Through such voyage, the filmmaker underscores the Arab youth's ability to (re)define his European–Maghrebi identity while also residing along the border of two contradicting cultures drawing a further comparison to Félix's condition.

Interestingly, nineteen of the twenty-one participants interviewed were familiar with Taïa's work, a likely result of the author and filmmaker's status as a growing icon among LGBTQ youth. The character of Abdellah was more recognised overall, owing in part to the film's 2013 release date.[14] Let us now return to Ducastel and Martineau's work in an effort to frame modes of desire and belonging as they relate to the Franco-Arabo queer encounter at the end of the tumultuous 1990s.

Inside-out: Marginalisation, Sexuality and *Différence* in *Le Drôle de Félix*

Le Drôle de Félix chronicles the struggles and triumphs of Félix, a gay French-Tunisian who resides in France. In addition to his status as an 'outsider', he is also HIV positive, a secondary motif that underscores the character's fragility at the margins of French society. But is he *marginal*? The fact that his mother is French does not appear to diminish his inferiority. His skin colour emphasises his minority status, particularly when he is confronted by the hostile white subject who is often portrayed as being both superior and more aggressive. It bears mentioning, and of central importance to the filmmakers' portrayal of Félix, that the character's health condition and outward appearance do not preclude him from living a relatively normal life. In this vein, I argue that Ducastel and Martineau are propelled here by their desire to challenge modes of homophobic discourse, including the presumption that HIV-positive characters are relegated to what could be described as an empty space of solitude.

Moreover, and as Alison Murray Levine points out, Félix's French shows no signs of *banlieue* slang (2008: 54), positioning him, at least from the inside looking out, as an average middle-class person, despite the fact that he has recently lost his job. Film critic Louis Guichard takes this argument one step further by suggesting that the character's sexuality and HIV status is of secondary concern: 'Cette vision non-problématique de l'homosexualité et cette dédramatisation du sida reflètent l'audace tranquille du film mais ne constituent pas pour autant le corps du récit' (Guichard 2013: n.p.).[15] Guichard's assertion that the filmmakers' de-dramatising of Félix's sexuality and HIV status underscores a proclivity to focus more acutely on what Orlando understands as the 'global' age. Instead, he believes, it draws upon a body of social–cultural questions related to national identity and trans-belonging in a multicultural and contemporary context. In their attempt to stabilise (and/or solidify) Félix's social condition, the filmmakers initiate a conversation that Abdellah Taïa will later draw upon in his own effort to underscore the Maghrebi youth traveller's ability to rewrite the outsider narrative. The question of language production resurfaces in *L'Armée du salut* when the young Abdellah questions the usefulness of the French language, a scene we will return to a bit later.

While *Le Drôle de Félix* contains a number of erotically charged scenes, the plot is anchored by Félix's journey toward self-discovery as he travels across France on a quest to locate his biological father who is Tunisian, whom he believes resides in Marseille. Each segment is framed by the qualifier *drôle* and builds upon one another in what is essentially a series of adventures that reinforce, and then deconstruct, a number of stereotypes, including characterisations of male (homo)sexuality. As such, and although erotic desire at times comes to the fore, the thematic of trans-identity informs the filmmakers' aesthetic in a way that continuously, and rather effortlessly, fosters reflection on the dual thematic regime of marginalisation and rejection without reducing the film to a series of erotic encounters *de passage* void of narrative substance.

In an early and pensive scene, Ducastel and Martineau construct Félix's sexuality and social condition by placing him in a slightly erotic yet politicised scenario with his French lover, Daniel, thereby blending race and culture in a prelude to what will unravel as an overarching theme of the film. Indeed, this moment could be interpreted as the antithesis of the character's ultimate struggle to be accepted as he embarks on a journey of self-discovery and affirmation. In this brief but revealing scene, the two characters are filmed while in bed. In what is arguably a quite banal scenario, such visual representation of the two lovers reduces the stigma of HIV to an almost non-existent factor as Guichard suggests. Moreover, and although it is apparent the two characters are nude under the sheets that function as a protective shield, we are not at this point exposed to their naked bodies, and any possible sexual act remains outside the purview of the camera's lens. Félix is portrayed as docile and submissive, and his body language suggests that he genuinely cares for his French lover, thereby signalling that he has neither solicited nor provided sexual services.[16] Such sentiment is further apparent in a scene that postfaces this encounter as the lovers once again interact with one another in a way that is neither overly eroticised nor dismissive. In so doing, Ducastel and Martineau 'rewrite' previous constructs of the Franco-Arabo queer encounter by de-sexualising the queer Arab body during such critical moments of transnational and homoerotic engagement.[17] This is not to say, however, that erotic desire is void of sexual imagery, a testament to the filmmakers' artistic prowess.

Despite a number of physical and social constraints, Félix's cross-country voyage gives way to new and unexpected unions in what is an apparent attempt by the filmmakers to reverse the traveller's presumed inferiority. Although Daniel makes plans to eventually join Félix in the south of France, the road trip becomes synonymous with the traveller's solo search for freedom, which is punctuated by a series of homoerotic encounters that, although at times erotically charged, do not reduce the film to a pornographic narrative.

As the film progresses, Félix's condition becomes further ensconced in the background that is metropolitan France. His status as an outsider is best examined in the context of a revealing scene in which he befriends Jules, a seventeen-year-old French *lycéen* with whom he refuses to have sex, despite the brief sexual tension that lingers in the background. While Jules appears to be unbothered by Félix's status as a non-conformist (it actually encourages the French adolescent), questions of race and ethnicity resurface when the French teen feels compelled to hide his new friend from his mother in what is an obvious reference to racism.[18] The following morning, the two characters decide to steal a car, permitting Ducastel and Martineau to once again blend race and ethnicity, as well as reverse social performances of 'expected' and/or implied behaviours. Indeed, one could argue that Jules is *as* marginal as Félix – if we measure marginality against the grain of expected behaviours that include not stealing.

During the road trip that ensues, Félix and Jules find solace in a gay dance club, which doubles as a safe zone where both characters are able to temporarily displace the trauma of isolation at the margins of society. Echoing early and widespread portrayals of such safe zones in queer cinema, particularly in Western contexts,[19] the gay dance club functions in this film as a utopian space, permitting the filmmakers to juxtapose the harshness of the 'outside' with the relative ease with which these two characters, despite their differences, form an effortless bond inside the club.

Each new acquaintance provides an important and sobering life lesson for both the traveller and his new companions, including Jules. I argue that such procedure is linked to a poetics of otherness and highlights the absurdity of stereotype. While Félix eventually abandons Jules as he continues on his way toward Marseille, their encounter is central to understanding the multidimensional aspect of the character's emergent self. While many of his liaisons may appear on the surface to be borne purely out of sexual tension for some audiences, they actually represent, in Félix's phantasmatic mind, the family that he so desperately desires, a further reflection of the immigrant's social condition as observed during my field research. These encounters permit Félix to construct a new identity while simultaneously rewriting his role in French society. Such a technique thus permits Ducastel and Martineau to transcend categories of race and ethnicity, two further politically charged inferences to the divisive nature that at times qualifies contemporary French society.[20]

As his journey south continues, Félix befriends another gay male (likely in his late thirties). As in earlier episodes, the male body is filmed in a way that does not overly eroticise the moment, thereby propelling us to more critically contemplate new and emerging modes of transnational engagement as seen through the eyes of the gay traveller. Although in this instance the camera's gaze eventually reveals shots of male genitalia, the scene somehow avoids the kind of raw sexuality that some audiences may anticipate due to the growing sexual tension that lingers in the background. Interestingly, a critical comparison can be made here with a scene that occurs near the beginning of the film in which Félix is accosted by a belligerent Caucasian motorist while driving. In what is a reversal of the hostility that qualifies this earlier frame, the example repositions the northerner as an accepting and non-judgemental character who is not blinded by racial and ethnic prejudices. The rainbow-coloured kite that Félix is flying during this 'stopover' (which he carries with him from point to point), unravels as a scene that is framed by an imposing shot of a meadow with flowers in full bloom. The shot is symbolic of the peaceful and multicultural exchange that has just taken place between the two characters.

While we have examined a number of scenes that point to the main character's *différence*, there are several defining moments in the film that bridge the divide between north and south, thereby rewriting in many ways the transnational narrative. One such scene occurs when Félix makes the acquaintance of Mathilde, an elderly French woman to whom he eventually refers as 'ma grand-mère,' played by French actress and singer Henriette Ragon.[21] Upon discovering Félix sleeping alone on a park bench, Mathilde proclaims, 'J'ai besoin de vous. Rendez-vous utile!'[22] He immediately responds and appears to be surprised that the woman has so openly engaged him. She indicates that she needs help carrying her groceries and motions for him to follow her. Félix is initially hesitant and his momentary pause at the entrance to her garden suggests that he is not accustomed to such an amicable welcome by a 'French' woman who appears to have no familial or genealogical ties to the Maghreb. Without second guessing her own motivation (yet another reference to the filmmakers' aesthetic), Mathilde welcomes Félix into her home where the traveller experiences the type of familial bond he so desperately seeks – and that we have been anxiously anticipating throughout his journey. Mathilde's home can easily be compared to the earlier scene in the gay dance club in that the elderly woman's house can also be described as a utopic space in which Félix experiences calm and tranquillity. The chance encounter gives way to an unexpected union in the context of a loving relationship between a grandmother and her adopted grandson. In a way, Mathilde poses as the film's matriarch and represents the traveller's growing and emergent family. Reminiscent of Félix's earlier and revealing encounter with Jules, and although these two characters, too, come from contrastingly different backgrounds and cultures, and despite their age difference, their presence in one another's lives fills a void that reverses in a rather ironical way the marginalisation and inferred isolation from which both Félix and Mathilde suffer. I would now like to turn to Taïa's film and consider how *L'Armée du salut* builds upon Ducastel and Martineau's work by further empowering the Maghrebi youth subject who is also caught between two cultures and worldviews.

The Emergent Traveller: Maghrebi Voices in Transition

L'Armée du salut was released in 2013. For avid readers of Taïa's work, the film's anticipated launch was lauded by many audiences, and was the subject of a number of critical discussions on the topic of 'open' homosexuality, particularly in the filmmaker's native Morocco. An adaptation of the 2006 novel of the same title, the film chronicles the coming-of-age story of a young Moroccan boy who is gay, yet not entirely sure that he wants to renounce his Muslim roots in order to embrace a homosexual lifestyle. The erotics of *Le Drôle de Félix* reappear here as allegories of resistance as the adolescent embraces his desire for the same sex, including an inferred sexual attraction to his older brother. While he may not be acutely aware that an attraction to his sibling is taboo (or at least he does not appear to care), he does express some initial concern over the aggrandising of European/northern culture, recalling Ducastel and Martineau's interwoven message on power dynamics.

The child's older sibling represents a colonial worldview and proclaims at one point that if one wants to ultimately succeed in life, it is necessary to travel to Europe. But at what cost? The young Abdellah is not initially convinced – *Is it possible to be both gay and Muslim?* Taïa's well-documented adoration for Morocco is apparent as his own worldview is voiced by way of the youth's hesitance in adopting his brother's insistence on migrating north. This primordial scene doubles as the boy's diegetic coming out.[23] Despite the possible stigma associated with incestuous and homosexual attraction, Abdellah's proclivity for rejecting modes of 'expected' social behaviour becomes increasingly apparent as he transforms from an innocent child into an outspoken young adult-traveller. As we will see momentarily, and central to the filmmaker's vision, the youth's initial reluctance to challenge the European *maître* translates into a renewed sense of self during a powerful moment of transnational engagement as colonial power structures are rewritten and redefined. One could argue that Abdellah's eventual travels north easily recall Félix's search for self as both characters balance various modes of identity, punctuated by the implications of travelling within spaces dominated by the motif of racism.

Among the subjects I interviewed, both male and female, all but one interviewee underscored a presence in their lives of the same social issues that are at stake in both films, including racist discourse and intermittent resistance to an open acceptance of minority youth populations. Of particular significance, and recalling a narrative procedure we observe in both *Le Drôle de Félix* and *L'Armée du salut*, the blending of cultures (north/south) often becomes linked to mere sexual liaisons, borne out of former colonial domination. While Félix may not be a 'sexual tourist' in the same way that Abdellah often becomes (either by default or intentionally), both characters are, at least initially, reduced to marginal status while in spaces dominated by the European *maître*.

Contrary to *Le Drôle de Félix*, which is set in metropolitan France, *L'Armée du salut* opens in North Africa, allowing us to develop an intimate relationship with Maghrebi culture as seen through the eyes of an innocent gay child. In opposition to the 'pure' love affair that Félix experiences with his French boyfriend, Daniel, the motif of sex-for-hire penetrates Taïa's imaginary in a rather opaque way, giving rise to the mentality that was apparent among the Maghrebi subjects interviewed for this study. In an initial scene of the film, the young Abdellah is 'sold' by his father to an older Arab man who uses the child for what we presume is a sexual encounter.[24] This moment easily recalls the *non-dit* or unspoken aspect of the homosexual encounter in North African culture as the father, without hesitating, negotiates this moment of sexual exploitation in the absence of fear or guilt. While we are unsure if the adolescent enjoys the implied sexual exchange, the character's outlook as captured in subsequent scenes suggests that he is quite complacent – and perhaps even takes pleasure in the experience despite the traumatic implications audiences may associate with the encounter.

As the film progresses, Abdellah's attraction to his older brother resurfaces during a trip to a seaside resort town. In a way recalling the *jouissance* Félix experiences while travelling across France, Abdellah, too, finds solace in escaping the mundane reality of his life at home. One of the adolescent's first moments of absolute freedom occurs during this trip in the context of an erotic encounter with another older male – this time of his own volition.[25] Recalling a procedure that qualifies *Le Drôle de Félix*, the erotics of this exchange are ultimately relegated to the viewer's imagination, thereby placing greater emphasis on the character's emergent self, as opposed to an adolescent's sexual impulse. Echoing Félix's melancholic search for a new beginning, Abdellah, too, appears to be caught in a fragile space of the in-between. As his older brother slips away into the arms of a new girlfriend, Abdellah is faced with his first loss of love, propelling him into an unsure future. Following this transition, the filmmaker renegotiates what it means to be both gay and Muslim in twenty-first century French and Maghrebi spaces.[26]

At this point, there is temporal shift in the film as we flash forward ten years. Abdellah is reintroduced as a young adult, and has entered into a relationship with Jean, an older European man. Unlike Félix who establishes relationships with both men and women, which are not always driven by erotics, including his union with his adopted French 'grandmother', Abdellah's link to the north is by way of the European male subject, who likely signifies the bond he felt for his older brother as a child – and who reduces him to the *éphèbe* status that he so desperately seeks to avoid. It is at this critical moment when the filmmaker frames what are evolving power dynamics among (and between) northern and southern subjects caught up in the motif of desire and sexuality – ensconced in the transnational encounter.

As the second half of the film opens, Abdellah's European lover orders tea service while at a hotel in Morocco, a multicultural exchange that draws attention to the fact that the European tourist is regarded as both wealthy and in many ways 'superior'. Jean's body language suggests that while he is quite likely 'in love' with Abdellah, he also maintains control over their union. The scene draws attention to the very north/south dichotomy that Taïa wishes to reverse and prefaces a final and pensive episode in which Abdellah challenges and rewrites the power dynamics of their transnational union. Prior to the character's complete disavowal of what could be described as colonial era power structures, he capitalises on this moment to draw attention to a similar struggle that Félix must also confront as he travels across France. While the European is often portrayed as a dominant and even mythical figure in Ducastel and Martineau's imaginaries, Taïa, too, empowers the young traveller to assume control over his own destiny, thereby rewriting the parameters of the transnational union.

A powerful and defining moment in the film occurs when Abdellah arrives in Europe and confronts his Swiss lover, Jean.[27] Having in many ways completed his journey toward a new form of self and being, Abdellah engages with his lover in a revealing exchange. At this moment, Jean confesses to Abdellah, 'You have changed; you have used me; it's all you have ever done.' Yet we may question *who has used whom?* Such modality recalls several instances in which the young Abdellah is interrogating his own at least apparent proximity to 'meta-prostitutional' intentions. The innocence of the young boy we witness at the film's opening is here rewritten as a self-serving and forceful character. But while the traveller's actions and demeanour may portray someone who is only concerned with his own well-being, this moment also incites reflection on the type of overarching freedom that both Abdellah and Félix seek. That is, the ability to navigate their own desire – on their own terms. Among the 'French' subjects I interviewed, and among those who recalled this scene of the film, all of them unanimously agreed that the film functions in part to dispel 'traditional' portrayals of the Franco-Maghrebi encounter.

To return to Altman's assertion that gay identities are becoming internationalised, it is important to reconcile the differences that define these highly unique cultures, thereby enabling us to better engage with questions of self and being along the north/south divide. The characters I have considered here are located in spaces of otherness that are at times singular, yet these voices in transition underscore an undercurrent of continuity that links *Le Drôle de Félix* and *L'Armée du salut*. In both films, we are confronted by a traveller who rejects colonial forms of domination that have historically divided north and south. As these French and Maghrebi subjects redefine their role in contemporary European society, new constructs of transnational engagement begin to take shape. In Ducastel and Martineau's work, the Maghrebi subject, although at times marginalised and seemingly powerless, constructs a locus of belonging despite his status as an 'outsider'. For Taïa's traveller, the transition from youth to young adulthood can be qualified by his ability to rewrite the power structures that until now have relegated him to a space of silence. As such, we are left to (re)consider how we view, manipulate, and (re)construct meanings of national identity and trans-belonging.

To conclude, these films reinforce a number of sentiments and concerns shared by the subjects who were interviewed as part of this study. There is much evidence to support the fact that minority LGBTQ and youth populations in France remain at a disadvantage, yet are able in many instances to at least partially rewrite their role in contemporary society. One must also consider, as does Bouhdiba, the delicate balance of respecting tradition while embracing new and emerging constructs of queer and transnational identities. To return to the notion of the utopic space, the characters in these films, as well as the participants who were interviewed as part of the field component of this study, underscore a quest for identity, while constructing their own realities. As such, the north/south dichotomy is being increasingly rewritten from the perspective of French and Maghrebi voices in transition. The films studied here contribute to an important and growing archive of contemporary queer films that further illuminate present-day debates on human rights, transnationalism and inclusion. Of equal importance, LGBTQ youth who reside in the trenches, including those interviewed for this project, highlight the fragility of a society of contradictions.

Notes

1. In November 1960, an indecent exposure ordinance was imposed in France, penalising homosexual erotic acts. In June 1980, new legislation was enacted, reversing previous definitions of homosexuality as a mental disease (see Corriveau 2011).
2. In her article 'Mapping *Beur* Cinema in the New Millennium', Alison Murray Levine comments on the implications of the 2005 riots in France and their effect on unemployment rates among migrant youth populations. Although her study focuses on intra-Arab cinema, she postulates that, 'Beur filmmakers working in France must work with French cultural institutions and appeal to a broad non-minority audience in order to make a case for the future financial

success of their works' (Murray Levine 2008: 56). Interestingly, Ducastel, Martineau and Taïa resist this type of visual discourse, and quite openly and overtly challenge what we might understand as a colonial and 'French' mindset by inverting 'traditional' Beur/French power dynamics. These films directly engage with minority populations in an effort to encourage dialogue with so-called 'mainstream' viewers.
3. In my work, the 'north/south' dichotomy is a reference to the Franco-Maghrebi transnational encounter.
4. Here, one is reminded of Joseph Massad's work *Desiring Arabs* (2007) and his premise that the imposition of Western constructs of sexuality are linked to what he argues to be a growing presence of the 'International Gay'. Such blending of Western and Oriental cultures in this regard imposes new challenges for Maghrebi gay youth as they attempt to assimilate into their native and adopted cultures. As such, constructs of sexuality in the twenty-first century appear much differently than they did prior to the so-called Western imposition associated with post-colonial transnationalism.
5. Interviews were conducted in the third, fourth and tenth arrondissements of Paris in June and July 2016. Questionnaires were distributed at a number of locations that cater to a diverse LGBTQ clientele. Sites were largely chosen at random, although some effort was made to visit establishments that are known to be 'traditionally' inclusive, and vice versa. The interviews and questionnaires were anonymous, although all twenty-one participants openly admitted their country of origin. Respondents were both male and female. Of the participants, 51 per cent were male.
6. Here, the qualifier 'relationship' refers to both platonic unions as well as intimate (including sexual) liaisons.
7. In this study, the qualifier 'French' refers to someone who was born in France, and who does not have racial, ethnic or familial ties to another country.
8. Know in English as 'The Lead Years', this period of King Hassan II's reign is associated with the years between 1963 and 1999.
9. Robert Salis's *Grande École* (2004) also underscores multiple instances of discrimination among French and Arab youth, as well as the thematic of queer desire in a bicultural and transnational context.
10. One should note that there are indeed exceptions to this observation. For example, Ben Attia's film *Le Fil*, which takes places in Tunisia and chronicles the sexual coming of age of a gay young man, was produced in 2010.
11. All participants interviewed for this study unanimously agreed that cinema is often the best outlet for voicing the plight of gay youth who reside at the margins of society. They each agreed that the medium of film can incite political action due to its ability to reach large audiences both at home and abroad.
12. Inclusion in this study was purely voluntary and anonymous. Participants ranged in age and were between nineteen and twenty-eight years old. The respondents hailed from Algeria, France, Morocco and Tunisia. Since my work is focused primarily on transnational relations between France and the

Maghreb, I included in my final analysis only those individuals with ties to these countries, and who view themselves as residing along what I refer to as the 'north/south' divide. Moreover, many of these participants struggle to find gainful employment, an interesting parallel to Ducastel and Martineau's film.

13. An important comparison can be made here to the final scene between Abdellah and his European lover, Jean, in *L'Armée du salut*.
14. *L'Armée du salut* is a visual interpretation and rewriting of the 2006 novel of the same title, also by Abdellah Taïa. The work has been awarded a number of accolades and has been translated into several languages, including Arabic, Dutch, English and Spanish.
15. 'This unproblematic vision of homosexuality, and this de-dramatising of AIDS, reflects the quiet audacity of the film, but does not, however, constitute the body of the story' (my translation).
16. Throughout the nineteenth and twentieth centuries, a number of French and North African writers portray the north/south encounter as an erotic exchange that is motivated primarily by the character's desire to leave one's country in search of new beginnings. Ducastel and Martineau rewrite such thematic by placing Félix's journey within metropolitan France, thereby permitting us to respond to these questions from an intra-France perspective.
17. In reference to a number of important literary works in which Franco/Arabo relations are often qualified by the *maître/éphèbe* liaison. Examples include homoerotic travel narratives by André Gide, Roland Barthes and Tony Duvert, among other writers.
18. This moment aptly reflects the kind of racism to which my subjects referred when expressing doubt about the viability of a transnational relationship.
19. Of the many titles that fit into this category of films, Rob Epstein and Jeffrey Friedman's *The Celluloid Closet* (1996) underscores the harshness of the gay lived experience during this time, particularly in regards to filming practices. As we will see later in this article, the very stereotypes that these early filmmakers underscore appear to haunt the postmodern youth's imaginary in French and Francophone contexts.
20. Such critical positioning of contemporary French society reinforces the divisiveness that is felt among youth populations in France, as noted among the subjects whom I interviewed for this project.
21. Henriette Ragon is also known as Patachou.
22. 'I need your help. Make yourself useful!' (my translation).
23. Taïa (2009) discusses the difficulties and struggles he experienced in regards to his decision to come out and live as an openly gay and Muslim man.
24. While this particular scene occurs in the context of an intra-Arab exchange, the moment is reinterpreted later in Geneva, and in the context of a transnational love affair.
25. In the 2006 novel, Taïa refers to this moment, which has been 'rewritten' in the film, by suggesting that Tangiers has 'quelque chose d'unique' (p. 53).

The seaside is acutely perceived by him as an almost foreign enclave and a liminal site. We locate here an interesting parallel to French writer Jean Genet (1949) who refers to Tangiers as a 'ville de tous les trafics'.
26. Interestingly, the title of the Dutch translation of the novel is *Brotherly Love*.
27. One should note here the meta-linguistic implication of the character's ability to speak the French language, which plays a significant role in his initial seduction strategy, as well as his willingness to challenge 'traditional' Franco-Maghrebi power structures in an intra-European setting.

Works Cited

Altman, Dennis (1996), 'Rupture of Continuity: The Internationalization of Gay Identities', *Social Text*, 48, pp. 77–94.

Bouhdiba, Abdelwahab [1975] (2014), *Sexuality in Islam*, London: Saqi Books.

Corriveau, Patrice (2011), *Judging Homosexuals: A History of Gay Persecution in France and Québec*, Vancouver: UBC Press.

Genet, Jean (1949), *Journal du voleur*, Paris: Gallimard.

Guichard, Louis (2013), 'Drôle de Félix', 13 April, <http://www.telerama.fr/cinema/films/drole-de-felix,49524.php> (last accessed 29 June 2016).

Massad, Joseph (2007), *Desiring Arabs*, Chicago: University of Chicago Press.

Murray Levine, Alison J. (2008), 'Mapping *Beur* Cinema in the New Millennium', *Journal of Film and Video*, 60:3, pp. 42–59.

Orlando, Valerie (2011), *Francophone Voices of the 'New Morocco' in Film and Print: (Re)presenting a Society in Transition*, Athens, OH: Ohio University Press.

Taïa, Abdellah (2006), *L'Armée du salut*, Paris: Éditions du Seuil.

Taïa, Abdellah (2009), 'L'homosexualité expliquée à ma mère', *Tel Quel*, pp. 82–8.

Films

L'Armée du salut, film, directed by Abdellah Taïa. France: Les Films de Pierre, 2013.

Le Drôle de Félix, film, directed by Olivier Ducastel and Jacques Martineau. France: Pyramide Distribution, 2000.

CHAPTER 8

'A Child of the Ruins': Youthful Disaffection and the 'Making Of' the Terrorist

Maria Flood

Cinema has a long-standing engagement with the disenchantments of adolescence and early adulthood, but rarely are films that deal with terrorism and the process of radicalisation treated as films about the dissatisfactions of youth. Terrorism is read as an identitarian, religious or civilisational clash, rather than as a manifestation of generational discontent. However, recent cinema from the Maghreb and the Middle East, a region with chronic unemployment and where over half the population are under thirty years of age, stresses the connections between radicalisation and the disenfranchisement of young people under global capitalism. This article, then, proposes an examination of the links between terrorism and youthful disaffection, focusing on the figure of the male protagonist drawn into fundamentalist violence in Nouri Bouzid's *Making Of* (2006). Unlike Western depictions of the terrorist, which have tended to present a univocal image of the terrorist as malignant and external force and a fully formed and utterly unscrupulous agent of violence, this film invites the spectator to encounter the terrorist as a humanised and vulnerable young man, screening the pivotal transition from broader political discontent to the channelling of that dissatisfaction into terrorist violence. The film also questions authoritarianism, indoctrination and intergenerational conflict through its use of documentary-style sequences, which pit the director's vision against the beliefs of the principal actor. My intervention seeks to interrogate the figure of the terrorist through the prism of youth, reading youth as an affective and biological category that encompasses and often magnifies many of the issues that are frequently cited as catalysts in the radicalisation process: idealism, rebellion, anti-authoritarianism, economic and social insecurity and disenfranchisement, and powerlessness.

Making Of is veteran Tunisian filmmaker Nouri Bouzid's sixth film, and it stages the themes of social, personal and political alienation and disenchantment that mark the entirety of his *œuvre*. Born in Sfax in 1945, Bouzid is a stalwart of cinematic production in North Africa, having directed nine feature films since 1986. Fully bilingual in French and Arabic, he trained at the Institut national supérieur des arts du spectacle (INSAS), the film school in Brussels, from 1968 to 1972. Bouzid has personally experienced the vigorous rebellion of early adulthood, and he writes, 'jeune, j'étais rebelle sans raison, et [je] vivais en plein mélodrame' ('as a young man, I was a rebel without a cause, and I lived in the midst of melodrama', quoted in Mimoun 2009). As a student, he considered himself a Marxist, and took part in left-wing student movements, and upon returning to Tunisia affiliated with the extreme left-wing group *Perspectives tunisiennes/ El Amal Ettounsi* (*The Tunisian Worker*). This movement radically opposed Habib Bourguiba's repressive government, and the director's writings and activities as part of *Perspectives* led to his arrest, torture and imprisonment by the state from 1973 to 1979.

Bouzid's work explores his personal familiarity with the intense desire for subjective and political action that marks youthful engagements with the world, and their occasionally dark consequences. Indeed, many of his films feature young characters hemmed in by difficult circumstances, often pertaining to social or political situations beyond their control. *Golden Horseshoes* (*Safa 'ih min dhahab*, 1989), for example, based on Bouzid's experience of imprisonment and torture, examines an older man's struggles with the memories that plague him of his youthful incarceration. *Man of Ashes* (*Rih essed*, 1986) tells the story of a young man who, in the days before his wedding, is tormented by the memory of sexual abuse he experienced as a child at the hands of a local carpenter, a respected member of the community. *Bezness* (1992) explores the moral and economic dilemmas of a young male prostitute, Roufa, and his burgeoning and potentially exploitative relationship with a French photographer in Tunis, probing European influence in Tunisia and the sex tourism industry. *Clay Dolls* (*Poupées d'argile*, 2002) examines the servitude and exploitation of young female domestic workers. Evidently, Bouzid does not shy away from difficult, controversial or unpopular subjects and his realist style and the overtly political themes explored in his works display a deep engagement with the effects of socio-economic policies on his protagonists. The fragile, haunted and perplexed young people that populate Bouzid's work are not the traditional young heroes or heroines of popular Hollywood cinema, who overcome a series of obstacles in order to achieve personal growth and adult understanding, but rather, as he describes, 'des héros d'un type nouveau . . . mes protagonistes portent en eux le conflit principal, originel dont ils ne pourront jamais se dépêtrer' ('heroes of a new kind . . . my protagonists carry inside themselves a primary, original conflict, that they can never extricate themselves from'; quoted in Mimoun 2009). Bouzid's characters, then, may appear to have much in common with the hero (and occasionally heroine) of classical Greek and Renaissance theatrical tragedy, who is marked or scarred by an internal 'fatal flaw' (*hamartia*), which propels them towards an inevitable and catastrophic outcome. In cinematic terms, his vulnerable and haunted personages can in many ways be aligned with the perplexed and disenfranchised characters of transnational cinema, with its 'desolate structures of feeling and lonely diegetic characters' (Naficy 1999: 55) and its staging of the 'people caught in the cracks of globalization' (Ezra and Rowden 2006: 7).

However, Bouzid situates his vision within a specifically Arab context of what he calls a 'defeat conscious cinema' or 'New Realism' (Bouzid 1995: 242), arising out of what he perceives as the politically and psychically catastrophic defeat of the Arab coalition against Israeli forces in the 'Six Day War' in June 1967, and the subsequent decline of Pan-Arabist ideals and ideology. The generation of young filmmakers who emerged at this time sought to create a cinema that interrogates these defeats, questioning the origins and possible solutions to the crises plaguing the region, and thus 'render cinema a vehicle for the spreading of awareness and a tool or forum for analysis or debate' (Bouzid 1995: 243). This is a cinema that should combine the 'greatness and impotence' (Bouzid 1994: 54) he perceives at the heart of the Arab impasse, and as the term 'impotence' suggests, this is a predominantly male predicament. Thus, these films feature a male character who is 'lost and confused . . . plagued with a set of dilemmas that shake him to the core' (Bouzid 1995: 249). Bouzid's work can also be situated within what documentary filmmaker Hichem Ben Ammar calls the 'New Tunisian Cinema' of the 1990s and 2000s, a movement characterised by 'une révolte contre l'injustice de la société' ('a revolt against the injustice of society', quoted in Elgaaïed 2007).

Making Of embodies all of the above characteristics of the 'defeat conscious cinema' in its staging of a youthful male protagonist, while the film references the aims of the 'New Tunisian Cinema' in its interrogation of a major contemporary social and political scourge. The film tells the story of Chokri, nicknamed Bahta (Lotfi Abdelli), a breakdancer who lives in the working-class neighbourhood of Radès, on the outskirts of Tunis. The opening sequences of the film depict a resourceful if misguided young man who spends time with his friends, listens to music and commits petty crimes, like drawing graffiti, theft and, according to the police, breakdancing. Incarnating the twin forces of greatness and impotence that Bouzid describes, Bahta is a talented dancer, who is kind and playful with his mother, Halima (Fatima Ben Saïdane), initially tender and teasing with his girlfriend Souad (Afef Ben Mahmoud) and caring towards his little brother (Mohamed Ali Boumnijel) but he is also impetuous, volatile, stubborn, and prone to verbal outbursts and moments of uncontrolled rage. Following an aborted attempt to travel clandestinely to Europe, Bahta's antics draw the attention of a group of fundamentalists. They indoctrinate him with the aim of turning him into a suicide bomber, although in the end, he only kills himself.

Bouzid began writing the script of *Making Of* in the immediate aftermath of the 9/11 attacks, while he was filming *Clay Dolls*. The film arose out of a profound desire to understand the causes of religious radicalisation among young Muslim men. The film's caption, a clear reference to Simone de Beauvoir's *Le Deuxième sexe* (1949), reads 'on ne naît pas terroriste, on le devient' ('one is not born, but rather becomes, a terrorist'). The title and subtitle stress the process of creating or 'making' the terrorist (although it also refers to the 'making of' the film itself, discussed in the closing sections). Bouzid conducted extensive research for the film, by reading the Koran in French and in Arabic, the writings of Osama Bin Laden, as well as theses written by doctoral students in Arabic countries (Mimoun 2009). He wanted to tell the story of a young man who ultimately does not commit a suicide attack, and he stresses the youthful naivety and despair of the individuals who are brainwashed and drawn into fundamentalist movements. He also highlights the social, economic, political and familial structures that have failed to provide young people with concrete, attractive and viable futures:

> I believe we are all responsible for this. The police, family structures, the education system, the lack of freedoms. We grew these suicide bombers – the Islamists only 'pluck' them from the tree. The Islamists couldn't do a thing if a youth weren't willing. (quoted in Bender 2007)

Bouzid's words highlight the web of complex push factors that can lead to radicalisation. Yet, more broadly, young people all over the world are struggling to situate themselves within a global social and economic environment that provides few certainties, limited and often unfairly skewed opportunities for advancement, and that appears increasingly to offer little in the way of political or ideological stability (Corlett 2017). In Tunisia in 2014, the youth unemployment rate was at 33 per cent (Anon. 2016). For Asef Bayat and Linda Herrera, a combination of the 'youth bulge' in Muslim majority countries, repressive and autocratic regimes, and Western xenophobia and racism render Muslim youth throughout the world particularly vulnerable to these profound socio-economic shifts:

> As a result of . . . the relentless process of neoliberal globalization, the geopolitics of neo-imperialism, the rise of a civilizational discourse in which 'Islam' is positioned in opposition to the 'West', and unprecedented levels of school and university graduates, combined with crises of unemployment, youth cultures are developing in novel ways with consequences of historical significance. (Bayat and Herrera 2010: 4)

Bayat and Herrera further suggest that young Muslim people 'respond to their situations and express their youthfulness in remarkably diverse ways' (Bayat and Herrera 2010: 4) and they are reluctant to offer any easy equivalence between fundamentalism and the other youthful movements of music, dance and peaceful piety in Islam that they explore in the rest of the volume. They further emphasise the fallacies of the glib and common neo-liberal equation of poverty and deviance, in relation to terrorism in this case, highlighting recent research which suggests that no reliable correlation can be found in Muslim populations between radicalisation and unemployment: 'no difference exists in the unemployment rate among the politically radicalized and moderates; both are approximately 20%' (Bayat and Herrera 2010: 6; Esposito and Mogahed 2007: 71).

However, attempts to correlate radicalisation with poverty serve a purpose beyond the bolstering of a neo-liberal narrative of personal responsibility and economic self-reliance. They trace an easy and comfortable source (the 'give them jobs' hypothesis) to what is fundamentally an extremely complex problem. Psychological abnormality theories no longer withstand longitudinal data based scrutiny (Hassan 2009), and as poverty falls out of favour as a satisfactory explicatory paradigm, researchers turn increasingly towards more nuanced models which take into account social and economic factors, while focusing primarily on the aspirations and affective urges of young people. Foremost among these theorists is Scott Atran, who describes the radicalisation of the young as 'the dark side of globalization': 'young people, unmoored from millennial traditions, flail about in search of a social identity that gives them personal significance and glory . . . they radicalize to find a firm identity in a flattened world' (Atran 2015). For Atran, the persistent and increasing draw of radicalisation is part of an age-old quest of the young for identity, achievement, belonging and, of course, rebellion.

However, are there ethical, moral or political hazards inherent in such a perspective? Do we risk negating the very real dangers and material consequences of terrorist violence by examining terrorism from the perspective of youth? In the following sections, I propose a consideration of terrorism and youth in Bouzid's *Making Of*, the work of a filmmaker who, as I have outlined above, has a long-standing personal and artistic engagement with political controversy and the torments of youth. In this account, I do not want to suggest that youthfulness might replace poverty or psychological deviance as another easy category that might neatly explain the phenomenon of radicalisation. Rather, through an analysis of *Making Of*, I address the multitude of social, psychological and environmental factors that contribute to radicalisation, issues and perspectives that are overwhelmingly the concerns and characteristics of youth. Bouzid's film addresses the complexity of the radicalisation process, by staging a series of 'tipping points', tributary factors that lead to Bahta's radicalisation. Without presenting one cause as predominant over the others, I suggest that the youthfulness of the central character binds these factors together.

The opening shots of the film underscore this central theme. As the credits roll, a close-up shot with the camera close to the ground registers the hectic pacing of anonymous feet, clad in the universally recognisable symbol of globalised youth: the branded trainer. The frantic movement of these feet, their frenzied pacing into and outside the frame, and the tears and scores that mark many of the shoes, broadly situate the film in temporal, spatial and thematic terms. This is the present day, and these young people, energetic and animated, desire trademarked goods, but they do not have the means to renew them constantly: the shoes are scuffed and worn.

The next scene highlights the young people's situation as both within and outside global capitalism, without the means of their Western contemporaries but adhering to the same cultural and affective codes and behaviours. The camera zooms out to reveal Tunis's port, La Guelette, and a youthful *bande à part*, a gang of male friends dressed in the baseball caps, singlets, football jerseys and tracksuits that typify one global mode of male youth culture (see Figure 8.1). Unsurprisingly, the ribald and vulgar chat is of girls, sex, music and manliness, as one of the younger boys is teased for his failure to grow a moustache. Bahta is at the centre of this group, and leads them to an underground passage where they turn on music and as some begin breakdancing, others spray anti-institutional graffiti on the walls. The police arrive, and as many of the other boys flee, Bahta challenges them, leading to his arrest.

Thus far, the film offers a familiar set of tropes and images concerning global youth culture: clothes, friends, music and hobbies that the older generation disapproves of have been important markers of early adulthood in the mid-to-late twentieth century. Yet like the ethnically and socially marked characters of films set in the *banlieue*, such as Mathieu Kassowitz's *La Haine* (1995) or Céline Sciamma's *Bande de filles* (2014), the youthful

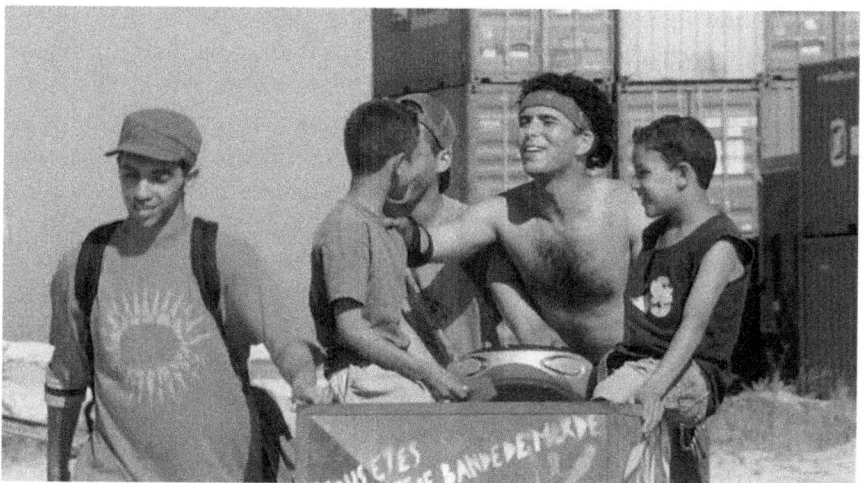

Figure 8.1 A youthful *bande à part*.

energy and misfortunes of the central characters, combined with the fact that the spectator is induced to identify with them through narrative perspective and cinematography, make the severity and frequency of the consequences appear disproportionate. The prohibition the police place on his breakdancing dramatises what Robert Lang calls 'the Tunisian police state's metastasizing reach into nearly every corner of social life' (Lang 2014: xiii). Bahta is arrested, beaten and only released because his cousin is a policeman: the punishment, in this case, in no way appears to fit the crime. In the police state that was Tunisia in 2006 under Ben Ali's regime, perceived aberrations could lead to dangerous, and potentially fatal, outcomes. Tearing off Bahta's bandana, the policeman asks him if he thinks he is Che Guevara, a nod to Bouzid's youthful Marxism certainly, but also an allusion that marks Bahta as a rebel, a young man who speaks a global counter-cultural language, and an individual who will reach a tragic, and politicised, end.

The fact that Bahta is a breakdancer situates him at a complex intersection of local and global trends. Breakdancing and hip hop rose out of the disenfranchisement of African Americans, but have been adopted by artists globally as a form through which local and regional discontents can be articulated (Morgan and Bennett 2011: 177). The suppression of Bahta's dance practice and music, therefore, can be read as part of a broader 'violation of rights to a lifestyle' (Bayat and Herrera 2010: 14) among Muslim youth populations, the suppression of their instinctual need for cultural and counter-cultural movements that capture their own particular needs, concerns and desires. Indeed, Bouzid is personally positioned to understand the significance of a youthful passion for art, as his love of film arose at an early age: even in primary school he was an avid cinemagoer. Like Bahta, his father disapproved of his choice of career, saying 'tout ça pour vendre des billets derrière un guichet!' ('All that to sell tickets at a box office!', quoted in Mimoun 2009). However, unlike his central character, Bouzid had the opportunity to pursue his passion, and he writes that, through cinema, he has 'worked through pain' (quoted in Stollery 2013).

Bahta never gets the chance to use his art as a means to expel some of the demons that haunt him, and what all of the negative authority figures in his life share, from his father, to the police, to Abdallah (Lofti Dziri) the fundamentalist, is the suppression of his desire to dance. Abdallah castigates Bahta for dancing, saying that it is a sin and that the young man should 'Watch out for those Sufis who lead us to decadence.' Sufi Islam is a mystical, spiritual and artistic expression of faith, embodied in the dances of the whirling dervishes or the poetry of Jalāl ad-Dīn Muhammad Rūmī. In contrast, the Wahhabi branch of Islam, preached by many fundamentalist groups and by Abdallah, believes dance, music and poetry to be *haram* (forbidden). This interpretation of Islam, which emerged in the territory now known as Saudi Arabia in the eighteenth century, focuses instead on the textual study and literal interpretation of the Koran in matters of behaviour, dress, lifestyle and faith. For Durre S. Ahmed, Wahhabism is a Saudi-Arabian export, one that has greatly impoverished indigenous cultures in the Muslim world because of its 'singular view of a culturally barren Islam' (Ahmed 2006: 23). He elaborates: 'efforts at hereticizing, decrying, stifling and marginalizing the mystical dimensions of Islam are intended . . . to obliterate the magnificent rainbow of its mystical tradition(s) renowned especially for music, poetry and dance' (Ahmed 2006: 22).

Of course, breakdancing is neither a traditional Tunisian nor a Sufi practice, but its suppression does point to deeper cultural losses felt across the Muslim world, and by young people most acutely. As Atran notes, 'violent extremism represents not the resurgence of traditional cultures, but their collapse' (Atran 2016: 8). Perhaps the most salient issue in this instance is not that Bahta cannot fulfil his dream of becoming a dancer, but rather the cultural and economic void that confronts him when the police prevent him from dancing: he has no job prospects and no artistic freedom. In one scene, this void is literally figured as the Mediterranean Sea, the expanse that separates the young man from Western Europe, where Bahta imagines his ambitions to dance could be fulfilled. Drunkenly, he shouts out to the dark water at night, rapping about an imagined future on the continent. Yet even his dreams of escape to Europe fail: the smuggler steals his money, and the man's henchmen beat him when he tries to recoup his losses. While it would clearly be erroneous to suggest that every young person whose visions of artistic glory fade turns to anger or violence, in Bahta's world, there is nothing to replace them. On the run from the police, he is isolated from his friends, who are all in similar positions of idleness, and although he longs to get a job, he has failed his baccalaureate, and without a job, as his girlfriend bitterly reminds him, he cannot get married. This leads to a situation where young people remain stuck in a permanent state of transition, where they have neither the insouciance of the teenager, nor the economic ability to progress to adulthood. As Bayat and Herrera summarise, 'the high cost of marriage in regions like the Middle East and North Africa, combined with lack of jobs and affordable housing, prevent the young from experiencing the transition from adulthood to independence' (Bayat and Herrera 2010: 13).

One key scene in the film captures Bahta's frustrations at a social and economic system that has denied him the right to progress to responsibility, authority and a version of manhood that he esteems. Stealing his cousin's police uniform, he enters the local café and launches into a swaggering, faux-authoritarian monologue in the guise of a police officer to the bemusement, anxiety and tentative amusement of the patrons. In his monologue, he repeats over and over again that all he needs to 'be a man' is a new outfit, performing a travesty of manliness in the shoddy veneer of power a uniform bestows in a police state (see Figure 8.2). This scene received a standing ovation at the 2006 Carthage premiere (Ruoff 2011: 27), and it shows a young man who is acting out the adulthood that has so far been denied to him. Moreover, it worryingly highlights his perception of maturity: it is nothing more than a new change of clothes, a few accessories. In a situation where figures of authority are respected simply on the basis of a uniform rather than for their actions, on external appearance rather than internal skills, knowledge or merit, it is easy to see why the fundamentalists hold such appeal: beards, veils, clothing and headdresses are easy outward manifestations of an apparently God-given system of authority and justification (see Ahmed 2006: 23).

In this scene, Bahta is not only performing adulthood, but also authority, and an authority that is fundamentally tied to the notions of masculinity. Indeed, the most repeated refrain of the film is Bahta's occasionally hysterical assertion that 'I am a man', and one of the most powerful insults that can be levelled at him, or his male friends, is an attack on their masculinity through accusations of weakness, cowardice, physical immaturity

Figure 8.2 Bahta performs authority in a police uniform.

or homosexuality. Masculinity, its fragility and inconsistencies, is a consistent feature of Tunisian filmmakers work (see Stollery 2001; Gana 2010), and Bouzid's cinema is no exception. He writes: 'the issue of filial duty and machismo has inspired me in all my films and scripts. I've always tried to catch out machismo, to corner man in his flaws' (Bouzid 1994: 56). Bahta's need to constantly reiterate his manliness, and to find new ways to prove its existence, is of course evidence of its tenuousness and brittleness, for, as he asks, 'what's the good of a man without money, who has nothing?'

For Bahta's father, dancing is not a 'manly' pursuit, because it will not lead to stable employment and subsequent marriage, yet the extent to which these trappings of adulthood remain inaccessible to Bahta and his generation appears to escape the adults in his life. Bouzid explicitly targets the older generation through the figure of Bahta's somewhat senile grandfather, who hoards a stash of money underneath his pillow, waiting to seduce the woman of his dreams, who in his advanced years, seems unlikely to materialise. When a woman does appear, it is in the figure of a prostitute who Bahta has brought to the house in order to force his grandfather to reveal where he guards his secret stash. This scene dramatises the farcical nature of the grip which older generations hold on political and economic power: the young man cannot get married because he has not the means, while the elderly hold onto wealth that they are not able to use. This scene is not merely indicative of Bahta's situation, but rather that of

Tunisia and Arab countries more broadly: 'whether in opposition movements or ruling parties, political elites do not have a good record of allowing the current younger generation, with the exception of their own kin, into the corridors of power, opportunity, and privilege' (Bayat and Herrera 2010: 10). In the case of Tunisia, the two rulers of the country since independence in 1956 to 2011, Habib Bourguiba and Zine El Abidine Ben Ali, were ousted or were deposed at the ages of eighty-four and seventy-two respectively (Bourguiba by Ben Ali in 1987 and Ben Ali by the Arab Spring revolutionaries). In this sense, Bouzid intertwines the personal and the political aspects of the intergenerational power imbalance, an injustice and inequity that Bahta experiences as deeply shameful.

Indeed, ideas of manliness in *Making Of* are powerfully tied to its negation, denial and subjugation, and this is evident in two concurrent sequences that dramatise Bahta's experience of shame as bound up in both personal and political humiliation. When his father discovers that the police have arrested him and that he has stolen his grandfather's money, he beats him with a leather belt. Filmed in long shot in the hazy darkness of their home, Bahta, his back hunched and his head bowed, allows himself to be whipped by his shorter and physically less powerful father. This scene cuts abruptly to the café, where a voice from the television intones, 'Why this humiliation? Submission, humiliation and defeat', a question that may have echoed in Bahta's mind as his father beat him. The grainy images on the screen show a war-torn and destroyed Baghdad, desecrated buildings, and the figures of two American soldiers who topple a statue of Saddam Hussein. 'From now on, everything will be American', the voice continues, the words resonating powerfully with Bahta who sits transfixed, mounting anger on his face. Lamenting the disenfranchisement and cultural monopoly of the West, the words echo the brutal appropriation of Bahta's own cultural landmarks, breakdancing and rap music, by violent, external forces of authority. Further intertwining the personal and the political, as the voice on the television asks, 'Arabs, where is your honour? Where is your dignity?', his brother rushes into the café to tell Bahta that he has spotted Souad with a 'wealthy Arab', compounding the young man's shame.

Thus far, I have examined what I have outlined the 'push' factors in relation to Bahta's radicalisation: the curtailments of cultural expression and artistic pursuits, extremely limited opportunities for employment and personal fulfilment through marriage, intergenerational power structures, and the experience of personal and political humiliation. But what can we learn in *Making Of* about the 'pull' factors, the draw of young people towards radical ideology? For Jeffrey Ruoff, the appeal of fundamentalism for Bahta, as presented in the film, is difficult to determine. He writes:

> The fundamentalist leader is a caricature, totally unsympathetic, as if he were an unfathomable other for director Bouzid. It is hard to understand why Bahta finds this indoctrination compelling, and equally difficult to see why the fundamentalists would target a wild card such as Bahta for a suicide mission. (Ruoff 2011: 28)

Ruoff raises several important concerns, and although he is a skilled emotional manipulator, the character of Abdallah is certainly monodimensional, and his speeches are verbose and dull, heavy with doctrinal references and circuitous, faux-theological arguments. Yet if we shift our focus away from his words and character, and from the explicitly religious aspect of what Abdallah appears to offer Bahta, the attractiveness of what he gives the young man becomes more apparent.

Bahta is twenty-five, mirroring the statistic that twenty-five to twenty-six years old is the average age of suicide bombers in Al Qaeda (Merari 2010: 72). This reflects the transitional, uncertain nature of this age category: if society is not offering a young person concrete and realisable opportunities for advancement and fulfilment after two and a half decades, many individuals feel understandable anger and frustration, which can turn to rebellion. As Atran outlines, the majority of foreign recruits to the Islamic State of Iraq and Syria (ISIS) in Iraq and Syria are 'youth in transitional stages in their lives: students, immigrants, between jobs or mates, having left or about to leave their native family and looking for a new family of friends and fellow travellers with whom they can find significance' (Atran 2015). The question of significance is a key element of Atran's thesis of radicalisation: young people want meaningful personal and creative engagements with the world. They want the chance to invest in social life, participating in cultural and political debates that, with the advent of the Internet, are increasingly global. Noorhaidi Hasan argues that the draw of Laskar Jihad for young Indonesians in the late 1990s was not the lust for violence or an escape from poverty, but rather a 'rational choice in their attempt to negotiate identity, and thus claim dignity' (Hasan 2010: 51).

Moreover, rebellion against authorities and the older generation is not only tied to radicalisation. A 2016 study undertaken by *The Economist* suggests that 'the Arab world's large youth bulge, and its rulers' failure to harness it for economic development' played a significant role in the uprisings of the Arab Spring in 2011 (Anon. 2016). Bahta has shown himself to be an insubordinate and unruly individual, and it is his anti-authoritarian rant in the café in the guise of a policeman that first attracts the fundamentalist's attention. The rebellious nature of adherence to radical Islam has proven to be one of its chief attractions, as older generations of Muslim parents and elders consistently prove bemused and appalled by their children's actions. ISIS targets young people specifically for this reason, and their manifesto, *Idaraat at-Tawahoush* ('The Management of Savagery') states that their global media programme should target young people because 'the youth of the nation are closer to the innate nature [of humans] on account of the rebelliousness within them' (quoted in Atran and Hamid 2015). Furthermore, as is the case of Bahta, the older generation is perceived as the cause of many of their woes, and the rejection of the political and religious ideologies of parents and authority figures, beliefs and practices that are perceived to have led to their own disenfranchisement, appears as a rational, defiant choice, a choice that manifests the independence and guidance so frequently denied to them.

Bahta calls himself on several occasions a 'child of the ruins', and indeed, it is among the ruins of a building, which could be a vestige of one of Tunisia's many colonial pasts (French, Ottoman or even Roman), that Bahta first encounters the fundamentalists. They have followed him there, and interrupt a moving moment when Bahta, exhausted by his continual flight from the authorities, lays his head on Souad's shoulder in tender quietude as she comforts him. It is as if, in the midst of the ruins of his dreams, Bahta has two choices, one which involves acceptance of his vulnerability, his losses, and the other, a denial of his fragility through becoming part of an organisation that will give him the 'manhood' and direction that engages his idealism. Bahta chooses idealism, and Atran has identified this striving for personal and political glory as a key attraction of *jihad* for globalised youth: 'jihad offers the group pride of great achievements for the underachieving: an englobing web of brave new hearts for an outworn world tearing at the seams' (Atran 2010: 42).

Indeed, one of the first questions that Abdallah asks Bahta is 'What do you dream of?', to which Bahta responds, 'I don't dream anymore'. Abdallah offers him a grandiose dream for a young mind of creating (perceived) political and social justice through personal self-sacrifice and glory in the name of a (posited) greater, universal good. Bahta has seen each one of his hopes shattered: his relationship with Souad and the possibility of marrying, his breakdancing, which he can no longer practice because of police interference, and finally, the possibility of escaping to Europe, when the trafficker steals his money. To this volatile cocktail might be added his sensitivity to the global and national injustices and the humiliation he experiences daily at the hands of his elders: this makes him, to recall Bouzid's words, a target ripe for indoctrination. As Bouzid summarises, 'there are . . . internal reasons: failure, desperation, the impossibility of going abroad . . . then there are also external factors, for example the Iraq War or Palestine' (quoted in Bender 2007).

On a basic material and psychological level, Abdallah offers Bahta a certainty and security that has been utterly absent from his life thus far. Bahta is on the run from the police, and Abdallah feeds him, clothes him and shelters him, and the young man says quietly, 'Nobody has ever helped me before', referring to the absence of state or social supports in his life thus far. Abdallah offers him employment, as an engraver of gravestones, a task with rather ominous and obvious symbolism, and the older man treats Bahta like an adult, speaking to him softly and calmly, and with outward respect for the young man's intelligence. More than this, Abdallah offers certainty, responsibility and adulthood to Bahta at a desperately uncertain time in the young man's life, saying 'I know you're a man, a real one.' The fundamentalist shows Bahta a way to master and channel his intense emotions: 'sit like a man . . . control your words and let your hands be still'. The texture of the film changes to reflect this shift from insecurity to certainty once Bahta is recruited; a contrasting of filmic form before and after radicalisation also occurs in Nabil Ayouch's *Les Chevaux de dieu* (2012). The frantic movement, short cuts and bright incandescence of Tunis cede to long takes, lengthy dialogues and muted interiors; in short, a heavy calm settles over both Bahta and the film's form.

Bouzid's films are filled with often cruel or inadequate father figures and for Ruoff, these flawed and sometimes violent paternal characters can be linked to the 'surrogate father figures found in authoritarian dictators' (Ruoff 2011: 22). Lang suggests that the despotic paternal figure in Tunisian society, from Bourguiba to Ben Ali, can be tied to 'disastrously infantilizing effects upon the population, particularly its male members' (Lang 2014: 5). On the psychological plane, Bouzid identifies a kind of Arab or Muslim *épistème*, where, in contrast to the Oedipal complex of the Western/Christian imaginary, there is Abraham, a father who was prepared to sacrifice his own son to the will of God. Rather than seeking to overcome the father and (literally or psychically) kill him and destroy his power, Bouzid writes that in the Arab context, 'the son submits to the father and serves him' (Bouzid 1994: 57). Bahta's biological father is a sinister and largely absent figure, whose only prolonged screen appearance is the scene in which he beats his son. Abdallah, whose care and attention lull Bahta into a false sense of trust, ultimately wants his surrogate son to sacrifice his life as a suicide bomber. At the end of the film, when Bahta begins to furiously resist this fatal destiny his would-be parent has planned for him, Abdallah tries to manipulate him, asking angrily, 'I let you into my house like a son. I made you a man. Aren't you grateful?' The adopted son, in this case, should be grateful for the opportunity the father has given him, that of sacrificing his own life.

The idea of filial submission and sacrifice can be further located in the third father figure depicted in *Making Of*. The film's title, as previously mentioned, refers to the indoctrination of the young man by radical ideology, but it also refers to the 'making of' the film itself. The chronological realist narrative of Bahta's downfall is interrupted on three occasions by short documentary sections that depict the principal actor, Lofti Abdelli, in tense and anxious discussions with Bouzid about the symbolism and morality of the film's content. Abdelli, who states that he thought he was making a film about a dancer (and Bouzid did hide the content of the film from him), objects with real confusion and anger to the depiction of Islam and Muslims in the film, shouting at Bouzid, 'You're using me in this film to attack Muslims.' Bouzid responds to Abdelli's concerns with the arguments of a secular rationalist, noting that 'the Koran contains everything', and the Sufi can find peace in it just as the fundamentalist can find war. What he is really against, he states, is the mixing of religion in politics, whether that religion is Christianity, Judaism or Islam, and this statement ties Bouzid to a fiercely secular political tradition in Tunisia, depicted in Nadia El Fani's *Laïcité, Inch'Allah!* (*Neither Allah, Nor Master!*, 2011). These sections, which Bouzid says were genuine moments on set, were implanted in the film for two reasons, according to the director. Firstly, he wanted to show that 'la lute contre le terrorisme doit aller de pair avec la lute pour la liberté d'expression' ('the fight against terrorism should go hand in hand with the fight for freedom of speech'; quoted in Mimoun 2009). Abdelli really was afraid, and his feelings deserved recognition and a public forum. Secondly, Bouzid states that he didn't want to 'limiter la conception de l'Islam à celle de l'intégriste' ('limit the conception of Islam to that of the fundamentalist'; Mimoun 2009), and thus by integrating Abdelli's thought and his own, he adds a greater number of perspectives to a thorny and difficult debate.

However, Bouzid's approach has been critiqued as 'too didactic', and lacking in subtlety (Ruoff 2011: 31), and certainly, on first appearance, jarring as they are, these sequences seem to do the work of thought and disentanglement for the viewer, by providing us with a neat exposition of the filmmaker's vision. Moreover, the words that the veteran director uses in persuading his young actor to continue making the film resonate uncomfortably with Abdallah's rhetorical tactics. Abdelli accuses Bouzid of 'playing with symbols', much as Abdallah, the director's dark other, manipulates Batha with words, metaphors and the meanings of paradise, virgins, suicide and martyrdom. Phrases like 'fais-moi confiance' ('trust me'), 'c'est un risque que tu prends, prends-le avec moi' ('you're taking a risk, take it with me') and 'calme-toi' ('calm yourself') might easily be transplanted into Abdallah's script. In addition, Bouzid employs an audio-visual vocabulary of gesture and spatiality that resounds strikingly with the actions of Abdallah. Just as the fundamentalist comforts his young charge, taking him by the shoulders and moving in intimately to occupy his personal space, Bouzid lays his hand on Abdelli's arm, takes his hands, brings his face close to the actor's and kisses him. These are gestures of affective control and manipulation that evidently persuade his young actor to continue making the film (see Figure 8.3). For Ruoff, Bouzid thus risks becoming 'as authoritarian as the fundamentalist, thus neutralizing his critique' (Ruoff 2011: 31).

In this way, Bouzid could be said to represent another ageing patriarch, manipulating and controlling the younger generation. Indeed, the director wanted the film to attract a younger cohort of cinemagoers, but there is evidence that his appeal is not fully trans-generational. In 2010, the radical Islamist rapper, Psycho M, sampled a clip from one of the documentary sequences of *Making Of*, using it to promote violence against secular intellectuals in Tunisia, Bouzid among them (Stollery 2013). There is evidence that this call to violence was heard: in April 2011, Bouzid was brutally assaulted by an unknown attacker with an iron bar (Stollery 2013). Given that *Making Of*'s subtitle is *The Last Film* (*Akher Film*), because of Bouzid's fears of reprisal, this incident shows how perilously close his premonition came to being realised. Bouzid also drew criticism from some sections of

Figure 8.3 Directorial gestures of control and manipulation.

the Tunisian Press for accepting to be promoted *Chevalier de la Légion d'honneur* at Cannes in 2011, because it was seen as currying favour with the old colonial power, a country that was slow to recognise the revolutionary ideals of the Tunisian population during the Arab Spring (Stollery 2013).

Yet given the undeniable similarities between Bouzid's words and gestures and those of his fundamentalist character, it seems unlikely that he is unaware of the impression he imparts in the documentary sections. Bouzid's own rebellious youth and his clear opposition to forms of state control instead make it probable that he is highlighting the need for everyone to remain attentive and vigilant in the face of any form of indoctrination: religious, secular or ideological. Writing in praise of three films of the New Arab Realist Cinema, Shadi Abdel Salam's *The Mummy* (*Al Mumia*, 1970), Tewfik Saleh's *The Duped* (*Al-makhdu'un*, 1973) and Youssef Chahine's *The Sparrow* (*Al-Asfour*, 1972), Bouzid locates his admiration for their work in the following shared theme:

> It is noteworthy that these three films converge on a single point: the ordinary citizen is deceived by those in charge, and his real defeat lies in the fact that he had handed over power to another and accepted guardianship from the authorities. They all warn against the danger of such guardianship. (Bouzid 1995: 245)

What Bouzid counsels against, then, is the relinquishing of the personal power of thought to any form of authority and control, and the final sequences of the film bear out this proposition. Bahta, imprisoned in an abandoned warehouse by the fundamentalists because of his psychological volatility, finds a few sticks of dynamite and a means of escape. He meanders through the streets and portside of Tunis, the explosives strapped to his chest on full display. He meets one of the bearded fundamentalists, and attacks him, shouting, 'Don't you want to be a martyr too?' Bahta ends up running from the police through the huge shipping containers of La Guelette, where he finally detonates the bomb, alone, deliberately killing himself.

Bahta's appearance has changed throughout the film as his worldview has been altered: a loose-curled hip-hop breakdancing street boy at the start, he adopts the posture of a policeman, the overalls of the engraver, before shaving his head and face and morphing into an austere radical. Bahta's final vestimentary incarnation can therefore be marked as particularly significant: as he trundles through the streets of the city, he sports a jacket marked 'Picasso', replete with sharp lines and haphazard red and yellow patches (see Figure 8.4). Picasso, an Andalucían with strong cultural and artistic links to the Maghreb, was also a tireless innovator and a ceaseless proponent of originality whose artistic evolution consistently questioned established disciplinary norms and doctrines, namely through in his practice of cubism. Clearly, Bouzid feels strong artistic and affective affinity with the Spanish painter. The blinding sunlight, the bright primary colours on Bahta's jacket and on the shipping containers he runs through to escape the police all recall Picasso's visual aesthetic of stark angles and bold blocks of bright colour.

Bouzid's attempt to engage in contemporary politics and to question dominant modes of perception around political violence further recall Picasso's *Guernica* (1937), where the image of the victims of the Nazi's Germany Luftwaffe bombings in Galicia was designed to bring attention to the first major targeting of defenceless civilians by a bombing campaign. By drawing links between the aerial destruction of the Spanish village and the self-destruction of Bahta, Bouzid appears to suggest that the young man is a victim of an external force, rooted in a radical ideology, resulting in a violence that, in the end, destroys only himself. Thus, Bouzid interweaves the fragmentation of the cubist form, the rubble of Guernica, and the shattering of Bahta's body, bringing together art, politics and individual fatality in one tragic conclusion.

The film closes circuitously with a shot of the group of friends, Souad now at the centre, trundling along at the edge of the port where the spectator first encountered them. The final musical score erupts immediately after the explosion, and the haunting refrain fills the audible field with the somewhat jarring and improbable lyrics, 'be who you want'. Recalling

Figure 8.4 Bahta's final incarnation, in a jacket marked 'Picasso'.

the cheap jingles of advertising or the catchy refrains of a pop song, these words lose all frivolity when paired with the sombre strains of the melody and the deep, plaintive male voice. At once an exhortation and an instance of tragic irony, the words summon Picasso's statement that 'every child is an artist, the problem is how to remain an artist once he grows up' (quoted in Buttignol 1999: 121). Bahta, this 'child of the ruins', has been lost in a hinterland between youth and adulthood, art and life. Like the crumbling old structures he frequented with Souad, forgotten and derelict, the vestiges of Bahta's artistic dreams, his imaginings of travel and flight, disintegrate amid the ruins of a society that offers him no social or economic future. All that is left of the young man is a broken and fragmented body, and a lonely refrain.

Works Cited

Ahmed, Durre S. (2006), 'Gender and Islamic Spirituality: A Psychological View of "Low" Fundamentalism', in Lahoucine Ouzgane (ed.), *Islamic Masculinities*, Chicago: University of Chicago Press, pp. 11–34.

Anon. (2016), 'Look Forward in Anger', *The Economist*, 6 August, <http://www.economist.com/news/briefing/21703362-treating-young-threat-arab-rulers-are-stoking-next-revolt-look-forward-anger> (last accessed 11 February 2017).

Atran, Scott (2010), *Talking to the Enemy: Religion, Brotherhood, and the (Un)Making of Terrorists*, London: Penguin.

Atran, Scott (2015), 'Address to UN Security Council Ministerial Debate on: "The Role of Youth in Countering Violent Extremism and Promoting Peace"', The Center on Terrorism, 23 April, <http://johnjayresearch.org/ct/2015/05/11/professor-scott-atrans-address-to-the-un-security-council/> (last accessed 12 August 2016).

Atran, Scott (2016), 'ISIS is a Revolution', *Aeon Essays*, 4 January, <https://chip-gagnon.files.wordpress.com/2016/01/atran-isis-is-a-revolution-2015.pdf> (last accessed 10 August 2016).

Atran, Scott and Nafees Hamid (2015), 'Paris: The War ISIS Wants', *The New York Review of Books*, 16 November, <http://www.nybooks.com/daily/2015/11/16/paris-attacks-isis-strategy-chaos/> (last accessed 14 August 2016).

Bayat, Asef and Linda Herrera (2010), 'Introduction: Being Young and Muslim in Neoliberal Times', in Asef Bayat and Linda Herrera (eds), *Young and Muslim: New Cultural Politics in the Global South and North*, New York and Oxford: Oxford University Press, pp. 3–26.

Bender, Larissa (2007), 'Interview with Nouri Bouzid: Preventing Youths from Becoming Terrorists', Qantara, <https://en.qantara.de/content/interview--with-nouri-bouzid-preventing-youths-from-becoming-terrorists> (last accessed 10 August 2016).

Bouzid, Nouri (1994), *Sources of Inspiration*, Amsterdam: SOURCES.

Bouzid, Nouri (1995), 'New Realism in Arab Cinema: The Defeat-Conscious Cinema', trans. Shereen el Ezabi, in *Alif: Journal of Comparative Poetics*, 15, pp. 242–50.

Buttignol, Margie (1999), 'Encountering Little Margie, My Child Self as Artist', *The Postmodern Educator*, 89, pp. 121–46.

Corlett, Adam (2017). 'As Time Goes By: Shifting Incomes and Inequality between and Within Generations', The Intergenerational Commission, February, <http://www.intergencommission.org/wp-content/uploads/2017/02/IC-intra-gen.pdf> (last accessed 11 February 2017).

De Beauvoir, Simone (1949), *Le Deuxième sexe*, Paris: Gallimard.

Elgaaïed, Leïla (2007), 'Le documentaire comme combat', *Africultures*, 22 January, <http://africultures.com/le-documentaire-comme-combat-4701/> (last accessed 10 February 2017).

Esposito, John L. and Dalia Mogahed (2007), *Who Speaks For Islam?: What a Billion Muslims Really Think*, New York: Gallup Press.

Ezra, Elizabeth and Terry Rowden (2006), 'Introduction: What is Transnational Cinema?', in Elizabeth Ezra and Terry Rowden (eds), *Transnational Cinema: The Film Reader*, London: Routledge, pp. 1–12.

Gana, Nouri (2010), 'Bourguiba's Sons: Melancholy Manhood in Modern Tunisian Cinema', *The Journal of North African Studies*, 15:1, pp. 105–26.

Hasan, Noorhaidi (2010), 'The Drama of Jihad: The Emergence of Salafi Youth in Indonesia', in Asef Bayat and Linda Herrera (eds), *Young and Muslim: New Cultural Politics in the Global South and North*, New York and Oxford: Oxford University Press, pp. 49–62.

Hassan, Riaz (2009), 'What Motivates the Suicide Bombers?', *Yale Global*, 3 September, <http://yaleglobal.yale.edu/content/what-motivates-suicide-bombers-0> (last accessed 13 August 2016).

Lang, Robert (2014), *New Tunisian Cinema: Allegories of Resistance*, New York: Columbia University Press.

Merari, Ariel (2010), *Driven to Death: Psychological and Social Aspects of Suicide Terrorism*, Oxford: Oxford University Press.

Mimoun, Mouloud (2009), 'Entretien avec Nouri Bouzid', *Maghreb des films*, 7 October, <http://www.maghrebdesfilms.fr/IMG/pdf/Dossier_de_Presse_Making_of.pdf> (last accessed 16 August 2016).

Morgan, Marcyliena and Dionne Bennett (2011), 'Hip-Hop & the Global Imprint of a Black Cultural Form', *Daedalus*, 140:2, pp. 176–96.

Naficy, Hamid (1999), *An Accented Cinema: Exilic and Diasporic Filmmaking*, Princeton: Princeton University Press.

Ruoff, Jeffrey (2011), 'The Gulf War, the Iraq War, and Nouri Bouzid's Cinema of Defeat: *It's Scherazade We're Killing* (1993) and *Making Of* (2006)', *South Central Review*, 28:1, pp. 18–35.

Stollery, Martin (2001), 'Masculinities, Generations, and Cultural Transformation in Contemporary Tunisian Cinema', *Screen*, 41:1, pp. 49–63.

Stollery, Martin (2013), 'Nouri Bouzid: Great Director Profile', *Senses of Cinema*, 68, <http://sensesofcinema.com/2013/great-directors/nouri-bouzid/> (last accessed 11 August 2016).

Film

Making Of, film, directed by Nouri Bouzid. Tunisia: Les Films de l'Atalante, 2006.

CHAPTER 9

Gender and Representations of the *Banlieue* in Abd Al Malik's *Qu'Allah bénisse la France!* and Sylvie Ohayon's *Papa Was Not a Rolling Stone*

Jocelyn A. Wright

The French *banlieue* is a space that, more often than not, evokes images of burning cars, violent youth and tall, imposing concrete buildings that stretch for miles in every direction. In the political sphere, it is the site of endless debates about immigration, integration, race relations, police brutality, the treatment of women and radical Islam in France.[1] Events such as the 2005 riots during which the *banlieue* exploded in flames, and the national scandal in the early 2000s about *tournantes*, the violent gang rape of young women recounted in fictive films such as Fabrice Genestal's *La Squale* (2000) and real-life testimonials such as Samira Bellil's *Dans l'enfer des tournantes* (2002), further reinforced these stereotypes with their heavily mediatised imagery of angry, violent men and vulnerable women who were the victims of their wrath.[2] Genestal's *La Squale* is not the only film to have participated in the creation and reinforcement of *banlieue* stereotypes. Male-authored *banlieue* films produced in the 1980s and 1990s, from Jean-Claude Brisseau's *De Bruit et de fureur* (1988) to Matthieu Kassovitz's *La Haine* (1995) and Jean-François Richet's *Ma 6-T va crack-er* (1997), routinely featured violent, law-breaking protagonists who had dropped out of school. Women were often totally absent from this male-authored filmic space. When women were featured, they were either relegated to domestic spaces as mothers and sisters with little to no agency, or, at the other extreme of the spectrum, they became the hyper-sexualised objects of male desire.

At the turn of the twenty-first century, however, these portrayals of the *banlieue* began to shift as male *banlieue* directors began to push back against these characterisations of violence and sexuality in films like Rabah Ameur-Zaïmeche's *Wesh wesh, qu'est-ce qui se passe?* (2001) and Abdellatif Kechiche's *L'Esquive* (2003) and, particularly, as women such as Zaïda Ghorab-Volta (*Jeunesse dorée*, 2001) and Géraldine Nakache (*Tout ce qui brille*, 2010) began directing their own *banlieue* films. This counter-discourse in *banlieue* films has continued into the 2010s as can be seen in two *banlieue* films released in 2014: Abd Al Malik's *Qu'Allah bénisse la France!* and Sylvie Ohayon's *Papa Was Not a Rolling Stone*. While Al Malik evokes *La Haine* to contest its imagery of violent, delinquent masculinity, Ohayon draws from a tradition of female-directed *banlieue* films started by Ghorab-Volta that avoids stereotypical plotlines altogether, electing instead to tell stories that connect to the more universal experience of being an adolescent girl.

This article takes into account the gendered positions of both Ohayon and Al Malik and how this influences their portrayals of adolescence in the *banlieue*. Al Malik, like many men representing the *banlieue* across media, presents a very dark, sombre portrait of Neuhof (a *banlieue* of Strasbourg), both visually, through his choice of black and white filmography, and at a narrative level, through his storyline in which Régis (Marc Zinga) is the only boy to escape the *banlieue*. Ohayon's portrait is much more lighthearted, both due to its bright visual palette and a storyline in which the *banlieue* is presented as a safe, happy space while the Paris across the Boulevard Périphérique, the highway that surrounds Paris and marks the border between the city and its suburbs, is painted as the dangerous no-go zone. Ohayon's decision to avoid a wretched and desolate characterisation of the *banlieue* is part of a larger trend among women writers, comic artists, and filmmakers who grew up in the *banlieue*. Across genres, and in spite of the very real adversities that many young women in the *banlieue* do face in the form of oppressive families and sexual violence, these female artists choose to present the aspects of puberty that could apply to any young woman, regardless of whether or not she grew up in the *banlieue*. Thus, gender plays a significant role in terms of how adolescence in the *banlieue* is characterised, not just in these two films, but in the genre of *banlieue* films more broadly.

The *banlieue* film was, until the 2000s, a very masculine world. *Banlieue* films were directed by men, and the stories centred on adolescent male protagonists and their friendships with other men. Narratives of unemployment, drugs, violence, police confrontation and crime dominated these early *banlieue* films, highlighting the street smarts of the young men who navigated these issues. Plots focused on crime and encounters with the police further fed stereotypes of *banlieue* inhabitants as delinquents, with over two-thirds of *banlieue* films before 2000 featuring delinquent protagonists (Wagner 2011: 92). Many of these films were shot on location with a shaky hand-held camera to enhance a feeling of realism, which was further evoked through the extensive use of slang. The importance of the family and family life typical of earlier *beur* films[3] was eclipsed in *banlieue* films by the strong bonds formed between young men in these films, creating a male-dominated space where women rarely figured.[4]

Banlieue films in this period privileged representations of male spaces, and the women who do figure in these spaces, according to Carrie Tarr in her seminal overview of *banlieue* filmmaking practices, are 'generally silenced, relegated to minor or secondary roles, and/or constructed through stereotypes' (Tarr 2005: 111). As Tarr observes, the masculine spaces favoured in the films, 'city streets and public spaces', were 'frequented by transgressive, sexualized women' such as prostitutes or drug-addicted dancers while the women featured in the domestic space are 'victims of the oppressive patriarchal Arabo-Islamic sex/gender system' (Tarr 2005: 112). These two extremes leave little room for female agency. Indeed, Tarr identifies only two films from the 1990s that constructed complex roles for their secondary female characters 'without simultaneously exploiting them as objects of the gaze': Malik Chibane's *Hexagone* (1994) and *Douce France* (1995) (Tarr 2005: 89).

There were, however, shifts in representations of both masculinity and femininity in the *banlieue* that began around the 2000s and have continued to shift in the decade and a half since then. In contrast to the pre-2000 period, David-Alexandre Wagner observes that only one of thirteen films released between 2001 and 2005 reproduced the same stereotype of delinquent protagonists (Wagner 2011: 92). Male directors such as Philippe Faucon in *Samia* (2000), Genestal in *La Squale* (2000) and Kechiche in *L'Esquive* (2003) also began featuring more complex female protagonists around this time.

While portrayals of women began shifting at the turn of the twenty-first century, there was not a single *banlieue* film that featured both a female protagonist and was directed by a woman until Zaïda Ghorab-Volta released her groundbreaking film, *Jeunesse dorée* in 2001. *Jeunesse dorée* was remarkable not only for being the first *banlieue* feature film directed by a *beur* (meaning of Arab descent) woman, but also for its plotline, which eschewed many of the conventions of the masculine *banlieue* genre. Instead of a violent tale of conflict set against a backdrop of tall, looming towers, Ghorab-Volta sends her two female protagonists, Gwénaëlle (Alexandra Jeudon) and Angela (Alexandra Laflandre), on a road trip around France, during which they meet and photograph the people they encounter. Unlike Faucon's Samia or Genestal's Désirée, Gwénaëlle and Angela are not subject to the policing authority of the men in the *banlieue*. They are free to move about Colombes, the *banlieue* where they grew up, and they also enjoy the freedom of mobility to leave the *banlieue* not because they want greater freedom or to escape from overbearing male figures, but because they want to explore their country. This worry-free portrayal of female adolescence instead touches on universal themes of girlhood that extend across the Boulevard Périphérique: friendship, the transition from adolescence to adulthood and young romance.

Jeunesse dorée led the charge in a tradition of female *banlieue* filmmaking that avoids stereotypes and offers more unusual *banlieue* narratives. Michael Gott notes that the release of female-directed *banlieue* films such as Karin Albou's *La Petite Jérsualem* (2005), Isabelle Czajka's *L'Année suivante* (2006), Audrey Estrougo's *Regarde-moi* (2007), Nora Hamdi's *Des Poupées et des anges* (2008) and Géraldine Nakache's *Tout ce qui brille* (2008) coincided with 'a diversification of cinematic images of the suburbs' and argues that they 'have clearly played a significant role in the enrichment of perspectives' of the *banlieue* (Gott 2013: 468). Indeed, this diversification of cinematic images has continued well into the 2010s, in both male-authored and female-authored films, as can be seen in both *Papa Was Not a Rolling Stone* and *Qu'Allah bénisse la France!*

Papa Was Not a Rolling Stone, which was released in August 2014, tells the story of Stéphanie (Doria Achour), a young girl with passions for both dance and advertising, who is coming of age in the 1980s in the Cité des 4000 in La Courneuve. In order to pursue her dream of working in advertising, Stéphanie must get a 'mention très bien' on her *baccalauréat*, a goal which she achieves in spite of the many odds against her: an abusive stepfather, an absent-minded mother, an unsupportive school system and an unplanned pregnancy that forces her to find money for an abortion. Stéphanie perseveres through it all, and the film ends with her smiling as she sits down to take her first class at La Sorbonne. The film, which is Ohayon's auto-adaptation of her 2011 autobiography, *Papa Was Not a Rolling Stone*, mostly follows Ohayon's life as written in her autobiography, although a few plot points, such as Stéphanie's pregnancy, were added to the film.

Released a few months later, in December 2014, *Qu'Allah bénisse la France!* tells the story of how Régis[5] (Mark Zinga), Al Malik's first name before he converted to Islam, was the only one from his *banlieue* of Neuhof, Strasbourg, to leave and start a legitimate, non-criminal career. Due to the combination of his romantic relationship with Nawel (Sabrina Ouazani), an Arab girl in his neighbourhood who teaches him about Sufi Islam, his talents for writing, music and philosophy, and a fair amount of luck, Régis escapes from the crime-fuelled exploits of his youth unscathed. Drawing closely from Al Malik's actual life and his 2004 autobiography of the same name, the film chronicles Régis's transformation from petty criminal to devout Muslim to the world-renowned rapper he is today.

Both films represent a counter-discourse in their portrayals of the *banlieue* and in their portrayals of adolescent sexuality. Ohayon's *Papa Was Not a Rolling Stone* capitalises on the neon hues and catchy pop songs of the 1980s to create an upbeat *banlieue* that does not resemble the gritty, miserable spaces of early *banlieue* films and actively works against characterisations of the *banlieue* as a desolate place devoid of hope. By contrast, Al Malik's film deliberately references *banlieue* films to produce a space that is visually evocative of these early *banlieue* films. Al Malik, however, complicates Kassovitz's portrayal to show the pitfalls and dangers of *banlieue* violence. These films also deal with sexuality in a very different manner. Al Malik avoids portrayals of sexuality to create a portrait of masculinity that is not based on the objectification of women while Ohayon capitalises on the sexuality in her film to present a positive portrait of Arab–Jewish relations and to talk about teenage abortion, two themes which are not typical of *banlieue* films. These are also situations that extend far beyond the *banlieue*, that connect the film to a more universal theme of experiences shared by women of all social classes and backgrounds.

While the visual representations of the *banlieue* in *Papa Was Not a Rolling Stone* and *Qu'Allah bénisse la France!* could not be more different, both represent important challenges to the stereotypical images of the *banlieue* as a gritty, dangerous space rife with crime and violence. Ohayon refuses the dark, sombre, shadowed imagery of the *banlieue* in favour of a bright portrayal of La Courneuve where shadows and the colour black are practically banished from the film and the characters move to a poppy, upbeat soundtrack of 1980s hits. By contrast, Al Malik adopts the same black and white of *La Haine* in order to critique and complicate portrayals of violent masculinity. Although Ohayon and Al Malik take two very different approaches, both films continue to complicate stereotypical portrayals of the *banlieue* and expand narrative possibilities for *banlieue* films.

The black and white cinematography in *Qu'Allah bénisse la France!* is a deliberate reference to Kassovitz's *La Haine*. The connection between the films is not accidental, as the impetus for Al Malik's decision to make the film came from a conversation he had with Kassovitz, who encouraged him to adapt his autobiography *Qu'Allah bénisse la France!* into a film (Al Malik and Azzouz, 2014). When Al Malik chose to do so, he used the same director of photography, Pierre Aïm, that Kassovitz used in *La Haine* (Coppermann 2014). Aside from the high-contrast cinematography, several shots from *Qu'Allah bénisse la France!* are also evocative of *La Haine*. For instance, the iconic *black-blanc-beur* shots depicting Vinz, Hubert and Saïd walking in *La Haine* are reworked in *Qu'Allah bénisse la France!* with Régis at the centre and his white and Arab friends walking on either side of him. The films also use many of the same framing devices; both begin with scenes of police in riot gear and both use the main character's voice-over (Hubert in *La Haine*; Régis in *Qu'Allah bénise la France!*) to guide the viewer through the film.

Al Malik's aim in referring to *La Haine*, however, is not to reproduce its gritty representations of violence and masculinity but rather to complicate these ideas. For instance, like *La Haine*, the soundtrack of *Qu'Allah bénisse la France!* is primarily rap, although, unlike in *La Haine*, the majority of the songs are written by Al Malik and performed by the actor Marc Zinga who plays Régis. Furthermore, if the rap used in *La Haine* was meant to enhance the backdrop of violent performances of masculinity, the songs in *Qu'Allah bénisse la France!* call this glorification of violence into question. For instance, 'Soldat de Plomb', a track from Al Malik's album, Gibraltar, that features prominently in the film, does not glamorise the life of violence and crime in the *banlieue* but rather emphasises the fear that these people feel in these situations. Régis is *tout maigre* in his *grosse veste* and soils his pants, a far cry from Vinz's iconic monologue in *La Haine* where he reinforces the stereotype of the *banlieue* gangster who is not afraid of anything in his reprise of Travis Bickle in Martin Scorcese's *Taxi Driver*, 'You talkin' to me?' monologue in the mirror. He laments, 'J'avais déjà vu trop de sang.'[6] At twelve years old, he has already seen too much death. Images such as this push back against a narrative of the glamour of crime, and the infallibility of those who sell drugs, either as small-time drug dealing *petits vendeurs* or as masterminding *caïds* by showing that they are not fearless gangsters but rather scared little boys who are likely to die well before their time.

The soundtrack is not the only way that Al Malik indicates the real dangers associated with criminal delinquency. As in the book, where an entire page is dedicated to listing the names and causes of death of the people Régis knew from his neighbourhood who died too young (Al Malik 2004: 51), the film likewise pays homage to the many people from Régis's youth who passed away. When Rachid, one of the many boys in the *banlieue* caught up in crime and selling drugs, is murdered in a drive by shooting, all of his family, friends and acquaintances from the neighbourhood gather to pay their respects by his grave. As the imam speaks about the afterlife, the camera focuses on two groups: the women and the men, who are standing in separate groups. First, one woman, Isabelle, disappears from the crowd. Her body disappears from the screen but her name and the reason for her death (an overdose) linger on the screen. The camera then focuses on the group of young men standing near her. First one young man disappears, then another and another. In the end, of the sixteen men who were initially standing, only nine remain, and the screen is covered with the names of not only those who stood among the original sixteen but also of the others who died from overdoses, car and motorcycle accidents, and shootings. A total of eighteen names appear on screen, a sobering reminder of the many youths who died before they could leave the *banlieue*. The men who remain range in age from young to old and are white, black and Arab. Some are religious figures, some have jobs and others are unemployed. The randomness with which the men disappear highlights the element of chance regarding who did or did not survive. The disappearing bodies and the lingering names are ghosts who haunt the screen, not just in this scene, but throughout the film, accentuating the truly exceptional nature of the simple fact that Al Malik escaped the *banlieue* alive, much less with a career. These ghosts remind viewers of the very real risks of the violent displays of masculinity glorified in many *banlieue* films, including *La Haine*.

Ohayon also uses the visual space of her film to critique the violent imagery of the *banlieue*, but in an entirely different fashion because, as a female director, Ohayon is connecting to and aligning herself with a different strain of *banlieue* filmmaking that defies the doomsday portraits of the *banlieue* found in male-authored narratives. Ohayon's film is set in the Cité des 4000 in La Courneuve, which is notorious, in both televised news reports and in feature films, as a grim place rife with lawless individuals. As David Garbin and Gareth Millington describe in their study of La Courneuve, the Cité des 4000 is 'one of the most infamous *grands ensembles* of mass housing built in the 1960s' while La Courneuve is 'perhaps the most stigmatized Parisian *banlieue*' (Garbin and Millington 2012: 2068). This can be seen in the vocabulary of news footage of La Courneuve during the 1980s, which calls it *dégénéré* and *insalubre*, deeming the Cité des 4000 a place where 'on ne vit pas, on survit' (INA Société 2012).[7] This was the same area where, in 2005, Nicolas Sarkozy infamously promised he would 'nettoyer les cités au Kärcher'.[8] Garbin and Millington's survey of the Cité des 4000's residents demonstrated that this place is so stigmatised that its inhabitants feel the associations with the housing estate negatively impact their opportunities for employment and promotion, even outside La Courneuve (Garbin and Millington 2012: 2068). This stigma is also reinforced by movies. Even from the very beginning, films set in La Courneuve, such as Jean-Luc Godard's *Deux ou trois choses que je sais d'elle* (1967), depicted it as an empty shell that lacked a cultural centre (Hensman 2013: 445). In more recent years, the choice to film polemical films such as *La Squale* (2000), which featured violent portrayals of gang rape, in the Cité des 4000 further reinforces the association between this place and the same stigmatising images of violence and lack of social mobility. Indeed, as Bruno Levasseur has argued, La Courneuve has become a 'cult place' of French *banlieue* cinema because of its proximity to Paris (it is one of the few *banlieues* with a metro stop) that makes it an ideal space to reinforce the contrast between centre and periphery (Levasseur 2008: 101).

Working directly against these stereotypes of the Cité des 4000 as a dark and desolate place lacking in opportunity, Ohayon paints the housing estate with a hyper-saturated colour palette, recasting the Cité des 4000 as bright, colourful and full of love. Even at night, the *banlieue* sky is not a hue of black but rather a soothing, dark, calming midnight blue. The majority of the characters wear neutral colours, making the bright sunny backgrounds of graffiti and wall murals, as well as the red doors on the apartment buildings, pop all the more. By choosing a cheery, luminous palette, Ohayon connects her film to a filmic tradition of counter-resistance against the grey, dark colours of *banlieue* films. A few early films, such as Bertrand Blier's *Un deux trois soleil* (1993), eschewed the dark palette of the *banlieue* in favour of one full of light, although Wagner argues that the black and white cinematography of *La Haine* led more filmmakers to contest the dark images of the *banlieue* that appeared on television with more colourful films (Wagner 2011: 316). For instance, in films such as *La Squale*, *Samia* and *Wesh wesh, qu'est-ce qui se passe?*, greys were replaced with vivid, multicoloured palettes, even when the narratives remained sombre, as is the case in *La Squale*. Likewise, the bright colours and catchy 1980s soundtrack in *Papa Was Not a Rolling Stone* welcome viewers into the space of the film, encouraging them to identify and sympathise with the people who live there.

This flood of colours also came from a desire on the part of the directors to humanise the *banlieue*. When speaking about her film, Ohayon emphasised her desire to show that 'si on apprenait à se connaître les uns les autres, on verrait que ce sont les mêmes ressorts qui font bouger l'humanité, quel que soit le milieu social' (quoted in Rousseau 2014).[9] Ohayon accentuates the human relationships that Stéphanie (Doria Achour) forms with the people who live in the Cité des 4000. The film highlights Stéphanie's friendship with Fatima, her close relationship with her grandmother, and her love story with Rabah, all of whom are sources of comfort to her, particularly since her mother and her stepfather are emotionally unavailable. Ohayon further contests the idea that there is nothing to do in the Cité des 4000 by showing that there are social programmes and opportunities available to La Courneuve's residents. Stéphanie takes dance courses, a social service she has been taking advantage of since childhood. As the montage goes back and forth between her abusive stepfather and her dance classes shows, these classes helped her to weather the aggressions of her abusive childhood.

Ohayon further drives home her portrait of La Courneuve as a safe and comforting space by visually contrasting it with a darker, moodier Paris that is full of browns and greys and artificial colours. The perceptible contrast between these spaces can be seen most intensely when characters are travelling between Paris and La Courneuve; as they head towards Paris the bright colours on the screen are replaced by darker, deeper hues and when they return to the *banlieue*, the colours intensify and brighten. For instance, when Stéphanie and her friends visit La Sorbonne to see how the students dress there so that Stéphanie can fit in better, the rich brown leather satchels and deep forest green and dark purple sweaters atop dark jeans of the Parisians at the Sorbonne contrasts with the bright, faded blue jeans of Stéphanie and her friends, whose shirts are in light, muted colours. This contrast reflects the film's play with assumptions about danger and safety, a concept that is reinforced by Fatima's advice to Stéphanie at the end of the film, when she tells her to be careful in Paris because 'C'est pas comme ici à la cité, c'est dangereux.'[10] In typical *banlieue* films, the *banlieue* is the dark moody, dangerous space while Paris is bright, colourful and full of life. By contrast, in *Papa Was Not a Rolling Stone*, Paris is the source of danger, an idea which is reinforced by a series of events where misfortune befalls those from La Courneuve who go to Paris: Stéphanie's mother has the sexual encounter on the Champs Élysées which gets her pregnant, Stéphanie discovers the positive results of her pregnancy test in a bathroom in Paris, and she and her mother witness her father-in-law cheating at a Parisian restaurant.

The difference in the visual textures of these two films spills over into a difference in the portrayals of sexuality. While Ohayon follows in the female filmmaking tradition of portraying female sexual agency more openly, Al Malik creates a vision of masculinity for Régis that is not dependent on sex. While sexuality is a central plotline in *Papa Was Not a Rolling Stone*, in *Qu'Allah bénisse la France!* there is no physical contact, not even hugs or hand-holding, between any of the male and female characters, including Régis and Nawel, whose wedding is shown at the end of the film. Ohayon follows in the footsteps of the still-nascent tradition of female *banlieue* filmmakers with a love story that shows female sexuality, and the pleasures and complications it can produce, while Al Malik breaks with the male-authored *banlieue* filmmaking tradition by telling a chaste love story in which the female love interest is never hyper-sexualised.

Just as Al Malik sought to combat traditionally violent visual imagery of the *banlieue*, he also contests stereotypical portrayals of women by not objectifying the women he portrays on screen. Most of his shots of women are medium shots that focus on their facial expressions, instead of their bodies; even love interests, such as Nawel, are not presented as physical objects of desire. The women in *Qu'Allah bénisse la France!* also do not fall to the other end of the spectrum of being depicted as victims, but rather are strong figures who are positive influences on Régis's life. Even in situations where women are typically objectified, such as the party scene, Al Malik still avoid sexual imagery, electing to convey the party atmosphere through images of party-goers injecting themselves with drugs in a smoke-filled, hazy room, instead of through voyeuristic shots of scantily clad women.

Al Malik drew his inspiration for the love story between Régis and Nawel from Norah Ephron's films, saying that he, too, wanted to tell a love story in a different, non-traditional way (Al Malik and Azzouz 2014). Much like the characters in Ephron's films, who are often friends for a long time before they become romantically involved (*When Harry Met Sally*) or who develop a relationship that is intellectual before it is physical (*You've Got Mail*), Régis and Nawel's relationship is unconventional. At first, they must meet in secret because Nawel's overbearing older brother, Rachid, has a tense and unfriendly relationship with Régis. On dates, the couple steals away to Petit Paris, a romantic oasis in Strasbourg where they walk and talk without interruption. On a physical level, Nawel and Regis's relationship as shown on screen is remarkably chaste. They do not hug and are never shown kissing, even at their wedding (the first time they are even shown holding hands is at their wedding.) Sex is never even a possibility. While Regis and Nawel are clearly charmed by each other, their affection for one another is never made physical, but is instead shown through shared smiles and intellectual discussions. Much of the relationship revolves around Nawel teaching Regis about Sufi Islam by sharing a book, Karim Ben Driss's *Le Renouveau du soufisme au Maroc*, with him.

Al Malik's portrayal of love and sexuality is a direct reaction to the many *banlieue* films that came out around the time of *La Haine* in which characters performed their masculinity through the hyper-sexualisation of women. As Tarr observes, these films were marked by 'the expression of macho yet largely impotent attitudes towards women' (Tarr 2005: 99–100). By contrast, Al Malik refuses this stereotype by removing sex from the equation entirely while still having a perfectly self-assured masculine character. Régis's identity and masculinity are not built on his ability to marry Nawel, but rather on the choices he makes over the course of the film. At his wedding, Régis announces 'J'ai plus peur',[11] a phrase which refers to the many choices that he made throughout the film that were motivated by fear: the fear of not having enough money (which led him to rob tourists in Strasbourg), the fear of death following Rachid's murder (which led him to, briefly, adopt an extreme version of Islam), the fear of not making it out of Neuhof (which led him to pursue his rap career but also to accept 'dirty' drug money in order to get there), to name a few. As Régis overcomes these fears, he also becomes more self-assured and confident that he can be the man Nawel deserves.

Unlike Al Malik, Ohayon has no qualms about placing sexuality at the heart of her narrative. In contrast to Regis and Nawel's cerebral relationship, Stéphanie and Rabah's connection is quite physical. Rabah (Rabah Faït Oufella) is drawn to Stéphanie after watching her in dance class, and their first romantic interaction takes place when they are dancing at a party. Unlike Régis and Nawel, Stéphanie and Rabah seem to have very little in common on an intellectual level; while Stéphanie is a top student, Rabah is already caught up in a life of petty crime and is sent to jail during Stéphanie's summer vacation. Rabah seems to have little interest in discussing Stéphanie's dream of pursuing a career in advertising, though he does try to help her by stealing trendy clothes for her to wear on her first day at the Sorbonne.

As a result of this lack of intellectual connection, Stéphanie and Rabah's relationship is mainly sexual. A large portion of the drama of their relationship centres on them trying to have sex for the first time, something they struggle with because their only sex education came from movies, leading to some misconceptions about how to approach the sexual act. When they do have sex, they do not use birth control and Stéphanie becomes pregnant. The remainder of their relationship centres on how this pregnancy could stop Stéphanie from achieving her dream of going to the Sorbonne or of becoming a professional dancer. Because of her pregnancy, Stéphanie falls during an ambitious move at a crucial dance competition she has spent the entire school year preparing for, effectively ruining her chances of being able to continue dancing at a professional level. She chooses to pursue her academic career, and is accepted to the Sorbonne after receiving the highest honours on her *baccalauréat*. At this point, Stéphanie is certain that she must get an abortion to take advantage of this once-in-a lifetime opportunity to go to the Sorbonne. However, she does not know how she will pay for the procedure. In a surprisingly touching moment, Stéphanie's absent-minded mother returns from an impromptu vacation just in time to give her money for her abortion and take her to the clinic, which requires a parent or guardian for minors needing the procedure.

The sexual scenes in the film between Stéphanie and Rabah are all the more remarkable because they show a romantic relationship between a Jew and an Arab in a relatively uncomplicated and unburdened manner, and their religious differences are not a source of tension. In fact, their difference in terms of religious upbringing is only ever brought up by Stéphanie's Arab friend Fatima, who dramatically gasps when she discovers that Stéphanie is attracted to Rabah. Nevertheless, she does so in a very light-hearted, jovial manner that is more reflective of the teasing banter between two friends than it is indicative of an actual conflict. More significantly, Stéphanie and Rabah do not have to hide their relationship, and they even get along well with one another's families; for instance, Rabah helps Stéphanie's grandmother with her bags as she crosses the street. This depiction of Arab–Jewish relations, however, is quite revolutionary, even for contemporary French films, where the complicated history between Jewish and Arab people is typically a point of tension. While a few films about Jewish–Arab relationships in contemporary France have been released in the past two decades (Karin Albou's *La Petite Jérsualem* in 2005 and Philippe Faucon's *Dans la vie* in 2008), *Papa Was Not a Rolling Stone* still stands out as the only one of these films in which the characters' religious differences are not a source of conflict. Even in *La Petite Jérusalem*, Laura's attraction to the illegal Arab-Muslim immigrant Djamel produces so many complications between their respective families that she leaves him. While they ultimately overcome these differences, at first religion is also a major source of conflict between Jewish Esther and *pied-noir* widow Halima, who is Muslim, in *Dans la vie*.

Interfaith relationships are not the only taboo topic Ohayon depicts in the film. Ohayon also openly discusses a topic that has traditionally received much less attention in French films, and, even less again in *banlieue* film: abortion. The film depicts the shame Stéphanie feels for being pregnant while also emphasising how essential an abortion is in order for Stéphanie to pursue her dreams. Stéphanie is terrified of people finding out she is pregnant; she goes all the way to Paris to take a pregnancy test and, afterwards, hides her condition from everyone, including close mentors like her dance teacher. Stéphanie wears loose clothing whenever possible to conceal her growing bump, as she is especially paranoid about being the subject of gossip at school. Throughout this time, Stéphanie never wavers from her conviction that she does not want to have the child. Shortly after the trip to Paris to procure the pregnancy test, Stéphanie sits in the locker room after one of her dance classes, and stares down at her growing stomach, punching it repeatedly, as though she could will the pregnancy to disappear. She understands how having a baby at such a young age could change the course of her own future, since this is what happened to her mother before her. As she explains to Rabah: 'Je peux faire des études à la Sorbonne [où] je suis prise en philosophie du langage. Après je vais faire un doctorat, mais si je garde ton enfant je fais rien du tout.'[12] When he suggests that she go back to Tunisia to have the baby, she responds, 'Non, je ne peux pas, je veux pas. Tu comprends je veux pas le garder je peux pas me faire ça.'[13] Stéphanie has made up her mind, and has no intention of keeping her baby, since doing so would keep her from achieving all the dreams for which she worked so hard. She is not afraid of the sacrifices this might entail and tells Rabah that if he does not support her decision and help her, he will never see her again.

Stéphanie is deeply aware of the potential implications of keeping her unwanted baby because of the way she came into the world, which was due to her own mother's unwanted pregnancy. As we are shown in the film's opening scene, Stéphanie was conceived in the front seat of a car on Christmas Eve, when her mother, a virgin, supposedly became pregnant from her father dry-humping her in the front seat of his car. As Stéphanie wryly explains in a voice-over at the beginning of the film, the *tache* of semen he left on her mother's leg 'c'est moi'. Though Stéphanie's mother decided to keep her child, it is clear that this pregnancy kept her from achieving any of her own dreams.[14] Thus, it is Stéphanie's mother who gives her the 5,000 francs she needs (which approximately corresponds to 800 euros) for the abortion and who accompanies her to the hospital to have the procedure done. When Stéphanie heads to the Sorbonne shortly thereafter, it is her mother who encourages her by saying 'fais toute la vie que moi je n'ai pas eue'.[15] Stéphanie's mother does not want her daughter to also have her life derailed by an unwanted pregnancy and does everything in her power to help her daughter avoid this. She procures the money Stéphanie needs while protecting Stéphanie's privacy by telling her family members she needs the money to pay for her own divorce. The abortion becomes a secret shared between Stéphanie and her mother, a formative moment in her life that brings them closer together.

In the interfaith love story and in the abortion plotline, Ohayon pushes the limits of conventional *banlieue* narratives, both by refusing to make religious differences an obstacle in the love story, and by describing thoughtfully and sympathetically why a young girl might choose to have an abortion. Furthermore, these are plotlines that are not restricted to *banlieue* films (many women experience unwanted pregnancies, and star-crossed lovers are as old as Romeo and Juliet), lending a universal quality to Stéphanie's story. Plotlines such as these are also reflective of a number of more open accounts of female sexuality in *banlieue* stories across a variety of mediums that came out in the 2000s and were authored by women. Doria, the protagonist in Faïza Guène's (2004) novel *Kiffe kiffe demain* talks about getting her period and being surprised that her blood was not blue, like it is in the commercials for Always pads (Guène 2004: 49). Nine Antico's (2012) autobiographical graphic novel about her childhood in Seine-Saint-Denis, *Le Goût du paradis*, focuses on her burgeoning sexuality, showing crushes and first kisses instead of gang violence and petty crime. As such, Ohayon is participating in a larger tradition of female-authored representations of the *banlieue*, not only in films but also in novels and graphic novels, in which the plotlines centre less on the violence commonly associated with the *banlieue*, and more so on universal aspects of girlhood and adolescence, from first periods to first kisses. Although these stories are set in the *banlieue*, the setting is ancillary, and the stories would still make sense even if they were set in the sixth arrondissement in the middle of Paris. As such, *Papa Was Not a Rolling Stone* marks an effort to normalise life in the *banlieue* and connect it to the universal experiences of female adolescence that extend beyond the Boulevard Périphérique.

Both *Papa Was Not a Rolling Stone* and *Qu'Allah bénisse la France!* are remarkable not only for their more nuanced portrayals of the *banlieue*, but also for the fact that they were not created by *beur* directors. While *beur*-authored films have long been recognised for what Carrie Tarr has called 'reframing difference', that is to say, 'reassuring majority audiences that fears about "otherness" are unfounded', the role of films created by non-*beurs* in complicating this dynamic has been less recognised (Tarr 2005: 210–11). In the same volume, Tarr contrasts white-authored *banlieue* films with *beur*-authored films, creating a binary between *beur* filmmakers and white filmmakers which excludes directors like Ohayon, a Jewish-Tunisian woman, and Al Malik, who is of Congolese origin. Ohayon and Al Malik's films complicate this binary by presenting equally humanising portraits of non-*beur* minorities that reframe difference in the *banlieue*.

Many other post-2010 films have continued to push the conventions of the *banlieue* genre and further complicate the white-authored/*beur*-authored *banlieue* film binary. In addition to Ohayon and Al Malik's films, films such as Céline Sciamma's *Bande de filles* (2014), which featured girls playing with the presentation of their femininity, and Faucon's *Fatima* (2015), which centres on a hard-working single Maghrebi mother's complicated relationship with her two daughters, represent other fresh portrayals of the *banlieue*. As such, they continue to broaden the concept of what is and is not an appropriate topic for a *banlieue* film, while showing how other, non-*beur* voices can present equally compelling and complex portraits of the *banlieue* and its inhabitants.

Notes

1. See Hargreaves (2007) and Bourdieu (1993).
2. For more on the how the *tournantes* created a national scandal fuelled by a combination of media reports, fictional films, and testimonials co-written with journalists, see Mucchielli (2007), especially 5–17.
3. *Beur* films refer to the films made by the children of Arab immigrants, most often in the 1980s and early 1990s. Tarr describes *beur* films as 'informed by the need to reassure majority audiences that fears about "otherness" are unfounded. Thus, they draw on realist modes of filmmaking to demonstrate the basic humanity of the *beurs*, placing them at the center of the diegesis, privileging points of view which make them the subjects rather than the objects of the gaze, and constructing them as complex individuals whose feels and emotions are likely to elicity sympathy' (Tarr 2005: 210–11).
4. For a general overview of the history of *banlieue* filmmaking, see Tarr (2005).
5. Since they share the same name, to differentiate between the film's protagonist and its director, I use Régis to designate the film character and Al Malik to refer to the film's director.
6. 'I have already seen too much blood.'
7. 'one does not live, one survives'.
8. 'to clean the housing projects with a Kärcher [power washing tool]'.
9. 'If we learn to get to know one another, we would see that people are motivated by the same causes and responsibilities, regardless of their social class.'
10. 'Life in the projects is different from here, it's dangerous.'
11. 'I am no longer afraid'.
12. 'I can study at the Sorbonne, where I have been accepted to study the philosophy of language. After, I am going to pursue a doctorate degree, but if I keep this child, I won't do anything at all.'
13. 'No, I cannot, I do not want to. Can't you understand I don't want to keep it, I can't do that to myself.'
14. This is a topic of lengthy discussion in Ohayon's autobiography, in which she recounts how her mother was shunned and shamed by the family for being pregnant (2011: 30–4) and how disappointed she was when she had a daughter instead of a son (ibid.: 37–8).
15. 'have the life I never had'.

Works Cited

Al Malik, Abd (2004), *Qu'Allah bénisse la France!*, Paris: Albin Michel.
Al Malik, Abd and Nawell Azzouz (2014), Audio Commentary. *Qu'Allah bénisse la France!*. Director Al Malik. Ad Vitam.
Antico, Nine [2008] (2012), *Le goût du paradis*, Bordeaux: Les Requins Marteaux.
Bourdieu, Pierre (1993), *La Misère du Monde*, Paris: Éditions du Seuil.

Coppermann, Annie (2014), '"Qu'Allah bénisse la France": Dans la cité, la paix après la haine?', *Les Échos*, 10 December, <http://blogs.lesechos.fr/annie-coppermann/qu-allah-benisse-la-france-dans-la-cite-la-paix-apres-la-haine-a15119.html> (last accessed 29 January 2018).

Garbin, David and Gareth Millington (2012), 'Territorial Stigma and the Politics of Resistance in a Parisian *Banlieue*: La Courneuve and Beyond', *Urban Studies*, 49:10, pp. 2067–83.

Gott, Michael (2013), '"Bouger pour voir les immeubles": *Jeunesse dorée* (2001), *L'année suivante* (2006) and the Creative Mobility of Women's *Banlieue* Cinema', *Modern & Contemporary France*, 21:4, pp. 453–72.

Guène, Faïza (2004), *Kiffe kiffe demain*, Paris: Hachette.

Hargreaves, Alec G. (2007), *Multi-Ethnic France: Immigration, Politics, Culture and Society*, New York: Routledge.

Hensman, Ravi (2013), 'Oracles of Suburbia: French Cinema and Portrayals of Paris *Banlieues*, 1958-1968', *Modern & Contemporary France*, 21:4, pp. 435–51.

INA Société (2012), 'Vivre à la cité des 4000 à La Courneuve en 1983 | Archive INA', 9 July, <http://www.youtube.com/watch?v=xRTHyqbJKJc> (last accessed 20 August 2018).

Levasseur, Bruno (2008), 'De-Essentializing the Banlieues, Reframing the Nation: Documentary Cinema in France in the Late 1990s', *New Cinemas: Journey of Contemporary Film*, 6:2, 97–109.

Mucchielli, Laurent (2005), *Le scandale des 'tournantes': dérives médiatiques, contre-enquête sociologique*, Paris: La Découverte.

Ohayon, Sylvie (2011), *Papa Was Not a Rolling Stone*, Paris: Robert Laffont.

Rousseau, Élodie (2014), 'De La Courneuve à Paris VIII: parcours de Sylvie Ohayon, héroïne et réalisatrice de "Papa was not a Rolling Stone"', 13 October, <http://www.aufeminin.com/sorties-cinema/sylvie-ohayon-rencontre-avec-la-real-de-papa-was-not-s1068910.html> (last accessed 29 January 2018).

Tarr, Carrie (2005), *Reframing Difference: Beur and Banlieue Filmmaking in France*, Manchester: Manchester University Press.

Wagner, David-Alexandre (2011), *De La Banlieue stigmatisée à la cité démystifiée: La Répresentation de la banlieue des grands ensembles dans le cinéma français de 1981 à 2005*, New York: Peter Lang.

Films

Papa Was Not a Rolling Stone!, film, directed by Sylvie Ohayon. France: Pathé Distribution, 2014.

Qu'Allah bénisse la France!, film, directed by Abd Al Malik. France: Ad Vitam, 2014.

CHAPTER 10

(Re)Framing Youth and Identity in the Classroom in *Être et avoir* and *Entre les murs*

Aubrey Korneta

Introduction

Separated by only six years, Nicolas Philibert's *Être et avoir* (*To Be and to Have*, 2002) and Laurent Cantet's *Entre les murs* (*The Class*, 2008) depict their setting, the classroom, as a space that invites reflection and debate about the school's role in shaping youth identity in France. These widely successful and critically acclaimed films explore similar themes, such as the complexities of language, the testing of boundaries, as well as the difficulties of learning, living in a community and growing up. However, in spite of their many similarities, these films illustrate strikingly different perspectives on youth in the context of a classroom.

How and to what end do these two films depict similar themes in such divergent ways? To respond to this question, I will briefly situate the films in their political and historical contexts. Then, I will examine the spatial representation of the schools, how the students and their communities are characterised and framed as well as the messages these images convey. Finally, I will analyse the relationships to language learning through the linguistic registers taught, praised and disparaged. My study of both the formal and thematic elements demonstrates that Philibert's attempt to capture 'something more universal' (Falcon 2003: 28), instead depicts a very particular educational experience; and that while Cantet portrays the untold stories of France's 'excluded' youth through a particular classroom (Vincendeau 2008: 30–1), he also asks broader questions regarding the definition of French identity and the role education plays in shaping it.

The Historical and Political Landscape

To better understand the themes and potential messages of these films, we will begin with a bit of context. The decade preceding the release of *Être et avoir* in August 2002 was marked by many changes. Europe was becoming an increasingly powerful political and economic entity with the ratification of the Treaty of Maastricht in 1992, which led to greater European integration, the eventual adoption of a single European currency (the euro) in 2002, and the disappearance of the French franc. However, France's relationship to Europe's expansion was complicated: while many politicians on the left and the right supported further European integration, not everyone was convinced of the benefits of a larger, more powerful Europe. Some saw it as a threat to French sovereignty or the expansion of neoliberal policies and globalisation, leading to uncertainty and even hostility vis-à-vis Europe.[1]

Additionally, France's domestic political landscape was in flux. In 1997, President Jacques Chirac's right-wing party lost the legislative elections. While the Socialists won a large majority, the National Front – an anti-Europe, anti-immigration and racist party – also made gains in this election due in large part to fears of economic liberalism and globalisation (Sowerwine 2009: 405). Chirac's loss led to a situation known as cohabitation, and resulted in the appointment of Socialist leader and former presidential candidate Lionel Jospin as Prime Minister. This cohabitation would last the remaining five years of Chirac's seven-year term. The late 1990s and early 2000s witnessed several positive social reforms;[2] however, this period continued to be marked by a sense of uneasiness regarding globalisation and the changing demographics of France.

This malaise led to what was arguably one of the more shocking events of the Fifth Republic: the 2002 presidential elections, during which sixteen candidates from the Workers' Struggle on the extreme left to Jean-Marie Le Pen's National Front on the extreme right appeared on the ballot in the first round.[3] Due to the fractured vote on the left and a higher than normal abstention rate, Lionel Jospin came in third, meaning that the far right National Front was represented in the second round of the presidential election. The reaction was immediate, with nearly every candidate calling for a vote for the Republic, that is, for Chirac, and against Le Pen's extremist politics. Chirac won, and while Le Pen did not reach his projected goal of 40 per cent in the second round, the fact that he was there at all was shocking and seemed to reveal a France divided in relation to its own image and identity (Chevallier et al. 2004: 496).

Philibert's documentary was released a mere four months after the first round of the 2002 election, and was greeted with both commercial and critical acclaim. With 1.8 million tickets sold in France alone, it was one of the most successful films in France that year. The film follows a *classe unique*, or one-room school, nestled in a small village in Auvergne. The class is composed of the teacher and his twelve students; the children form a heterogeneous group in some respects, ranging from four to eleven years of age and with different ability levels. However, they share largely similar backgrounds: they come from the same geographic region, speak standard French and, as we see throughout the film, many of their families work in agriculture. This student body is a far cry from the demographic composition of many French schools, particularly those in Parisian suburbs or other large cities. Yet, this low-budget documentary seems to have struck a chord with the general public in France. One might ask why this film, which Philibert asserts was his 'attempt to capture something more universal: what it is to learn, to acquire knowledge and social skills, which are the building blocks of civilisation' (Falcon 2003: 28), was so successful? Perhaps it is because the film presents the image of a unified community, a France removed from the effects of globalisation, or a more hopeful vision of education. We will return to these questions shortly.

The six years separating *Être et avoir* and *Entre les murs* were no less tumultuous than the previous decade. Following the 9/11 terrorist attacks in 2001, Muslims in many countries, including France, came under increased scrutiny. According to Charles Sowerwine, 'Islam challenged the notion of republican universality, the Muslim seeming to be . . . the individual who could not be abstracted into the citizen' (Sowerwine 2009: 421–2). This perceived challenge to republicanism provoked the *foulard* controversy, spearheaded by then-Interior Minister, Nicolas Sarkozy, and led to the eventual ban of headscarves in schools in 2004. While many people on the left and the right commended this law as progress toward integration, others saw it as an infringement on personal liberties, culturally disrespectful and a sign that France was uncomfortable with its increasing diversity (Sowerwine 2009: 422–3).

Tensions surrounding France's republican model of integration rose even higher in 2005. In June, following the shooting death of a child, Nicolas Sarkozy promised to 'nettoyer au Kärcher' the Parisian suburb La Courneuve. According to the Magistrates Union 'nettoyer' (to clean) has 'heavy historical connotations, and its use should be avoided'; while 'Kärcher' refers to a high pressure cleaning system that literally and violently blasts away dirt. The Human Rights League of France swiftly denounced the comments as 'troubling', while the anti-racist organisation Mrap deemed them 'unacceptable' and accused Sarkozy of conflating immigrants with criminals and stigmatising an entire group of people. Politicians on the left, such as François Hollande, said his language was 'shocking' and lacking in any substantive policy.[4] A few months later, during a turbulent visit to Argenteuil, Sarkozy said he would 'get rid of the "*racaille*"' (often translated as 'scum').[5] While difficult to translate directly, '*racaille*' is an intensely pejorative and even dehumanising term when applied to a group of people.[6] Though Sarkozy doubled down on the use of '*racaille*',[7] his language was widely criticised as inflammatory and provocative on both sides of the political spectrum.[8]

The following day, two teenagers from another *banlieue* were electrocuted after running from the police.[9] The most violent riots in forty years began and spread throughout France, lasting for several weeks in October and November. Some in the media blamed the riots on immigrants and Muslims[10] when, in fact, most of the rioters were not recent immigrants, but a group Azouz Begag termed 'young ethnics' (Sowerwine 2009: 427). Historians regard this moment as the height of the malaise that had been developing since the 2002 elections and the start of the Iraq war in 2003, or as Vincent Tiberj put it, the '*crispation*' (cited in Sowerwine 2009: 428). France's model of republican integration was breaking down for many in the suburbs:

> The second and third generations of minority ethnic groups – from whose ranks the rioters have come – have overwhelmingly assimilated to the cultural norms dominant in France. In this respect, the French model of integration has been highly successful . . . [These young ethnics] share the same aspirations as their majority ethnic peers but are being denied equal opportunities to participate in French society. What generates the resentment in the *banlieues* is social exclusion, unemployment as high as 40 percent, ghetto-like housing projects, and police harassment. That is the failure of the republic. (Alec Hargreaves, quoted in Sowerwine 2009: 427)

The residents of the *banlieues* felt increasingly excluded and unwelcome, while a majority of poll respondents said there were 'too many immigrants in France'. These figures illustrate fractures on the issues of multiculturalism and immigration, which still exist today.[11] The riots resulted in severe property damage and one death; however, the wounds to the French psyche were much deeper.

These fractures would play a role in the 2007 presidential elections, which pitted the right-wing candidate, Nicolas Sarkozy, against the Socialist candidate, Ségolène Royal. While this election was not as shocking as the previous one, Sarkozy assimilated much of the National Front's rhetoric. He spoke often of a 'crisis of identity and values', which he termed 'serious', 'profound' and 'dangerous'. He also insisted that France did not need to apologise for its Vichy or Algerian past, and that May 1968 'had destroyed French values' (Sowerwine 2009: 432–3). This provocative language proved successful though: Sarkozy won the election with a strong mandate. His victory and tough on immigration campaign emphasised France's increasingly tense relationship with its colonial past and changing demography and its difficulty reconciling republican values with rising immigration.

Laurent Cantet's drama was released in September 2008, a year into Sarkozy's presidency and at a time when the youth in France – and in particular youth from diverse backgrounds – were feeling increasingly marginalised and precarious.[12] Like *Être et avoir*, it was met with enthusiasm from the public: box office sales exceeded 1.5 million tickets in France alone. The reaction from the critics was almost unanimously positive; however, the release of the film did provoke debate. *Les Cahiers du Cinéma* (Renzi 2008), *Le Monde* (Douin 2008), *Libération* (Péron 2008) and *Télérama* lauded the film as nuanced, poignant, balanced, whereas the critics from *Le Figaro* (Wachthausen 2008) were less impressed. Many educators criticised it for being 'too bleak' or for showing a dysfunctional classroom, while some scholars saw it as stereotyping the minority groups it portrayed.[13] Nonetheless, it was the surprise winner of the 2008 Cannes Film Festival Palme d'Or, and was nominated for the Best Foreign Film Award at the Academy Awards.

Taking a different approach from Philibert's educational fable, Cantet explicitly set out to show the very *mixité* or diversity that makes France uncomfortable: 'This sort of school is one of the last places where there is a social mix in France. I wanted to give a voice to those excluded by this system' (Cantet, quoted in Vincendeau 2008: 30–1). Cantet's decision to represent France's 'excluded' youth in the school should be read in dialogue with contemporary events:

> In 2005 many of us noticed that the rioters particularly targeted educational establishments. They were expressing anger and a feeling of injustice toward the school. Yet, failure in school, which begins in nursery school, has not become the important national issue that it should be. (Hache 2015; translation mine)

While France's schools were fully integrated by class and gender with the 1975 Haby Law (Almeida 2015), numerous studies indicate that the school system does not lead to the same outcomes for all groups.[14] According to the results of the Program for International Student Assessment (PISA) Study published in December 2016, France's educational system remains 'profoundly unequal'. Nearly 40 per cent of students from socially disadvantaged backgrounds struggle academically compared to only 5 per cent of their peers from more privileged backgrounds. For immigrant children, the situation is even direr. The system is 'dichotomous': there are of course very talented students, but a major factor in academic trajectory remains socio-economic background. And the social determinism of the French school system distinguishes it from its peer group. France struggles more than most other countries in the study to reach students from diverse backgrounds 'despite changes in power and successive reforms' (Battaglia and Collas 2016; translation mine). This inequality leads to serious problems, such as teacher dissatisfaction and turnover in disadvantaged areas, de facto segregation and a sense of exclusion,[15] and even violence.[16] Cantet's decision to focus on this population is political. As another director, Abdellatif Kechiche, notes, there is a lack of representation of minorities in the arts,[17] and the representations that do exist in politics and the media are often negative.

To make his film more representative, Cantet's *Entre les murs* focuses on a middle-school French class in a priority education zone (*les zones d'éducation prioritaires*; ZEP) in Paris's 20th district.[18] The group of students, comprised of non-professional actors who participated in workshops for a year before filming, presents a different picture of France from the children in *Être et avoir*. The students come from Mali, Morocco, the Antilles, China and the Hexagon, and the majority of the discussions revolve around their cultural and ethnic backgrounds and their more ambiguous relationship to French language and identity. Unlike in Philibert's documentary, which downplays individual identities in order to focus on the more general question of what it means to be a French republican, the diversity of Cantet's characters occupies the foreground and calls into question the universality of the Republic.

Two Schools

In multiple reviews and interviews, Cantet characterises the school as 'une caisse de résonance', an echo chamber for contemporary questions.[19] Both *Être et avoir* and *Entre les murs* take place largely within the walls of two classrooms, and the French school system, as one of the pillars of the Republic, is far from a neutral setting. It provokes intense debate, and the framing of these spaces influences our perception of the communities within them.

From the opening scenes, Philibert creates distinctions between interior and exterior spaces, and these divisions convey a positive message about the school. During the credits, before we see anything, we hear the wind whistling through the trees, birds chirping, cows mooing and a man's booming voice. The first image we encounter is not of a classroom or of children, as we might expect; instead the camera is centred on livestock being herded in the middle of a stark, wintery countryside. The environment appears brutally cold and uncontrollable. The numerous cows are loud and difficult to manage, but the farmers skilfully direct (and redirect) their movements. The first few minutes, consisting of harsh exterior shots, are immediately juxtaposed with interior shots of a quiet, warmly lit classroom. Once inside, the camera directs our gaze out the windows, so we, the spectators, can see and hear the outside world. The snowstorm we witness is muffled – we are protected from it. The camera remains fixed on these windows, and for nearly twenty seconds we are left to ponder the disparity between the interior and the exterior. In *Framing Attention: Windows on Modern German Culture* (2007), Lutz Koepnick describes the function of windows and asserts that they are difficult to conceptualise precisely because they both connect and divide. They allow us to see different worlds, but they also separate those worlds (Koepnick 2007: 1). Philibert cultivates the distinction between the warm, safe interior and the harsh, white, violent exterior, stating, 'We open with the snow, the whistling wind and the cows being herded; we thus recognise the school as a refuge from the violence of the world outside' (Philibert cited in Falcon 2003: 29).

The camera then cuts to show us more of the classroom. The chairs are stacked, the notebooks organised. The only movement and sound are two turtles slowly making their way across the floor. The camera tracks these turtles, at first from far away, and then in a close-up. While we might wonder how these turtles got into this classroom (and out of their terrarium), their presence and the emphasis on their movement symbolises steadiness, endurance and taking one's time.[20] These characteristics describe the time it takes for children to grow, the rhythm of learning, even the pace of the film. The camera then assumes the turtle's gaze in a point-of-view shot and looks at an overturned globe before cutting to an exterior shot of immense trees swaying ominously in the wind. These establishing shots situate the spectator geographically and socially: this is a sparsely populated, rural area primarily supported by agriculture. But these scenes could also be read as a statement: the outside world is threatening and spinning so fast, that like the overturned globe, it has literally come unhinged. The school, on the other hand, is depicted as distinctly removed from these threats. It is a haven, an insular, safe and orderly space that provides protection from the dangers outside.

The opening scenes of *Entre les murs* set an entirely different tone for the film and convey a much more ambiguous image of the school. The first sequence starts with a medium close-up on the neck of a man in a café with the sounds of cars rushing past and silverware clanging in the background. The camera focuses on this man lost in contemplation, leaving everything around him out of focus. He suddenly throws back his coffee and quickly departs. Once outside, we realise that we are in Paris, and that the man is a teacher about to start a new school year. The camera tracks his movements as he walks away from the café, past the prison-like windows of the school and into the staffroom. These tracking shots take us 'through a series of doors, passages, stairs, corridors, and classrooms being prepared by cleaners, a journey that demands an appreciation of space both as literal form of enclosure and, on a metaphorical level, as a negotiation of limits and borders' (Williams 2011: 61–2).

These first few minutes set the stage for the action to come: as the title suggests, this will be a story almost entirely confined to the walls of this school (the first shots are the only ones that take place outside its walls). However, just because one is on the inside does not imply belonging or inclusion. The interior of this school, contrary to that of *Être et avoir*, is not inviting: the opening sequence presents a labyrinthine space, with empty white walls, long hallways, and many doors, stairways and barred windows, all of which are means of excluding rather than including. This representation does not make us feel safe; on the contrary it refutes the idea that a school is a place of inclusion. According to Cantet, this feeling of exclusion or of fragmentation was intentional: 'School is a space where wonderful things can happen, as we show in the film, but it is also a segregating machine' (cited in Vincendeau 2009: 36). Through his use of space, Cantet makes a statement about the fractures in the republican model of education: this institution does not always fulfil its role of integration; instead of removing barriers, in many ways it creates them.

Within the Walls

The spaces of these schools stand in stark contrast, as do the interactions within them. A comparison of the first exchanges reveals two distinct visions of youth in a classroom: one predicated on community and respect for authority, the other emphasising individuality and contestation. In *Être et avoir*, following the establishing shots of the landscape and a long voyage, the children arrive at school through the gate. The teacher, M. Lopez, waits by the door to greet his students, ushering them into the large entrance. As the students file past him in a line, they each say 'Bonjour, Monsieur!' Later in the film, the students will stand quietly behind their desks, waiting for the teacher to tell them to take their seats. The repetition of these behaviours signals a routine, a prescribed way to enter the building and to address the teacher.

Philibert then cuts abruptly from the entryway to the classroom. This is the first time we see it occupied and in use. In a medium close-up shot of three children, the camera shows their small hands holding large, colourful markers. They are practicing writing, and the hands take centre stage. The camera zooms in on two pairs of hands, one larger, one smaller. The teacher is helping one of the youngest students, Jojo, write the letters by indicating where he should start. There is a model of the word 'maman' in the teacher's handwriting that the students are supposed to follow. In the background, we see another student, Jessie, also following the model, and the teacher's hand covers hers as they trace the letters together. There is no extra-diegetic sound, just hushed conversation between the students and the teacher. The camera remains angled at the students' level, close to them, focusing on the effort required to complete their tasks. We hear the teacher's words of encouragement, explanations or gentle admonishments, depending on the quality of the students' writing, and the students asking for his attention or approval. The camera pans around the table to show each student working and then zooms out to show the whole group. This circular movement captures the work of each individual but also the community working in concert with the teacher's help. M. Lopez then asks the students to share their work and to critique their classmates. Students respond with 'good' or 'not good' based on how well their peers replicated the model.

This scene is repeated with the older students as they complete a dictation on the imperfect tense. At one point, the teacher rebukes a student for using the wrong verb ending. There is no discussion about why they use this ending instead of another, even though they sound similar, or why they use the imperfect tense in the first place. In fact, there is little discussion at all during this interaction. In both sequences, the teacher establishes a very calm tone, but he is also authoritative. In his review, Jean-Claude Loiseau described the instructor Georges Lopez as 'the centre around which the children gravitate' (Loiseau 2003; translation mine). He sets the norms that the students must follow; he gives a model, and the students reproduce it; he dictates, and the students listen and write. The activities they engage in are not creative. They all write the same thing and follow the same rules. The space and the children within it are depicted as disciplined and orderly; there is harmony, but also uniformity.

By contrast, the first classroom scene in *Entre les murs* is boisterous and even confrontational. The students file past the professor and enter the class talking noisily, jostling each other and taking their seats without invitation. The camera energetically pans around the room, not lingering for long on any individual but showing an ethnically diverse group of students. As the teacher tries to gain control, a verbal joust regarding wasted class time ensues between him and two students. From this first exchange, the teacher attempts to assert his authority, but at every turn, the students push back. When he asks them to write their names, Esmeralda counters that they should not have to write unless he does. Though the assignment is simple, writing a first and a last name, the camera zooms in on several names as well as items of clothing; each one distinct, hinting at the owner's personality or background. A person's name confers a status and an identity; the graphic details that accompany the written names, such as a drawing of a flag, make the nametags even more personal. The act of asserting a different identity suggests a potential disconnect between the students and the Republic, making this initial image of the classroom and the students distinctly less harmonious and less uniform than in *Être et avoir*.

Moreover, the framing of the interactions in *Entre les murs* leaves us off-balance. According to James Williams, Cantet used three high-definition digital cameras; one was always on the instructor, one was on the speaker and one was on the observers who were about to (re)act. The cameras were often hand-held and give the spectators a sense of being a fly on the wall; it is as if we were 'caught in the action' (Williams 2011: 65). The use of three cameras avoids the traditional shot/counter-shot model, which typically facilitates identification and creates power dynamics. According to Cantet, '[my] central goals in replacing the conventional shot/reverse shot structure with the more fluid point of view offered by the use of three cameras was to put the teacher and students on an equal footing' (Strand 2009: 259). The three cameras ensure that the instructor's perspective is not favoured; and in many scenes like this one, the camera draws our attention to the reaction of his students and away from him. Thus, the very way in which Cantet shoots the film destabilises our perspective, making it more egalitarian and more difficult for us to know with whom we are supposed to identify.

Linguistic Politics

If Cantet works to destabilise the spectator, Philibert cultivates stability and unity. The language the students use and the activities they engage in at the rural school further emphasise this harmony. Apart from a light southern accent, the French in *Être et avoir* is standard. We do not hear slang in the classroom, familiar language is relegated to the home[21] and no foreign language is spoken. M. Lopez mediates the students' relationship to French, and he sets clear limits on what is linguistically acceptable.

While teaching his youngest students about noun genders, the children take turns creating sentences using the word 'ami(e)'. When Johann inserts 'copain', a more familiar way to say friend, M. Lopez immediately corrects him, and the other students chime in with the correct word.

Johann tries again, and repeats 'copain'. While we do not see M. Lopez, his tone suggests that he is not pleased, and he prompts Johann to say it again. Once Johann correctly repeats the sentence using 'ami', M. Lopez asks him what would happen if we substituted the word 'mom' for 'dad'; in other words, how to change from the masculine to the feminine form. He expects Johann to add an 'e' to 'ami'. Instead Johann says 'copine', which suggests that Johann understands the concept of masculine and feminine nouns, and even that he can apply this distinction to other words. However, M. Lopez expects Johann to use the word he gave the students, and instead of praising Johann's correct use of this grammatical structure, he insists on the word 'ami'. M. Lopez's insistence that all the students conform to his choice underscores his authority and emphasises linguistic homogeneity at the expense of diversity. All students write the same sentence, and any deviation is swiftly corrected.

The unity of this group is echoed in the classroom activities. In another sequence, the students all work together to make crêpes: in a medium close-up, the youngest students (with M. Lopez's help) measure the flour, add the sugar, crack the eggs and stir the batter. Then we see the older students, standing in a group as they practice flipping the crêpes, while the younger children shout 'bravo'. Each student completes a portion of the recipe, working in concert and encouraging each other, so that everyone can enjoy the meal. They are part of a whole, which functions best when everyone works together.

While this classroom is by and large a harmonious little world, there are occasional disputes, but even then, the emphasis is placed on the group. During a conversation about a fight between Julian and Olivier, M. Lopez explains that they must learn to get along and support each other for the sake of the example they set for the younger students. He also mentions that next year they will leave their small school for a much larger middle school, where they will be two amongst many strangers. During this discussion, M. Lopez remains off-screen, while the two boys, even though they are fighting, are framed together, as if on the same side.

When we finally visit the middle school, it is a field trip for the entire class. The new school is much less inviting: white, empty walls (in contrast to the yellow walls of our one-room class); an assembly-line cafeteria; and a noisy lunchroom filled with indistinguishable children. In a long shot of the lunchroom, we very quickly lose the ability to distinguish individual students, focusing instead on the large mass. The shot scale reinforces the distance: in the small classroom, the camera stays close to the children, so that we can identify (with) them. Here, the children become anonymous. Read as a microcosm of the Republic, the one-room school provides a safe, communal environment for the students to explore, to learn to work together and to make mistakes. However, it is also an insular space, one that is wary of the outside world.

In contrast, the school in Cantet's drama is an unwelcoming environment. In his review, Jean-Luc Douin (2008) describes *Entre les murs* as a veritable 'war of words'. The subject of nearly the entire film is discussions and debates between the students and the teacher: everything revolves around language. Cantet explains that language was a major issue in the film because he wanted to show 'how language is a tool of integration' (Vincendeau 2009: 35). Throughout the film, the students seem to be asking, 'Whose French are we speaking, and why are we speaking it?' while the teacher, M. Marin, wants to show them that the command of standard French signifies social mobility. Being able to shift registers will give them access to power: they can use the language of the *quartier*, which contains a great deal of *argot* (slang) or *verlan* (slang that inverts the order of syllables), but they must also be able to switch to standard French when necessary. The film depicts students learning how to navigate these different linguistic registers, such as when Khoumba uses the word 'vénère' (*verlan* for 'énervé') to describe Marin's irritated response to her insolence, and when Rabah characterises people at a party as 'jambon-beurres', slang for French. They are testing limits and at the same time portraying a much more multicultural and fluid image of the French language.

Moreover, the students do not passively accept what is taught: while Marin privileges standard French in the classroom, they openly question the value of what they consider to be 'white' French. They are aware that their cultures are not represented in the language of the classroom. During a vocabulary lesson, the students wonder why Marin only uses 'bizarre' names, like Bill, instead of names that sound like theirs. While not French, Bill communicates a certain vision of Western civilisation as white and Americanised. A similar dispute occurs following a quiz on the imperfect tense. Esmeralda questions why they say the imperfect indicative instead of just the imperfect; another student responds that there are different imperfect tenses, like the imperfect subjunctive. Marin gives an example of how one might use this tense, which is met with resistance from the students. They argue that it is from the Middle Ages, and no one 'normal' uses it anymore. While Marin agrees that this is very high register language, he explains that it is important to first learn the rules of the game before breaking them. For Marin, language is a powerful tool that they can learn to use and manipulate, but for the students, this tool is problematic. They do not see themselves reflected in its use: their families and friends do not use this register, and they are unsure of its value to them. These interactions illustrate a dialogue between teachers and students about the value and power of language, but they also depict students confronting and challenging a language they view as exclusive and distant.

One of the focal points of the film concerns the students' *autoportraits*, a written exercise with artistic and literary connotations. When the students present their *autoportraits*, they choose different mediums to tell their stories, the formal diversity echoing the plurality that exists in the classroom. Some students choose more traditional means: Wei, a recent immigrant from China, describes his solitary personality and his difficulty expressing himself in French in prose. Others push back on the codes of written French: Esmeralda incorporates *verlan* in hers, using the word 'tiéquar' for 'quartier', and is immediately corrected. Rabah touches on some potentially sensitive subjects, including teenage sexuality and desire. Some students avoid prose altogether: Karl, standing alone in a medium close-up and looking directly at the camera, reads his *autoportrait* aloud, the anaphora of 'I like' and 'I don't like' making it more of a poem. Souleymane, the most reticent and difficult student, initially refuses to write about himself, challenging the constraints of the activity altogether. He eventually completes the assignment successfully, but instead of writing, he tells his story through captioned photographs, which are displayed like portraits in a gallery. Unlike the writing activities in *Être et avoir* that stress uniformity and adherence to rules, writing in *Entre les murs*, as with the nametags at the beginning, emphasises self-expression, creativity and pluralism and depicts a multicultural and multilingual group of adolescents attempting to construct and affirm their individual identities.

While there is richness in these exchanges, there is also conflict. Cantet has described *Entre les murs* as both utopian and dystopian, and as such, its message is sometimes ambiguous and its characters not entirely sympathetic. While we often see students and teachers engaged in lively though mostly respectful conversation, boundaries are transgressed on both sides. From high-angle shots reminiscent of surveillance footage, we witness students sort out their differences in the *cour de récréation*. There is an unequal power dynamic inscribed in these sequences: we survey them. However, these disputes do not always end outside. One of the main characters, Souleymane, becomes increasingly disruptive. He vulgarly insults his classmates and even uses the informal 'tu' with M. Marin, resulting in a trip to the principal's office. As the principal questions him, the camera lingers on Souleymane's face. He remains silent, shifting uncomfortably, a sharp contrast to his demeanour in class. The lengthy close-up and his silence remind us that his transgression of linguistic norms has led to vulnerability and exclusion.

After a faculty meeting during which teachers discussed students' progress, Souleymane asserts that he knows Marin insulted him. This accusation leads to a heated argument in which Marin tells the class delegates that they had displayed 'une attitude de pétasse'. The class erupts in angry protests, Souleymane again uses the informal 'tu' with Marin, and they nearly come to blows. Souleymane then storms out of the room, accidentally hitting Khoumba in the face with his bag. The use of the word 'pétasse' is highly contested: the subtitles translate it as 'skank', Marin later defends himself saying it means more or less 'bimbo', and the students declare that to them it means 'prostitute'. What is clear is that Marin's impetuous word choice has crossed a line. In her review of *Entre les murs*, Ginette Vincendeau highlights the immense and sometimes destructive power of language, asserting that it 'divides and rules' (Vincendeau 2009: 35). In a claustrophobic shot of Marin surrounded by students in the courtyard, this time on their level and not from a high angle, we feel the tension and the difficulty of contending with many voices. There is no consensus, no unity, but instead misunderstandings and a heated argument about who can use such words and their very meaning.

The consequences for these transgressions are far from equal. While Marin's image suffers, he comes away from this experience otherwise unscathed. Professionally, he is not punished. The other teachers are sympathetic, stating that they have 'all gone too far with students' on occasion. All he must do is include what he said in his incident report. However, the principal cautions him from going into too much detail. In the end, he does not write the actual word 'pétasse'; he obfuscates, writing instead: 'The professor used slightly harsh words' (translation mine). The incident report is opaque, impersonal and cleansed of any trace of the violence of the verbal exchanges.

The story ends quite differently for Souleymane. Because of his outburst, Souleymane is brought to a disciplinary hearing, which we learn have always ended in expulsions. He must translate for the teachers and his mother because she does not speak French, and the school did not provide a translator. Souleymane's mother lacks the words to adequately defend her son in French, and Souleymane does not defend himself, responding, 'What can I say?' He seems to know that 'everything is already decided' and that his language cannot be powerful enough to rewrite his ending. The camera frames mother and son as separate from the rest of the committee, reinforcing the notion that their language marks them as 'other'.

We follow Souleymane and his mother into the empty hallway; like them, we are excluded from the deliberations. A giant, clear box is passed around the table and disembodied hands cast their votes: Souleymane is expelled; a decision we know may lead his father to send Souleymane back to Mali. The ridiculously oversized, transparent box ironically emphasises the opacity of this situation as if to ask, 'Why are we *really* expelling Souleymane?' Is it because he broke the rules, transgressed a norm? Or is it because he pointed to fractures and shortcomings in the republican school system as it grapples with increasing diversity?

Conclusion(s)

I would like to conclude with a discussion of the film's dénouements. *Être et avoir* ends with the last days of school and a series of conversations between M. Lopez and the older students about their next steps. During a discussion with Julian and Olivier, the teacher reminds them that they will be together in their new school. Julian affirms, 'We'll stick together', to which the M. Lopez responds that they must not forget themselves, as they may have to defend each other from bullies in this new environment. When speaking with a distraught Natalie about leaving the school, he reassures her that she can always return for support. Though they discuss individual trajectories, the focus is always drawn back to the community, one that is supportive and unified but also apprehensive about what lies beyond the walls of the classroom. On the last day, the students are assembled around M. Lopez, who orchestrates a choir of 'oui' and 'Au revoir, monsieur'. It is one of the more touching moments of the film, and the children's voices all speak as one, underscoring both harmony and uniformity.

In *Entre les murs*, we end on a more confrontational note. Marin asks students to talk about what they learned that year, and every student has something different to contribute. Esmeralda, however, says she did not learn anything in school, but instead read Plato's *Republic*. Visibly surprised that she has read this book, Marin asks her to explain it to the class. She says that Socrates asks people to question what they know about 'love, God, everything'. While the text's dialogic nature and emphasis on debate remind us of the pluralism in this classroom, the fact remains that Esmeralda associates this inquisitive and challenging text with the world outside the school. When the bell rings, Marin distributes a class book in which he has assembled their *autoportraits*. On the one hand, the book is a physical representation of their diverse stories; on the other, it is a collection that has been organised, codified and bound by the teacher. They wrote their individual accounts, but he asserts authority over those narratives and creates one book to represent them all. As the students say goodbye, Henriette admits that, compared to the others, she did not learn anything. They both look devastated, Marin because of a sense of failure in the present, Henriette because of apprehension about her future. In these final exchanges, Cantet reinforces several tensions that have been present throughout the film between linguistic creativity and authority, dialogue and silence, inclusion and exclusion.

The camera cuts to the courtyard, and we witness a friendly football match between students and teachers. Different groups cheer as the students score a goal. Finally, the camera transitions back and lingers on the vacant classroom, but we can still hear the exuberant cheers off-screen. Many scholars have commented on the unsettling image of an empty classroom in disarray,[22] yet as the camera moves, we hear voices echoing in this space. As with the rest of the film, Cantet's ending is ambiguous. The final image depicts a troubled space to be sure; we see its limits in the windows and walls, the dysfunction in the desks and chairs strewn about chaotically. However, for the first time in the film, we hear the outside world through those barred windows. Cantet transforms the classroom into a literal 'caisse de résonance' for today's questions while at the same time opening the space ever so slightly to include new voices.

If the school is an echo chamber for contemporary questions as Cantet suggests, then the representation of youth within it should be read in dialogue with its context. Philibert explicitly chose to avoid filming in a Parisian *banlieue* in order to focus on the 'universal' characteristics of learning. At a time when France was deeply divided by questions surrounding its national identity, his film was comforting, presenting hopeful images of a unified and largely harmonious community. However, the school and the students' interactions with each other, their teacher and their language emphasise harmony over plurality, uniformity and insularity over creativity and openness. He is celebrating a school, but one with a very different 'surface texture' (Philibert cited in Falcon 2003: 29) and relationship to language than most students encounter today.

Cantet on the other hand destabilises our perspective by confronting us with a multitude of cultures, languages and voices, which remind us 'that it is not easy to be young in France' today (Harris 2008: 102). When speaking about the film's tone, he asserted, 'It shows the richness of multiculturalism rather than its weaknesses ... The film is utopian about the possibilities this setting offers, but pessimistic about the school system in general' (Vincendeau 2008: 31). *Entre les murs* makes us uncomfortable because of this ambiguity, because of the tension between hopeful possibilities and at times disturbing realities. While not always a reassuring image, the film reflects on the role of education in forming France's multicultural youth and challenges us to do the same.

Notes

1. The Treaty of Maastricht was divisive with both politicians and the public. The centre and traditional left political parties supported European integration, while communists and the extreme right were opposed. The traditional right was divided (Chevallier et al. 2004: 401). In the end, the referendum won a narrow victory with only 51 per cent of French voters supporting it (Sowerwine 2009: 389). Once passed, the austerity measures proposed to meet Maastricht criteria provoked the biggest strike wave since May 1968 (Sowerwine 2009: 403).
2. During the Chirac/Jospin cohabitation, universal health coverage, the thirty-five-hour work week, the PaCS (Pacte civil de solidarité) and the parity law took effect (Sowerwine 2009: 406–13).
3. See Chevallier et al. (2004: 487–96) for a detailed analysis of this election.
4. Anon. (2005a), translations mine.
5. 'Vous en avez assez de cette bande de racailles? On va vous en débarrasser' (Anon. 2005b).
6. See Pulham (2005) for an etymological history of 'racaille' and a discussion of its connotations today.
7. During a television interview in November 2005, Sarkozy stood by his use of the offensive terms: 'I maintain that they are thugs and rabble' (Anon. 2005c; translation mine). In June 2016, he again expressed pride in his use of 'la racaille' and 'le Kärcher' (Girard 2016).
8. Doug Ireland, a leftist activist and journalist, likened Sarkozy's language to 'pouring verbal kerosene on the flames' (Pulham 2005). Azouz Begag, the delegate Minister for equal opportunities and a former member of Sarkozy's own party, was one of the Interior Minister's staunchest critics (Bacqué and Jakubyszyn 2005).
9. An investigation later determined that the teenagers had committed no crime, and that they ran simply because they saw the police, speaking to the level of distrust between suburban youth and the authorities. The officers were eventually brought to trial for failure to provide assistance (Chrisafis 2015).
10. Alain Finkielkraut claimed, 'The real problem is that most [of the rioters] are blacks or Arabs, with a Muslim identity' (Sowerwine 2009: 427).
11. On the ten-year anniversary of the riots, Claire Hache from the magazine *L'Express* interviewed sociologist Laurent Mucchielli, author of *Quand les banlieues brûlent: Retour sur les émeutes de novembre 2005* (2006). Regarding the image of the suburbs, he states that these areas still face issues of 'crime, unemployment, communitarianism', but to reduce the suburbs to this negative description, 'contributes to knocking down the people in working class neighbourhoods, who are clearly the scapegoats for all of our problems and fears'. He also asserted that the problematic relationships with the police have not improved, in part because there is no community policing and no trust built between residents and authorities. Overall, he describes the 'sentiment

d'abandon' many residents feel, the fact that Parisian elites are unaware of the full scope of inequalities residents of the suburbs face, and how the situation has in many ways worsened (Hache 2015; translations mine).
12. In 2006, Prime Minister Dominique de Villepin proposed the 'first job contract' (*contrat première embauche*; CPE), which was supposed to address the elevated rate of unemployment for eighteen- to twenty-five-year-olds. This proposal meant that employees under twenty-six 'would have no employment protection for the first two years of employment' (Sowerwine 2009: 428). It was seen as a neo-liberal strategy and was met with demonstrations and the occupation of universities, including the Sorbonne, eventually prompting Villepin's withdrawal of the bill.
13. See Gueye (2010), Vincendeau (2009) and Williams (2011) for detailed discussions of the film's reception.
14. For a discussion of the inequalities of opportunity and theories of social reproduction see Bourdieu and Passeron (1964, 1970). For analysis of how the French education system affects different groups see Baudelot and Establet (1992), Prost (1997), Merle (2002) and Beaud (2002).
15. See Valls (2006) and Viguier (2006) for a discussion of the challenges faced in suburban schools.
16. The journal *L'Express* published an entire dossier on school violence entitled 'Lutte contre la violence scolaire' with articles concerning (cyber) bullying, verbal and physical aggression, attacks on teachers and so on (*L'Express* n.d.).
17. Speaking about his own film *L'Esquive* (2003), Abdellatif Kechiche explained his motivation for filming in the *banlieues*: 'I also wanted to show that there exists true artistic potential in this immigrant community. Generally, they come up against a lack of consideration; they aren't integrated in the media landscape. Perhaps it is this injustice that motivates me the most to make films . . . What matters is this place that must be obtained. It's an opportunity for the media to be able to count on these talents because this youth and population are not simply a source of problems. Also representation is very important in the perception of the "other", especially for those who vote and make decisions' (Lalane 2004; translation mine).
18. ZEP refers to 'a program started in 1982 that channels additional resources to schools in disadvantaged areas and encourages the development of new teaching projects' (Bénabou et al. 2008).
19. See Borde (2008).
20. The turtles remind us of a fable, a story often used in a classroom setting, La Fontaine's 'The Tortoise and the Hare'.
21. During one sequence, an entire family crowds around a table to help Julian with his maths homework. The language is of a lower register; it is more colloquial and at times difficult to understand.
22. See Williams (2011: 72).

Works Cited

Almeida, Justine de (2015), 'Le collège unique a 40 ans, *La Croix*, 18 September, <http://www.la-croix.com/Actualite/France/Le-college-unique-a-40-ans-2015-09-18-1357912> (last accessed March 2017).

Anon. (2005a), 'Les propos de Nicolas Sarkozy sur le "nettoyage" de la Courneuve provoquent l'indignation', *Le Monde*, 21 June, <https://www.lemonde.fr/societe/article/2005/06/21/les-propos-de-m-sarkozy-sur-le-nettoyage-de-la-courneuve-provoquent-l-indignation_664721_3224.html> (last accessed March 2017).

Anon. (2005b), 'Visite de Nicolas Sarkozy à Argenteuil', *Institut national de l'audiovisuel*, 26 October, <http://www.ina.fr/video/2951569001019> (last accessed March 2017).

Anon. (2005c), 'Nicolas Sarkozy continue de vilipender "racailles et voyous"', *Le Monde*, 11 November, <https://www.lemonde.fr/societe/article/2005/11/11/nicolas-sarkozy-persiste-et-signe-contre-les-racailles_709112_3224.html> (last accessed March 2017).

Bacqué, Raphaëlle and Christophe Jakubyszyn (2005), 'Azouz Begag, principal opposant à Nicolas Sarkozy', *Le Monde*, 1 November, <https://www.lemonde.fr/societe/article/2005/11/01/azouz-begag-en-premiere-ligne-face-a-nicolas-sarkozy_705366_3224.html> (last accessed March 2017).

Battaglia, Mattea and Aurélie Collas (2016), 'Enquête PISA: les élèves français dans la moyenne', *Le Monde*, 6 December, <https://www.lemonde.fr/education/article/2016/12/06/enquete-pisa-les-eleves-francais-dans-la-moyenne_5044175_1473685.html> (last accessed March 2017).

Baudelot, Christian and Roger Establet (1992), *Allez les filles!* Paris: Éditions du Seuil.

Beaud, Stéphane (2002), *80% au bac . . . et après: Les Enfants de la démocratisation scolaire*. Paris: Éditions La Découverte.

Bénabou, Roland, Francis Kramarz and Corinne Prost (2008), 'The French zones d'éducation prioritaire: Much ado about nothing?', *Economics of Education Review*, 28, pp. 347–56.

Borde, Dominique (2008), 'Laurent Cantet à l'école de la vie', *Le Figaro*, 23 September, <http://www.lefigaro.fr/cinema/2008/09/23/03002-20080923ARTFIG00575-laurent-cantet-a-l-ecole-de-la-vie-.php> (last accessed March 2017).

Bourdieu, Pierre and Jean-Claude Passeron (1964), *Les Héritiers: Les étudiants et la culture*, Paris: Les Éditions de Minuit.

Bourdieu, Pierre and Jean-Claude Passeron (1970), *La Reproduction: Éléments pour une théorie du système d'enseignement*, Paris: Éditions de minuit.

Burdeau, Emmanuel (2008), 'Entretien Avec Laurent Cantet', *Les Cahiers du cinéma*, 637, pp. 10–18.

Chevallier, Jean, Guy Carcassonne and Olivier Duhamel (2004), *La Ve République, 1958–2004: Histoire des Institutions et des régimes politiques de la France*, Paris: Dalloz, Armand Colin.

Chrisafis, Angelique (2015), 'The Trial that Could Lay Bare France's Racial Divide', *The Guardian*, 15 March, <https://www.theguardian.com/world/2015/mar/15/trial-france-racialdivide> (last accessed March 2017).
Douin, Jean-Luc (2008), '*Entre les murs:* La guerre des mots au collège', *Le Monde*, 23 September, <https://www.lemonde.fr/cinema/article/2008/09/23/entre-les-murs-la-guerre-des-mots-au-college_1098573_3476.html> (last accessed March 2017).
Falcon, Richard (2003), 'Back to Basics', *Sight and Sound*, 13:7, pp. 28–9.
Girard, Étienne (2016), 'Nicolas Sarkozy fier de ses propos sur "la racaille" et "le Kärcher"', *Le Lab Europe 1*, 26 June, <http://lelab.europe1.fr/nicolas-sarkozy-fier-de-ses-propos-sur-la-racaille-et-le-karcher-2782717> (last accessed March 2017).
Gueye, Abdoulaye (2010), 'The Color of Unworthiness: Understanding Blacks in France and the French Visual Media through Laurent Cantet's *The Class* (2008)', *Transition: An International Review*, 102, pp. 158–71.
Hache, Claire (2015), '10 ans après les émeutes, "la situation des banlieues est encore plus mauvaise"', *L'Express*, 27 October, <https://www.lexpress.fr/actualite/societe/10-ans-apres-les-emeutes-la-situation-des-banlieues-est-encore-plus-mauvaise_1729611.html> (last accessed March 2017).
Harris, Brandon (2008), 'Social Studies', *Filmmaker: The Magazine of Independent Film*, 17:1, pp. 100–6.
Koepnick, Lutz P. (2007), *Framing Attention: Windows on Modern German Culture*, Baltimore: Johns Hopkins University Press.
La Fontaine, Jean de (1997), *Selected Fables, Fables choisies*, edited and trans. Stanley Applebaum, Mineola, NY: Dover Publications, Inc.
Lalane, Jean-Marc (2004), '"L'Esquive": entretien avec Abdellatif Kechiche', *Les Inrocks*, 7 January, <https://www.lesinrocks.com/2004/01/07/cinema/actualite-cinema/entretien-abdellatif-kechiche-lesquive-0104-1185003/> (last accessed March 2017).
L'Express (n.d.) 'Lutte contre la violence scolaire', *L'Express*, <https://www.lexpress.fr/education/lutte-contre-la-violence-scolaire_1616281.html> (last accessed March 2017).
Loiseau, Jean-Claude (2003), '*Être et avoir*', *Télérama*, 28 August, <https://www.telerama.fr/cinema/films/etre-et-avoir,61211.php> (last accessed March 2017).
Merle, Pierre (2002), *La démocratisation de l'enseignement*. Paris: Éditions La Découverte.
Péron, Didier (2008), 'Captation d'énergie scolaire', *Libération*, 22 September, <https://www.liberation.fr/evenement/2008/09/22/captation-d-energie-scolaire_80744> (last accessed March 2017).
Prost, Antoine (1997), *Education, société et politiques: Une histoire de l'éducation depuis 1945*, Paris: Éditions du Seuil.
Pulham, Sheila (2005), 'Inflammatory Language', *The Guardian*, 8 November, <https://www.theguardian.com/news/blog/2005/nov/08/inflammatoryla> (last accessed March 2017).

Renzi, Eugenio (2008), 'À Égalité', *Cahiers du cinéma*, 637, pp. 19–21.

Sowerwine, Charles (2009), *France since 1870: Culture, Society and the Making of the Republic*, Basingstoke and New York: Palgrave Macmillan.

Strand, Dana (2009), '*Être et Parler*: Being and Speaking French in Abdellatif Kechiche's *L'Esquive* (2004) and Laurent Cantet's *Entre Les Murs* (2008)', *Studies in French Cinema*, 9:3, pp. 259–72.

Valls, Manuel (2006), 'Violence dans les banlieues: Quel bilan un an après les émeutes?' *Le Monde*, 26 October, <https://www.lemonde.fr/societe/chat/2006/10/23/violence-dans-les-banlieues-quel-bilan-un-an-apres-les-emeutes_825976_3224.html> (last accessed March 2017).

Viguier, Frédéric (2006), 'Maintaining the Class: Teachers in the New High Schools of the Banlieues', *French Politics, Culture and Society, Special Issue: Lost Banlieues of the Republic?*, 24:3, pp. 58–80.

Vincendeau, Ginette (2008), 'The Times BFI 52nd London Film Festival *The Class*: Interview', *Sight and Sound*, 18:11, pp. 30–1.

Vincendeau, Ginette (2009), 'The Rules of the Game', *Sight and Sound*, 19:3, pp. 34–6.

Wachthausen, Jean-Luc (2008), '*Entre les murs*', *Le Figaro*, 24 September, <https://www.lefigaro.fr/scope/articles-cinema/2008/09/24/08005-20080924ART-FIG00015--entre-les-murs-.php> (last accessed March 2017).

Williams, James (2011), 'Framing Exclusion: The Politics of Space in Laurent Cantet's *Entre Les Murs*', *French Studies*, 65:1, pp. 61–73.

Films

Entre les murs, film, directed by Laurent Cantet. France: Haut et Court, 2008.

Être et avoir, film, directed by Nicolas Philibert. France: Canal Plus, 2002.

CHAPTER 11

Young Love and Everyday Freedom: Abdellatif Kechiche's *La Faute à Voltaire* and *La Vie d'Adèle*

Kathryn Chaffee

Tunisian-French director Abdellatif Kechiche writes love stories about misfits and outsiders: a clandestine migrant from Tunisia in *La Faute à Voltaire* (2000), a group of teenagers practicing a Marivaux play in the *banlieue* in *L'Esquive* (2003), a young girl discovering her queer sexuality in *La Vie d'Adèle* (2013). At the same time, he is also heralded as one of France's foremost political filmmakers.[1] How do Kechiche's love stories become political? What type of politics do his films represent? These are some of the questions that will inform our analysis. While his films usually avoid explicit political declarations, his stories are set against the backdrop of significant political events, including the severe deportation policies in France in the late 1990s and the legalisation of gay marriage in 2013.[2] The philosopher Emmanuel Barot highlights the useful distinction between '*la* politique', the sphere of governmental influence and state power, and '*le* politique', the community and shared space of the *polis*. Barot goes on to suggest that 'every image in a film (documentary or fiction) captures and transmits social realities', reconstructing the ways in which we conceive of the *polis* itself (Barot 2009: 27).[3] Similarly, Jacques Rancière argues that, through a fictionalised representation of reality, a '*réel de la fiction*', cinema uncovers a political significance that would otherwise remain hidden in our own world (Rancière 2000a: 62).

I argue that Kechiche's films represent an everyday freedom – as opposed to political freedom – for his characters, bringing to the forefront seemingly inconsequential moments of love and everyday life. For Kechiche's characters, the ability to make choices over their daily reality and to live a love story becomes a form of agency that offers an alternative to *la politique*. In his first film, *La Faute à Voltaire*, Kechiche tells the story of a young Tunisian man who comes to France seeking opportunity. While we might expect a story about a migrant worker to extol the virtues of political freedom available in France, Jallel (Sami Bouajila) actually finds freedom through his relationship with Lucie (Élodie Bouchez), a lascivious French girl with a history of mental illness. *La Vie d'Adèle* – a love story between two young women – was released in theatres immediately before the legalisation of gay marriage in France.[4] However, instead of an overt defence of homosexuality, the film gives us intimate moments in the lives of two young women: a desiring gaze when crossing a city street, a conversation about existentialism, and heartbreak. In both of these films, any type of freedom his characters experience comes through love.

The first sequence of *La Faute à Voltaire* begins with an illuminated image of Jules Dalou's statue, *Le Triomphe de la République*, erected to commemorate the centennial anniversary of the 1789 Revolution. As Colin Nettelbeck and others have noted, the statue located in Place de la Nation in Paris is one of the most heavily symbolic locations in the film, and even the title of the statue and the name of the Paris intersection at which it is located work to introduce key themes presented by Kechiche throughout *La Faute à Voltaire* (Nettelbeck 2007: 309–19). In the opening shot, Kechiche's camera looks up towards the statue: we see a woman's outstretched arm holding flowers down towards the viewer. The low-level, upward camera angle exaggerates the already large scale of the statue itself, and her bouquet of flowers prefigures the selling of roses by Jallel and the liberty he feels when wandering the streets of Paris.

This opening shot not only displays the title of the film, but also Kechiche's *visa d'exploitation*, the administrative permission necessary in order to show a film in a theatre. The visa, given by the French Ministry of Culture, confirms that a film follows the *Code du cinéma et de l'image animée* and usually appears after the credits at the end of the film in an extremely small font. Curiously, 'Visa d'exploitation n° 94323' reads like a subtitle in smaller font under the film's main title, *La Faute à Voltaire*. In the first shot of his film, Kechiche offers a not so subtle reference to his own ability to make and show films in France. The term *visa d'exploitation* takes on a second meaning as the sequence progresses, and a sound bridge links the image of the *Triomphe de la République* statue to the cacophony of languages heard at the immigration centre. Thus, the voices of those looking for legal grounds for a temporary stay in France are grafted on to the naked female statue and her offering of flowers and the republican values it conveys. Moreover, as suggested in the first shot, the temporary visas sought by the group of migrants are quite probably visas *d'exploitation*. Kechiche, through the inclusion of his own *visa d'exploitation*, deliberately conflates the film's diegesis with his own experience as a migrant. On the one hand, at a diegetic level, the migrants are poised to become a part of an exploitative system, but at an extra-diegetic level, Kechiche alludes to his own freedom to make films about love as he does in his cinematic *oeuvre*.

After the opening image of the *Triomphe de la République* we see a tracking shot at the immigration centre. The camera moves across the room filled with migrants completing the same administrative form, and comes to rest on Jallel and his uncle. Jallel reads in French: 'Reason . . . for the request . . . for political asylum. Why . . . did you leave your country? Why did you choose France?' The only viable reasons for coming to France are political. Poverty, as in Jallel's case, is not enough. When his uncle Mostfa (Mustapha Adouani) repeats that the question on the form is about his reason for leaving Tunisia, Jallel replies in Tunisian Arabic: 'To come to France!' His reasons for immigration are not actually political. He continues: 'For work . . . for money . . . you know why.' For his uncle, who already seems to know how to effectively navigate the system, none of Jallel's answers are satisfactory: 'Are you crazy? There are five million people unemployed here. How is your application political?' In his answer, Jallel again resists a political explanation for his desire to come to France: 'Oh, no, I'm just trying to survive.' He explains his difficult situation back in Tunisia where he became responsible for his many younger siblings following his father's death. The urgency of his family situation at home outweighs any potential political grievances and reasons for seeking political asylum. Mostfa's response is one of the most telling lines in the film: 'Why would they care about the novel of your life?' In this response, Mostfa asserts that one's story is either political, it is *la politique*, or it is narrative. To shape one's own social reality in *le politique*, or to render one's experiences into a story or into art, is not enough. This line in the film can also be interpreted as an insight into the ways in which Kechiche plays with aspects of what is political or not in his own filmmaking, and the question posed by Mostfa could also be a question for the film's spectator. Why would we care about a film about a Tunisian migrant and other characters, all in some way marginal, if the film isn't in some way political?

As the opening scene progresses, in an effort to create an appropriately political reason for Jallel to stay in France, the story of Jallel's life is first 'erased' before being 'rewritten' by Mostfa. He indicates it would be better for Jallel not to give his real name and to say that his papers have been stolen, before suggesting that Jallel could also adopt a more politically convenient national identity: 'Tell them you're Algerian.' The possibility of being Algerian also necessarily comes with a specific background story: 'The past . . . the weight of guilt . . .' Jallel's fictional past, freshly crafted by Mostfa, is also strategic insofar as it plays into the particular way in which the French would like to see themselves: 'France, the country of freedom. The homeland of 'Voltaire and human rights! Liberty, equality, fraternity and *tutti quanti* . . . They think they're the inventors of freedom!' In the following scene, Jallel 'plays the role' created for him by Mostfa. In his brief conversation with the immigration officer, he relates an unconvincing tale of hiding a cousin from the police back in Algeria, before clearly stating the invented cousin's crime: 'He was doing politics.' Doing politics, in the most abstract sense, is Jallel's ticket to a temporary stay in France and to his fictional political novel. While it is clear in Mostfa's advice that the proper reason for coming to France is necessarily political (again, poverty and a desire to build a better life for one's family isn't enough), the details about the connection between liberty and politics in France – themes introduced in the opening dialogue – are never clearly articulated for Jallel or for the viewer.

Yet, even as the opening minutes of the film both establish and complicate the themes of politics and freedom, Kechiche will nonetheless plant clues for the viewers, allowing them to begin interpreting these overarching ideas. With his new, temporary work visa in hand, Jallel is free to benefit from the existing political system and infrastructure available in France, albeit in unexpected ways. After obtaining his three-month temporary work visa and taking a quick ride on the metro, Jallel's first stop is the *foyer gratuit* (free shelter) mentioned in the opening sequence. While the film's opening dialogue reinforces France's image of itself as a country of freedom, at the shelter, Jallel is presented with all of the comforts of everyday life without charge. Jallel enters the foyer, and a continuity shot shows us Jallel's point of view as he looks around his new temporary home. We see a comfortable living area, a bookshelf with plenty of reading materials, and groups of friends drinking wine and playing cards. Jallel's introduction to the foyer continues as one of the shelter's employees shows Jallel where to find the laundry room, various toiletries and introduces him to Frank (Bruno Lochet), who shows him his room and presents Jallel to the other residents, with whom he will become close friends. The *foyer* offers an abundance of free, necessary, quotidian resources for the small price of inventing a new background story.

As Claudia Esposito notes, Jallel transforms spaces, like the *foyer*, which are typically seen as 'problematic or of marginal interest and transforms them into central places of everyday practices' (Esposito 2011: 223). The streets of Paris become the ideal location for the newspapers, various types of fruit, and roses he sells in order to send money to his family in Tunisia. Like the *foyer*, which becomes a functional space for Jallel as soon as he receives his new, fictional identity as Algerian political refugee, Jallel also successfully recreates various legal documents. A friend's driver's licence allows Jallel to evade the police while illegally selling fruit. And, after the end of his relationship with the beautiful *beurette* waitress, a friend's medical card gives him access to the psychiatric hospital where he recovers from depression.

I suggest that the freedom Jallel experiences in France throughout the majority of the film comes from his ability to navigate government-funded spaces and legal documents, granting him the time and resources to write his own story after his actual past is 'erased' in the film's opening sequence. He transforms *la politique* into *le politique*, repurposing political and government structures through the way in which he uses the shared spaces of the *foyer*, the psychiatric hospital, and the streets of Paris. The novel Jallel writes for himself in France is also a love story. Although the shelter provides friendship and everyday necessities, the one resource missing from Jallel's life in the *foyer* is romance.

The beginning of Jallel's stay in the mental hospital begins much like the beginning of his time in the *foyer*, and, with his borrowed *carte vitale* in hand, his stay in the hospital is also free. Jallel is greeted by other patients who are also *placement obligatoire* (required to stay in the hospital) and given a tour of his new, temporary home, which includes a television room complete with cable TV, and an introduction to Lucie, another patient who sleeps with the men in the psychiatric ward for a small fee. The way in which Jallel is presented to Lucie is much like his tour of where to find the laundry room and various toiletries on his first day in the shelter. Lucie offers love, a 'resource' available to Jallel during his time in the hospital.

In one scene, Lucie, who is spying Jallel as he reads Ronsard's *Les Amours*, makes her way into his room to proposition him for sex. She approaches, coming uncomfortably close to Jallel as he lights her cigarette. Jallel, still seated on his bed, looks up at her face before his eyes scan over the rest of her body standing over him. In the frame, Jallel's view of Lucie is much like the spectator's view of the naked statue in the opening shot of the film. While the first sequence of the film suggests that the *Triomphe de la République* is political freedom, the freedom Jallel actually finds in France comes through his relationship with Lucie. We learn that, unlike Jallel and the majority of other patients who are required to stay in the hospital, Lucie is there by choice – *placement libre*. 'I'm free. I'm PL', she mentions. Kechiche's camera shows us Jallel's view of her derrière as she gets up to leave the room, and Lucie, aware of Jallel's gaze on her body, takes her time exiting.

Lucie also introduces two of the most overt references to politics, a theme that remains mostly implied throughout the narrative. Spying Jallel alone in his room, Lucie makes herself available for sex, this time offering to waive the small fee she charges the other patients. Jallel refuses her offer, explaining that before sex, one must talk about 'everything'. 'Everything', he says, '. . . about life, poetry . . . like everyone else. About what's happening in the world, about . . . politics.' 'And after politics we make love?' Lucie asks. Her question for Jallel should also be read as a question for Kechiche's audience. If we make films about politics, when do we make films about love? Lucie implicitly answers her own question: we should make love first, and we can make love now. Later, when Lucie and Jallel are alone for the night in a hotel room, she rephrases her earlier question, asking: 'Would you like to talk about politics?' Faced with the curves of Lucie's half naked body, Jallel takes off his jacket. His emphatic, unspoken answer is no, politics can wait.

The beginning of Jallel's relationship with Lucie coincides with his newfound sense of freedom wandering the streets of Paris selling roses instead of peddling avocados in the metro: 'Roses are better', he explains: '. . . I'm working, and at the same time, I stroll around. I go where I want, I'm more free.' If France is indeed the 'country of freedom' as proposed in the film's opening scene, the type of freedom Jallel experiences is ultimately characterised by his ability to move around Paris, unconfined to a rigid work schedule. Ironically, the character of Franck, a French citizen who has managed to 'properly' integrate himself into French society, finding a stable job and a place to live outside the *foyer*, is less free than Jallel. Franck's job as a hotel night clerk is tedious. He is confined to the hotel front desk at all hours of the night and tasked with the repetitive job of handing keys and towels to guests.

The freedom Jallel experiences during his last days in Paris is again linked to his relationship with Lucie in one of the final scenes of the film. Lucie sits at the base of the *Triomphe de la République* statue we first saw in the opening shot of the film. While Kechiche uses close-ups of Jallel and Lucie in order to film the majority of their time together, this shot uses a deep space composition, allowing the entirety of the massive female statue to remain in the frame. Jallel stands with his roses looking down towards Lucie, essentially reproducing, on a smaller scale, the statue offering her flowers. In contrast, the film's opening image of the statue comes immediately before we see Jallel filling out his demand for political asylum, and we assume that the freedom he finds in France will be through the country's political system. However, for Jallel, freedom does not come through politics, but through love.

Ultimately, the freedom Jallel experiences in his relationship with Lucie is only a temporary one. And, while politics remain an implicit theme throughout the narrative, the ending of the film is explicitly political.

In the final scene, the camera uses deep focus to show the statue as well as the entrance to the Nation metro station. The camera remains stationary as we watch Jallel, flowers in hand, run across the grassy park before descending the steps to the metro. Moments later, he emerges in police custody, the Nation sign marking the entrance to the station and the *Triomphe de la République* remaining visible in the shot. A police officer carries his bouquet of roses, and Jallel is effectively stripped of the freedom once available to him. In the next shot, Jallel is quite literally extracted from the Nation – he is escorted from a police van onto an airplane back to Tunisia.

In this last sequence of the film, we are struck by the rapidity with which the new story Jallel has been writing for himself comes to a violent conclusion, and the parallel between the beginning and the end of the 'novel' of his life in France. Jallel awakes in his hotel room with Lucie, and seemingly moments later, he is on an airplane leaving the country. In the closing credits, we again see the statue in the *Place de la Nation*. This time, however, her back is turned, and her flowers are no longer visible in the frame. In contrast with the opening image of the statue, linked by a sound bridge of migrant voices filling out paperwork for political asylum to the following tracking shot in the immigration centre, the ending sequence takes place without dialogue. Instead of the voices of those seeking political freedom in France, we hear traffic around the metro station, then the noise of the airplane's engine, then the final image of the statue appears in complete silence. Although Jallel is, at first, able to use various political structures and government-funded programmes available in France to his advantage through the assumption of various alternate identities, at the end of the film, he remains silent and powerless. Migrants like Jallel are ultimately voiceless in the face of the French politics of immigration and deportation policies of the 1990s.[5]

The film's decidedly political ending, a powerful critique of *la politique*, recontextualises Lucie's assertion that we should make love before we talk about politics. If the ending to Jallel's story is already, in a way, written for him by the political climate in France, his relationship with Lucie is the part of his story he writes for himself. Kechiche, through the way in which he structures the film's narrative, also follows Lucie's advice to make love before 'talking politics', making a film about love with an unambiguously political conclusion. After the film's opening dialogue, we expect a more or less political story of a migrant's arrival in France, but for the majority of the film, Kechiche focuses on Jallel's romantic relationships. He suggests that, in the absence of true political freedom, the most we can hope for is the type of everyday freedom Jallel experiences with Lucie.

In his film *La Vie d'Adèle*, Kechiche once again offers us a love story. This time, instead of a portrait of a Tunisian migrant, Kechiche's camera focuses on a young, working-class girl from the outskirts of Lille discovering her sexual identity.[6] As in *La Faute à Voltaire*, Kechiche gives a specific name and a story to his critique of *la politique*, and while Adèle's (Adèle Exarchopoulos) economic background becomes an insurmountable hurdle in her relationship, she does experience a type of everyday freedom through her choice to pursue a queer relationship with a blue-haired girl who catches her eye.

Like Jallel, who rewrites his own story throughout *La Faute à Voltaire*, *La Vie d'Adèle* begins with an emphasis on the stories we write for ourselves. While the opening dialogue of *La Faute à Voltaire* asserts that no one should be interested in the 'novel' of Jallel's life, *La Vie d'Adèle* begins quite literally with a novel. A sound bridge links the opening images of Adèle arriving at school with the following scene in Adèle's French classroom. Kechiche's camera follows Adèle down the school hallways then, in the next shot, we see a student read a passage from Marivaux's *La Vie de Marianne* aloud: 'Je suis femme et je conte mon histoire.' From the opening sequence, it is clear that Kechiche's film is about Adèle telling her own story. The class continues to read the passage from Marivaux's text, which describes a shared gaze between the novel's protagonist and a potential love interest, on whom Marianne's eyes falls 'more willingly' than on her other suitors. In return, he sees her in a completely different way. In the subsequent class discussion, the French teacher reinforces the idea of predestination in Marianne's encounter with the young man who holds the potential to fill the missing part of her heart. Throughout the classroom dialogue, shots of students reading passages of the text are interspersed with continuity shots of Adèle as she listens to the story, hoping for a predestined, chance encounter of her own.

At first, Thomas (Jérémie Laheurte), one of Adèle's classmates, is positioned as a potential love interest, but their exchange of glances across the cafeteria lacks the intensity of the scene analysed in the passage from *La Vie de Marianne*. In contrast, everything about her first encounter with Emma (Léa Seydoux) suggests that she is the one Adèle is predestined to find. The scene begins in the same way as the opening sequence of the film, with a view of Adèle shot from behind. Instead of the sounds of traffic we hear in the opening sequence, this view of Adèle is linked to the subsequent shots through a sound bridge of the steel hand drums played in the city centre where she sees Emma for the first time. Upon her arrival in the city centre, she looks around, caught up in the movement of bodies around her, before her eyes come to rest firmly on something on the other side of the intersection.

In the reverse shot, Kechiche's camera shows us the focus of Adèle's gaze: the blue-haired girl in the middle of the intersection (Figure 11.1). The shot is particularly striking, and Emma herself is squarely centred in the camera's frame. The widescreen aspect ratio of 2.35:1 used throughout the film gives us extreme close-ups of characters' faces while also allowing portions of the background to remain in view. The use of the aspect ratio in this scene allows for a large portion of Lille's city centre to remain in the frame, while only Emma and her girlfriend are in focus in the camera's lens. The city centre is crowded with pedestrians, but Emma is the only person Adèle sees.

In this moment, Adèle sees the potential for a life very different from the one she had imagined for herself, and the great love she is predestined to find is a woman. I argue that Kechiche's film becomes political the minute Adèle sees Emma crossing the street. In *Politics of Aesthetics*, Rancière argues that politics and aesthetics come together through a 'distribution of the sensible: through shared spaces and activities that determine the ways in which we "participate" in the common' (Rancière 2000b: 12). In *La Vie d'Adèle*, Kechiche illustrates how the public space of downtown Lille becomes a shared experience for the two women, a moment which will fundamentally transform Adèle's view of her own sexuality and, therefore, change the way she participates in society. Suddenly, she looks at the other girls in her high school differently, dares to head to a gay bar for the first time and, later in the film, openly admires the female statues in the *Palais des Beaux-Arts de Lille*. Following Rancière's logic, for Kechiche to film

Figure 11.1 Adèle's first view of Emma in downtown Lille.

the ways in which Adèle begins to participate in communal spaces as a visible sexual minority would constitute a political act.

Adèle also has a certain amount of agency over *le politique*, her social reality, through the way in which she makes her choices throughout the film. Suddenly aware of her attraction to Emma, Adèle sees events around her differently. She realises her lack of desire for Thomas and seeks out her first potential female love interest. On a night out with a gay friend, we see Adèle's eyes scan the environment around her, noticing the freedom with which the men kiss, dance and interact. Shots of Adèle observing her surroundings are interspersed with her glances toward women in the bar next door, seen through the window. Looking for the same freedom for herself, she leaves Valentin (Sandor Funtek) behind, and heads to the lesbian bar. Like the scene in which Adèle first sees Emma crossing the street, the narrative is driven forward solely by the exchange of glances as she first enters the bar. Instead of a chance encounter on the streets of Lille, however, Adèle chooses to enter the bar where she is openly observed by the women around her, and where she once again finds Emma. When Adèle insists that she found her way into the bar 'by chance', Emma counters with the assertion that chance does not exist: her entrance into the lesbian bar is an affirmation of her sexuality, and her own freedom of sexual preference.

The scene is a representation of the way in which Kechiche uses everyday politics in his film. Instead of grand political gestures, or overt declarations of a specific political ideology, he captures moments of everyday life in which characters are able to push back against the limits imposed by *la politique*, changing their own stories, writing their own narrative. In the opening of the scene following her second encounter with Emma, we see Adèle writing in her diary, quite literally writing her own love story (Figure 11.2).

In the following scene, Kechiche introduces the notion of personal liberty into the film. Emma discusses Sartre and the way in which his philosophy helped in the 'affirmation of her freedom and her own values', but as the love story between the two women continues to develop, it becomes evident that some limiting social factors are beyond personal choice.

The way in which Kechiche represents politics in the film is linked to a notion of personal freedom and the ability to write one's own story, but the *polis*, the spaces we share with others in society, can be brutal for a young girl discovering her sexuality. While Emma's homosexuality is readily accepted by her fellow artists and her well-educated, bourgeois family, Adèle is violently harassed by her peers. On her first day back at school

YOUNG LOVE AND EVERYDAY FREEDOM 183

Figure 11.2 Adèle writes in her diary after meeting Emma for the second time.

following her date with Emma in the park, Adèle is immediately interrogated: 'Who was that girl who came to get you last time? The dykey one with the blue hair? . . . It's obvious she eats pussy.' Adèle denies her trip to the gay bar, but the insults from her friends become increasingly vicious: 'Did you already eat her pussy? . . . I can't believe you've slept naked in my bed . . . you'll never eat my pussy . . .', 'She sleeps in my bed naked, checks out my ass . . . Whores like you are into ass . . . Does your bitch also have a blue pussy?' The language used by the group of young students is violent, and the scene raises questions about the relevance of asserting your own 'freedom and values' – as suggested by Emma – when we are faced with such intolerance from those around us.

Throughout the film, Adèle remains more at ease in her relationship with Emma than she does openly asserting her queerness around others. At the gay pride parade in the centre of Lille, Adèle is visibly uncomfortable in the massive crowd. In contrast, during the public service workers' union strike earlier in the film, she actively chants 'No to privatisation! No to job cuts! No to austerity measures! More money for education!' She sings along to a popular protest song decrying the injustice of the economic system and demanding change for the working class.[7] In the first protest scene, the camera moves backwards as she moves forward, filming a close-up of her face while she actively protests. In this shot, the passion Adèle feels is clearly visible on her face: she is completely committed to the ideas held by the strikers.

At the later pride parade, the scene begins with an aerial shot that captures the crowd from above, followed by shots of various partyers. We catch a glimpse of Emma's blue hair before we find Adèle herself, and when we do finally spot her in the crowd, she bobs her head to the music apathetically. Totally overwhelmed by the environment around her, she stays close to Emma, who notices her discomfort. In contrast with Adèle's obvious unease at the pride parade, the next scene shows her alone with Emma, completely comfortable, kissing on a park bench. Even from the beginning stages of their relationship, Emma openly asserts her sexuality and her politics surrounding gay marriage while Adèle prefers to focus on her connection with Emma. I suggest that her reticence to publicly affirm her sexuality is not only the result of the violent reactions of her classmates as shown earlier in film, but also, in part, a response to continued social intolerance.[8]

In the following scenes, as Linda Williams notes, the relationship 'goes bad' for the 'time-honored reasons of class and age' (Williams 2014: 12). The way in which Kechiche represents politics takes the form of an economic critique, and the insurmountable differences in background between the two women become increasingly apparent. At dinner with Emma's parents, Adèle is presented as Emma's girlfriend, and the family's education as well as their social status are obvious though the choice of wine, the type of food and the discussion about art. Adèle confirms the quality of the wine: 'I don't know wine very well, but it's good', and immediately realises the differences between Emma's upbringing and her own. Social differences between Adèle and Emma's family are reinforced as she explains her plans to become an elementary school teacher, a statement met with momentary silence and visible disdain from Emma's parents. Adèle's plans for the future are also guided by economic reasons. She hopes to finish school and begin working as soon as possible, an implicit reference to her own family's inability to support her financially after she completes her studies.

The subsequent dinner with Adèle's family also reveals class differences. It becomes obvious that Adèle's parents have only very recently learned about Emma's presence in their daughter's life, and they understand the relationship to be based around philosophy tutoring instead of romance. Emma, suddenly aware that their relationship is still a secret, sends a betrayed glance to Adèle across the table. As the conversation turns to plans for the future, her parents are unenthusiastic about Emma's hope for a career in the fine arts, suggesting the importance of a 'real job' or a boyfriend to offer financial support. Already, the social and economic differences between the two women – at times painfully obvious – appear difficult to overcome.

Adèle takes naturally to teaching while Emma prepares to finish her master's programme in painting, and the differences between the two women are more pronounced as they become established in their careers.

Adèle keeps her relationship hidden from her colleagues, and although Emma prominently features Adèle in her paintings, Emma's friends know nothing about Adèle outside her physical appearance. Their dissimilarities once again become apparent at the party thrown by Adèle for Emma at the end of her time in art school. During the scene, Emma is quick to insist that Adèle is a talented writer, while Adèle asserts she only keeps personal journals. Her own story, emphasised in the opening scene and in the shots of her writing throughout film, is a love story she writes for herself and chooses to keep private, partly because she fears her relationship will not be accepted by her family and peers.

As the party continues, Adèle is increasingly isolated while others converse around her, discussing painters whom she has never heard of before. Throughout the scene, we are struck by how alone she feels around Emma's social circle comprised of other well-educated artists with bourgeois upbringings. Emma, engrossed in conversation, does not notice Adèle has yet to eat anything for herself, and the party illustrates the growing divide between the two women. Their differences in class and education lead to increasing loneliness for Adèle, who seeks companionship through infidelity with a male colleague. Her affair is the final blow to a relationship that is already broken.

What kind of political statement does Kechiche make through a queer love story that ends not because of social stigma but because of socioeconomic differences? Throughout *La Vie d'Adèle*, Kechiche suggests that while queer love is a passionate force, relationships are still subject to the external forces of the background and upbringing of those involved. Even with legalisation of gay marriage in France and the increasing social acceptance of homosexual couples, relationships, especially queer ones, are more difficult, especially for women whose careers and social settings lead them to radically different places. Kechiche's film is as much an economic critique as it is a love story. Similarly, in *La Faute à Voltaire*, Jallel's love story ends because of political forces beyond his control. Although he is temporarily able to use the French political system to his advantage and finds a type of freedom in his relationship with Lucie, Jallel's small moments of agency do nothing to prevent his abrupt and jarring deportation at the end of the film. Ultimately, the type of everyday freedom Jallel discovers wandering the streets of Paris and Adèle finds in her decision to enter a lesbian bar are paltry compensations for a lack of *actual freedom*: sustained and meaningful agency over *la politique*. Even if his characters' stories end for political reasons, Kechiche's films suggest that while we work towards greater equality for those who are marginalised, we can make and watch films about love.

Notes

1. Norindr (2012: 56); Higbee (2013: 97); Besson (2016: 1).
2. A *Le Monde* article from 2002 outlines key dates in France's immigration history, including the Pasqua laws of 1992, which made residence permits more difficult to obtain, and under certain circumstances, withdrew permits issued to refugees and facilitated deportation. After a campaign spearheaded by the Minister of Justice, Christine Taubira, gay marriage was legalised in France on 17 May 2013. Before legalisation, the 'mariage pour tous' movement experienced particularly strong resistance from the Catholic Church (see Duportail (2013); Gouvernement.fr (2017)).
3. The translation from the original French is my own.
4. Kechiche's forthcoming film, *Mektoub, My Love*, is scheduled to be released in theatres in the US in 2018.
5. The Quilès law of July 1992 created *zones d'attentes* in ports and airports in order to detain foreigners and those seeking political asylum. The Pasqua laws of August 1992 facilitated various forms of identity checks, made residence permits more difficult to obtain, added new conditions for family reunification and, in some cases, withdrew residence permits already issued. In April 1997, the Debré law facilitated the detention deportation of undocumented migrants, enforced border controls and regulated procedures for issuing housing certificates. While restrictive policies temporarily reduced migration in 1994, 1995 and 1999, official immigration numbers continued to rise, with Algerians and Moroccans constituting the two biggest groups of immigrants to France, respectively (Thierry and Rogers 2004: 638–44).
6. The release in France took place only five months after gay marriage was legalised in the country in May 2013.
7. The song is 'On Lâche Rien' by HK et Les Saltimbanks, a music group from the outskirts of Lille known for their politically engaged lyrics.
8. Even as gay marriage was legalised in France, the protests surrounding the gay rights movement and scepticism around the 'American invasion' of gender theory illustrate persistent social resistance for gay couples (Perreau 2016: 2). Bruno Perreau also notes that the marriage-for-all law was not 'a complete success for sexual minorities', but rather a 'concession to their struggle, just as civil unions had been in the past, legalised by the legislature only after many years of lobbying by organisations that defended homosexuals' (Perreau 2016: 5).

Works Cited

Barot, Emmanuel (2009), *Camera politica : Dialectique du réalisme dans le cinéma politique et militant*, Paris: Vrin.

Besson, Rémy (2016), 'Abdellatif Kechiche: un filmeur aux points de vue politique', *Cinemadoc*, <https://cinemadoc.hypotheses.org/3616> (last accessed 12 January 2018).
Duportail, Judith (2013), 'Mariage homosexuel: moins de remous à l'étranger', *Le Figaro*, 1 February, <http://www.lefigaro.fr/international/2013/02/01/01003-20130201ARTFIG00451-mariage-homosexuel-moins-de-remous-a-l-etranger.php> (last accessed 9 March 2018).
Esposito, Claudia (2011), 'Ronsard in the Metro: Abdellatif Kechiche and the Poetics of Space', *Studies in French Cinema*, 11:3, pp. 223–34.
Gouvernement.fr (2017), 'Le mariage pour tous', Gouvernement.fr, 15 May, <https://www.gouvernement.fr/action/le-mariage-pour-tous> (last accessed 10 March 2018).
Higbee, Will (2013), *Post-beur Cinema: North African Émigré and Maghrebi-French and Filmmaking in France since 2000*, Edinburgh: Edinburgh University Press.
Le Monde (2002), 'Les dates-clés de l'immigration en France', *Le Monde*, 12 June, <https://www.lemonde.fr/societe/article/2002/12/06/les-dates-cles-de-l-immigration-en-france_301216_3224.html> (last accessed 9 March 2018).
Nettelbeck, Colin (2007), 'Kechiche and the French Classics', *French Cultural Studies*, 18:3, pp. 307–19.
Norindr, Panivong (2012), 'The Cinematic Practice of a "Cinéaste Ordinaire": Abdellatif Kechiche and French Political Cinema', *Contemporary French and Francophone Studies*, 16:1, pp. 55–68.
Perreau, Bruno (2016), *Queer Theory: The French Response*, Stanford: Stanford University Press.
Rancière, Jacques (2000a), 'Il est arrivé quelque chose au réel', *Cahiers du cinéma*, 545, pp. 62–4.
Rancière, Jacques (2000b), *Le Partage du sensible : esthétique et politique*, Paris: La Fabrique Éditions.
Thierry, Xavier and Godfrey I. Rogers (2004), 'Recent Immigration Trends in France and Elements for a Comparison with the United Kingdom', *Population (English Edition, 2002–)*, 59:5, pp. 635–72.
Williams, Linda (2014), 'Cinema's Sex Acts', *Film Quarterly*, 67:4, pp. 9–25.

Films

La Faute à Voltaire, film, directed by Abdellatif Kechiche. France: Rezo Films, 2000.
La Vie d'Adèle: Chapitres 1 et 2, film, directed by Abdellatif Kechiche. France: Wild Bunch Distribution, 2013.

CHAPTER 12

Anthem for (Doomed) Youth: War, AIDS and the Queer Autobiographical Cinema of André Téchiné

Claire Boyle

Wilfred Owen wrote his poem 'Anthem for Doomed Youth' during his service as a British army officer during World War I, which he did not survive (he died in battle at the age of twenty-four). The poem is a searing indictment of the routine squandering of soldiers' young lives on the front line – this at the behest of an establishment that oversees this profligate expenditure of life without even the most rudimentary rites to recognise the ultimate sacrifice being made. 'What passing bells for those who die as cattle?' asks Owen in the first line of his poem (2013: 96). The answer? 'Only the monstrous anger of the guns.' Owen's poem speaks of a broken compact between the young soldiery on the front line, and the old, who occupy positions of political and military power, and thus hold young destinies in their hands.

In alluding to Owen's poem through this essay's title, my intention is to draw attention to something previously unremarked about how the French film director André Téchiné approaches the subject of youth in his cinema. Themes of youth and adolescence are recurrent preoccupations in his cinematic *œuvre*, which now stretches back five decades; the director himself acknowledges that '[l]'adolescence reste un terrain privilégié pour moi . . . pour moi, il y a dans la jeunesse quelque chose de magique, qui peut donner au cinéma une valeur enchantée' (Téchiné 2016: n.p.). In films throughout his career, such as *J'embrasse pas* (1991), *Les Roseaux sauvages* (1994), *Les Égarés* (2003), *Les Témoins* (2007), and in one of his most recent films at the time of writing, *Quand on a 17 ans* (2016), Téchiné explores the trials and the thrills involved in the process of growing up, showing particular understanding of the intense emotional experiences and sexual awakenings typically associated with coming of age. Sensitive to the explosion of new emotions and desires that characterise the teenage years and young adulthood, Téchiné's films illuminate the force and ferocity that drive youthful friendships and passions, often focusing particularly on the development of sexual subjectivities. Queer themes are recurrent in his films and, latterly in his career, Téchiné has paid regular attention to the experience of the young adolescent who grows up realising he is gay (most of the five films named above include such a protagonist). Alongside preoccupations of an emotional or physical nature, Téchiné also works through adolescent concerns of an ethical nature. Recurrent quandaries in Téchiné's cinematic treatments of adolescence include the following: how to set about starting to shape one's own destiny? How to respond to a developing ethical (and potentially political) awareness, and how to frame one's actions accordingly?

Yet what might be called Téchiné's 'cinema of adolescence' is not, I shall argue, only focused on young people. In what follows, I shall suggest that Téchiné's depictions of adolescence are in truth studies in intergenerational relations, for the capacity of young people to shape their own destinies is shown in Téchiné's cinema to be highly dependent on what possibilities are left open to them in the world that they are bequeathed by their elders. As we shall see, Téchiné's young protagonists often find themselves also confronted with the question of how to reconcile their desires and aspirations for the future with the conditions that prevail in the world that they inhabit.

This focus on the material circumstances of adolescence is an important but overlooked aspect of Téchiné's filmmaking. Whilst his emphasis on youthful becoming in films such as *Les Roseaux sauvages* has been explored in previous scholarship (Everett 1999: 47–57; Marshall 2007: 87–94), there has yet to be a broader study of a notable tendency discernible in Téchiné's cinema over the last twenty-five years or so: his habit of interweaving narratives that chart youthful progress toward coming of age with depictions of episodes from French history having major significance in the life of the French nation. This distinctive bi-focal approach to representing the process of growing up is seen in films such as *Les Roseaux sauvages*, *Les Égarés* and *Les Témoins*, which frame the evolutions of maturing adolescents against the backdrops, respectively, of the Algerian War; the *débâcle* of 1940 that heralded the armistice, Occupation and the inception of the Vichy regime; and the AIDS epidemic of the early 1980s. What is striking is that all these historical episodes are ones that have given rise to a collective, indeed national, trauma. Furthermore, as we shall see, the first and last named of this trio of films are also autobiographical in inspiration. Nonetheless, Téchiné's move in *Les Égarés* to represent the perilous and chaotic period preceding the armistice in 1940 (which precedes his birth) indicates that his predilection for combining momentous historical events and personal histories of growing up cannot simply be attributed to a penchant for autobiography. One clear advantage of choosing very clearly historicised settings for films that explore the travails of teenage development is that Téchiné thus avoids an abstracted treatment of this phase of life. Such an approach might run the risk of descending into an idealised or exaggerated portrayal of youthful existence without any anchorage in the material world. By contrast, Téchiné's young protagonists are perpetually responding to the conditions they encounter in their particular environment.

In this essay, I shall be probing further the effects produced by this combination of youthful subjectivities and traumatic historical events in Téchiné's cinema. My focus will be the autobiographical diptych formed by *Les Roseaux sauvages* and *Les Témoins*. As the following discussion will show, these two films illustrate the many uses of testimony. Yet we shall also see that they are less concerned with overtly bearing witness to the director's own past in an autobiographical mode than they are with using historical episodes of collective trauma as reference points to spotlight the admirable optimism of young people, and their resilience when confronted with formidable pressures and challenges not of their own making; but also the tragedy that befalls them when they are conquered by crises of an inescapable magnitude, for which they were never responsible. Téchiné's historical cinema of adolescence may thus be read as a series of studies bearing witness to the effects that are produced in the young as a result of living in a world belonging to adults: configured by them, complete with their institutions and rules, which too often disregard the interests of the young. Accordingly, in what follows, I will analyse *Les Roseaux sauvages* and *Les Témoins* with a focus on questions of memory, testimony, intergenerational relations and the obligations that one generation owes to another.

Les Roseaux sauvages traces the nascent aspirations and new discoveries of a group of *lycéens* growing up in the south-west of France in 1962, as France's long colonial war in Algeria is drawing to a close and the prospect of Algerian independence is coming into view. Here, the history of the period is no mere backdrop to actions and developments that might equally well occur independently of the specific historical circumstances depicted: it is the disorder of war itself that spurs on evolution and change in the film's young protagonists. Contemporaneous events in Algeria, especially the terrorist attacks being carried out by the OAS paramilitary group in a last-ditch attempt to restore 'L'Algérie française', force a political consciousness on Serge, Maïté and François; so does the abrupt arrival of a new addition to their class, Henri, a *pied noir* sent to complete his schooling in safety in France: his sympathies lie with the OAS and their aspiration to keep Algeria French. However, one of the OAS attacks takes the life of Serge's older brother Pierre, who had been posted to Algeria for his compulsory military service. These circumstances will require the young protagonists to consider how to reconcile their political awareness and the ethical positions they adopt with their desires for sexual intimacy and companionship (Everett 1999: 49–52). Téchiné shows evolution and change (and the requirement to adapt to these) to be the lot of young people growing into maturity, but not solely theirs: adults too must learn the lesson of the fable by La Fontaine referenced in the film, *Le Chêne et le roseau*, and find ways to deal with the challenges brought about by rapidly changing circumstances evolving in unanticipated ways. However, in contrast to the example set by the adolescent protagonists of *Les Roseaux sauvages*, the capacity of adults to negotiate these challenges successfully is cast into doubt. As Wendy Everett observes (1999: 51–2), Maïté shows greater capacity to evolve and see past a polarised conception of the politics of the Algerian War than does her mother, Mme Alvarez (coincidentally the class teacher to the three male protagonists). She descends into crisis and is taken into residential care in a psychiatric institution following the assassination of Pierre, the doomed soldier (and Mme Alvarez's ex-pupil), whose pleas for help to desert from the army she had refused during his brief visit home for his wedding. Mme Alvarez's breakdown leaves Maïté alone to fend for herself without a parent at home – her father, she reports to François, has left her mother because she was 'trop rigide'. Her conversation with François illustrates that, by contrast with her mother, Maïté possesses the necessary reserves of emotional resilience and determination to accept her new situation: she expresses to him her determination not to 'jouer les orphelines' in the face of this parental abandonment. Furthermore, like Henri, she will ultimately evolve too in her attitudes to political difference, which will allow the pair of them to revel in sensuality and sexual discovery together (Everett 1999: 52).

There are multiple autobiographical strands to *Les Roseaux sauvages* (Everett 1999: 47). As Bill Marshall notes, Téchiné grew up in the Midi-Pyrénées region of south-west France, the son of parents who ran their own manufacturing business in the agricultural sector there, and attended secondary school in the region during the period of the Algerian War (Marshall 2007: 2). He thus shares key characteristics with François, the main protagonist of *Les Roseaux sauvages*. This includes a youthful cinephilia: Marshall describes the teenage Téchiné's film-going habits and his taste as a young man for the cinema of Swedish filmmaker Ingmar Bergman in particular; in *Les Roseaux sauvages*, we see François and Maïté exiting the cinema and discussing a Bergman film they have just watched, *À travers le miroir* (*Through A Glass Darkly*) (Marshall 2007: 2–3). Téchiné himself has described the autobiographical inspiration behind the plot of

Les Roseaux sauvages, commenting on the way that he learned about the reality of the conflict in Algeria in a similar way to François and his friends in *Les Roseaux sauvages*, and that it was this war that spurred him to make the film: 'je me suis souvenu de ça et j'avais envie d'en parler' (Téchiné 2004: n.p.). Alongside its refracted personal testimony about growing up in a land at war, the film testifies (as has been observed elsewhere (Everett 1999: 49; Marshall 2007: 86–9)) to the popular cultural landscape of France in 1962 – particularly through its use of American rock 'n' roll music on its soundtrack and references to films of the era, including Jacques Demy's New Wave release *Lola*. The film's work of bearing witness to the period extends to references to key moments of the war. Notably, Henri cites the famous line 'Je vous ai compris!' from President de Gaulle's conciliatory speech of June 1958 to the French settlers of Algeria, following it up with a scornful, 'Tu parles!' Allusions to other happenings in the Algerian War are often made via the periodic episodes in *Les Roseaux sauvages* when Henri is shown watching television programmes or listening to radio broadcasts reporting news from Algeria. This is the narrative pretext for a distinctive visual device that foregrounds the testimonial function of the film: the use of archival sound and film footage relating to the Algerian War within *Les Roseaux sauvages* itself, a device which Téchiné will also employ in *Les Témoins*.

Yet perhaps the most striking way in which *Les Roseaux sauvages* frames itself as a personal testimony to formative moments experienced in youth comes in a sequence unconnected to the significant historical events that weigh so heavily on the day-to-day lives of the film's various characters. I am referring to the brief (and unrepeated) interlude in the film when an initially non-diegetic first-person voice-over, representing the consciousness of François, suddenly obtrudes into the soundscape one hour and thirty seconds into the film. Until this moment, all dialogue and music in the film has been clearly diegetic, and what makes François's voice-over narration stand out even more is that it has a non-diegetic musical accompaniment: a romantic refrain played on stringed instruments, which introduces and then attends his words until a cut reinstates them to the diegetic sphere. The voice-over begins just after a tracking shot captures Serge and François on the latter's *mobylette* riding through the verdant agricultural landscape of Téchiné's native French countryside. François rides as Serge's pillion passenger, clasping him tightly around the waist. A lengthy lateral tracking shot gives equal visual weight to François and Serge on the *mobylette* as it does to their surroundings, capturing the yellow highlights of a strong overhead sun as they reflect off the lush trees and undergrowth bordering the road. This sunlight illuminates the blissful expression etched on François's face during this sequence, which extends to nearly forty seconds. What spurs this unanticipated aural intrusion is François's ecstatic reminiscence of the day and night he spent alone with Serge in Toulouse, an experience rendered all the more intense following the brief sexual turn that their friendship took previously in the film. This is the one occasion in *Les Roseaux sauvages* when we viewers are able to access directly the interiority of any of the characters, rather than having to rely on how they articulate their thoughts and feelings to those around them. What strengthens the potency of this sequence all the more is the way that the images accompanying the voice-over convey visually the enduring affective charge of the experience that is being narrated retrospectively by François. Indeed, *Les Roseaux sauvages* consistently pays close attention to the emotional roller coaster that ensues from François's realisation of his homosexuality (at a time when this was still illegal). The film charts the highs of his short-lived 'friendship with benefits' with Serge, and the lows of his subsequent sense of social isolation and feeling that homosexuality is (as he puts to Maïté) a curse. This leads him to attempt to seek counsel from the only other person in the locality he knows to be gay, M. Cassagne, and the memorable 'mirror-stage' sequence in the toilets where François invokes the language of everyday homophobia to recognise in himself that 'Je suis un pédé'. *Les Roseaux sauvages* may bear witness to an episode of French history that continues to be of vital national importance, yet the strongest, most emotionally charged testimonial act in the whole film is the one that recalls a young gay man's giddy joy at the sensation of a one-time lover's physical proximity. In this way, the importance of the film's queer testimony is underscored.

If *Les Roseaux sauvages* offers a paean to youth – an anthemic celebration of the energy, flexibility and resourcefulness of adolescents, even in the face of setbacks and devastating events on a scale far beyond their capacity to influence, let alone control – and a celebration of gay youth in particular, then this is even more strongly apparent in *Les Témoins*. This film recounts the experiences of Manu, a young man who (in an echo of Pierre in the earlier *J'embrasse pas*) has left the mountains of his native Pyrénées and arrives in Paris determined to forge a new beginning for himself. He is especially keen to seize the opportunities that the capital offers to live out a life where his homosexuality can be given free expression. In the course of making a fresh path for himself and finding other like-minded men, he makes various new acquaintances, including two men who rival with each other for his affections, and who are, coincidentally, connected to each other by the ties of marriage and friendship. They are Mehdi, a closeted bisexual policeman who will start a secret affair with

Manu; and Adrien, a gay doctor who is best friends with Mehdi's wife Sarah, and whose attraction to Manu and feelings for him will go unrequited. Unfortunately, Manu's quest for a new life that has room for love and sexual awakening coincides with the AIDS epidemic that hit France in the early 1980s, and whose gravity in that country was amplified by a series of actions of the French government that led to the risk of infection being increased rather than diminished (Martel 2000: 322–68). In the course of the film's narrative, Manu becomes infected with HIV and subsequently dies of AIDS; the last part of the film concerns the efforts Sarah makes – with very little help from Medhi and Adrien – to write up and publish the autobiographical testimony that Manu had recorded on her Dictaphone. Just as with the teenagers Téchiné depicts as coming of age during the Algerian War in *Les Roseaux sauvages*, in *Les Témoins*, the main protagonist's process of growing into mature adulthood coincides with a national catastrophe. The similarities do not stop there, for *Les Témoins*, as we shall see, shows how AIDS was a man-made disaster as well as an epidemiological one. Also like *Les Roseaux sauvages*, *Les Témoins* explores the subjectivity of a young gay man, although in *Les Témoins* this will not be an intermittent preoccupation, as in the earlier film, but the dominant one, as Manu (even more than François in *Les Roseaux sauvages*) becomes the point of intersection linking all the other characters to each other.

However, unlike François in *Les Roseaux sauvages*, the character of Manu in this later film is seemingly not weighed down by his homosexuality. From his first appearance in the film's narrative, his same-sex orientation is shown as an established fact known to himself and others, as his first on-screen conversation with his sister Julie makes clear. He is charismatic and appears comfortable in his own skin – quite literally, as shown by his total lack of inhibition about walking around naked in front of Julie in the cramped room they share together in Paris. Similarly, outside his home, in the first part of the film, he is frequently to be seen bare-chested, or with his chest plainly visible through his unbuttoned shirt. Reinforcing this sense of Manu being charming and at ease with the world, he is often showing smiling and cheerily conversing with others in the first part of the film (such as his sister's landlord, whom he quickly befriends upon his unannounced initial arrival at Julie's address).

Given the presentation of Manu as charismatic and physically attractive, it therefore comes as little surprise that in the early days of Manu's acquaintance with Adrien, the older man quickly falls for him. The third-person voice-over narration delivered intermittently by Sarah during the film reports that, as Adrien shows Manu the sights of Paris, 'l'éclat de l'été était au rendez-vous'. The film suggests, in fact, that Manu *is* this sunny 'éclat de l'été', clothing him consistently in yellow tones throughout (thus pairing him subtly with Sarah herself, whose dyed blonde hair creates a more conspicuous association with the colour yellow, reinforced by the hues of her clothing and the household objects we often see her use). The implied sense of vitality in Manu is clear not only from his easy-going, confident disposition: it emerges also in the portrait of his youthful physicality that *Les Témoins* paints, showing him dancing enthusiastically with Sarah, and also spotlighting his strength and stamina in a striking tracking shot a minute later that depicts him running exploratively along the rocky *calanques* of the Mediterranean shoreline, where Sarah's family home is situated. At one point Manu runs up a shallow gradient created by the oblique angle at which a bent-over, wind-ravaged small tree grows out of the white rock, continuing his workout by using his arms to hoist his whole body up onto a low-lying branch of this tree, in order to perch there under the admiring gaze of Adrien, who is shown in the next shot staring down at him, enraptured, from the villa above. The strong critique he had previously uttered of the cult of youth within the gay community (Rees-Roberts 2008: 119), and the age discrimination which is its by-product, is for the birds. Thus, it is through Adrien's besotted eyes that we will see Manu in this first chapter of *Les Témoins*, which emphasises his physical attributes and energy, and the way that this energy carries over into a pronounced *joie de vivre* and evident appetite, as a young man just starting out on an independent existence, to make something of his own life. Manu is a passionate and consummate cook, who dreams of one day owning his own restaurant. Téchiné's anthem to youth is an anthem to the verve, the drive, the passion, the openness to opportunity and the determination to enjoy life that we see in Manu.

Although Téchiné has stated that Manu is a fictitious character, the autobiographical element is nevertheless strong in *Les Témoins* (Téchiné 2007: n.p.). Notably, the preoccupation with bearing witness is even more pronounced in this later film. Before the release of *Les Témoins*, Téchiné's intimate familiarity with the gay nightclub scene in Paris in the early 1980s, prior to the explosion of the AIDS epidemic, had already been attested by Frédéric Martel in his study of homosexuality in contemporary France (Martel 2000: 325). Speaking in an interview about *Les Témoins*, Téchiné makes it clear that his work of recounting through his film the French lived experience of a gay *hécatombe* caused by AIDS is, as he puts it, a 'devoir de mémoire' (Téchiné 2007: n.p.). This vocabulary sheds an interesting light on Téchiné's cinematic autobiographical act in this film: it frames *Les Témoins* as driven by an ethical imperative to produce testimony for others; it implies a commitment to contributing to cultural memory by generating a cinema of witness devoted to AIDS, and in particular the French experience of its initial eruption, when it was a mysterious and fatal illness – 'comme la lèpre ou la peste', as Manu observes when revealing his diagnosis to Mehdi.

The testimonial drive animating *Les Témoins* is indicated by the film's very name, and is expressed as early as the title sequence of the film, which depicts Sarah furiously typing a manuscript on a manual typewriter. Sarah is a published author, and we will later learn that this manuscript is destined to become a book that recounts the life of Manu. As the visual depiction of Sarah's act of creating testimony indicates, Téchiné's film is not concerned solely with delivering its own testimony to the disastrous outbreak of AIDS, and how it claims Manu's life. In addition, it thematises and interrogates the very act of bearing witness.[1]

Les Témoins bears witness to the (then) deadly phenomenon of AIDS in two ways. Firstly, it represents a young gay man's experience of coming to terms with his sexuality and living it out freely for the first time in the eye of the storm of the 1980s AIDS crisis, until he falls ill and ultimately dies. However, Téchiné's emphasis on situating Manu as part of a social group made up of his friends and (would-be) lovers means that his story can never be a singular one: not just because those in his network are susceptible to infection too, but because his testimony can survive him through others. It will fall to this group of older adults that have befriended him to take up the testimonial baton on behalf of the deceased Manu, who had started but been unable to finish this work.

Secondly, *Les Témoins* exploits its position as an inevitably retrospective act of witnessing by using its chronological distance from the initial outbreak to offer an insight into AIDS as a cultural phenomenon, and the kinds of discourses on AIDS that emerged with the epidemic. The film thus takes pains to bear witness to the discursive climate of the time in relation to AIDS, deploying archive footage to remind (or educate) its audience about the shocking prejudice and dehumanisation encountered by those dying of AIDS – very many of whom, in these early days of the illness, were gay men.[2] This archive footage is used to particularly strong effect when we see Manu watching contemporaneous television news reports of the outbreak of AIDS in the United States, which record (amongst other things) how undertakers refused to handle the AIDS dead.

Archive footage is used again later in the film to challenge testimonial discourse itself, at the point where we see Mehdi distractedly viewing television coverage of the annual 14 July commemorative military parade held in Paris under the observation of the French President. The inclusion of images from the period of President Mitterrand participating in this solemn rite to honour France's war dead – then and now a perennial feature in the television and media calendar – points up the reverence with which these dead are honoured and kept in the national memory. The conspicuous reference in the film to the Bastille Day parade as a commemorative act to preserve the memory of soldiers' lives lost at war shows that the lesson of the poem by Owen with which this essay began has, to a degree, been learnt. Yet, in the light of the dehumanising treatment meted out to the AIDS dead at the height of the epidemic, it also raises, by implication, the question of how the AIDS dead are to be remembered (Pratt 2008: 256). This becomes an especially pertinent consideration at a time when, in France and the West more broadly, HIV has become a treatable chronic health condition rather than the vehicle of a mortal illness. With these evolutions, and the concomitant cultural shifts, the risk is that their deaths will be consigned to oblivion (Hallas 2009: 5). *Les Témoins* itself tries to provide a more positive response to this question via its reverent treatment of young Manu, whose life, the film leaves us in no doubt, is definitely grievable (to borrow the phraseology of Judith Butler (2009)) and will not be forgotten.

Whether we think of Téchiné's *Les Roseaux sauvages* and *Les Témoins* as works of testimony themselves – as film testimonies bearing witness to some of the experiences that have especially marked their director – or else as works depicting acts of testimony, as *Les Témoins* does, it is clear that Téchiné's treatment of youth in these films is inseparable from the act of witnessing. This might seem a curious detail, and the thematic preoccupation with young people somewhat arbitrarily aligned with the theme of testimony. Yet giving testimony to a personal experience of a past moment, connecting the past self to the present one, is an inevitably retrospective act *that is also future-directed*. A testimony to one's own experience is something that one generation hands on to the next. The testimonial act is an act that addresses a future generation and thus binds different generations together. As such, Téchiné's conflagration of youth and testimony should not surprise us, for it is one aspect of a broader interest in intergenerational relations that renders his body of work distinctive within French cinema. It is to this intergenerational dynamic in Téchiné's cinema that I will now turn in the final part of this essay.

The adolescents of *Les Roseaux sauvages* are depicted as being without the support of their elders, even in cases where the latter are not absent completely, as is the situation with Henri's parents (his father has been killed and his mother is living in Marseille; although she writes to him – expressing hopefulness that this time, he will finally be successful in obtaining his *bac* – he does not respond). François's father and Serge's parents appear only very fleetingly; narratively, they are insignificant, and seem unaware of the turmoil each of their sons is going through. Maïté's mother is the parent – and indeed the adult – who is most visible in the film. However, although she is a teacher, she is not a supportive presence, confronting Henri in class over his politics on the question of the Algerian War, and tending to evaluate even the schoolwork of François, who is enthusiastic, gifted and committed to his studies, in scornful tones. Once she succumbs to a devastating psychological breakdown, she is no longer able to fulfil her role as mother to Maïté either. It is notable that the film attributes this crisis very precisely to Mme Alvarez's guilt over her refusal to assist her ex-pupil Pierre (Serge's brother) to desert from the French army. In a later scene showing Mme Alvarez in hospital, we see an image correlating with her subjective vision that shows Pierre in his military uniform, looming over his former teacher with a reproachful stare in an iconography that anticipates that of *Caché*, Michael Haneke's acclaimed filmic treatment of the return of the Algerian repressed to the French bourgeois consciousness. Pierre's head is bound with a white bandage that is marked with a large spot of blood, which is all the more striking due to the palette of neutral grey-brown tones that otherwise fill the frame at this point. If this image symbolises Mme Alvarez's belated recognition of her role in Pierre's death, then – like the similar bloodied body in Haneke's *Caché* – it also stands for something larger: the responsibility of the French nation for the bloodshed of the Algerian War, and particularly the responsibility of its leaders, who sent so many young, non-professional soldiers on compulsory military service into this traumatic colonial war. If the imaging of Pierre in a supernatural state echoes Christian iconography of martyrdom in this sequence, then he is a martyr to the political priorities and ideologies of an older generation that pays the debt of its colonial war in the lives of Algerians, and those of young French soldiers too.

Manu in *Les Témoins* is another of Téchiné's martyrs.[3] As AIDS takes greater hold over Manu's body, Johan Libéreau's performance charts Manu's physical sufferings: his weakness, diarrhoea, tremors induced by the constant sensation of cold, and finally – after the virus has reached his brain – his AIDS-induced visual impairment. *Les Témoins* also attends to Manu's emotional suffering as a young man denied his future due to the irrepressible ravages of a disease which (at the time when the film is set) is little understood by the medical profession, and of which Manu himself knew nothing prior to his diagnosis ('je ne savais même pas que ça existait', he tells Mehdi). The emotional torment is more subtly conveyed than the physical, drawing on a logic of indirectness in its representation that includes the use of what we might, after Karl Schoonover and Rosalind Galt, call 'queer register' (Schoonover and Galt 2016: 215). The cruelty with which AIDS thwarts Manu's ambitions for the life to come are brought out through the brutal contrast between the sense of possibility underlying his sister Julie's determined and tireless pursuit of her dream for the future – to become an opera singer – and his own situation. Like Julie, Manu (as previously mentioned) has clear professional ambitions: specifically, to become a restaurateur. Julie single-mindedly pours all her talent and energy into advancing her prospects of succeeding in her career goal – working long hours; accepting a life of living on meagre means (to keep her living costs down, she moves into the same *hôtel de passe* inhabited by Manu's friend, the prostitute Sandra); taking a day-job that pays the bills, but offers her little reward (she teaches singing but finds her pupils lack her commitment). Manu emulates her approach, taking on a job at a holiday camp that provides a good opening for him, but involves long hours and low pay. However, whereas Julie's future-oriented approach is rewarded with an opportunity to perform professionally and take the first steps in launching her singing career, AIDS means that Manu's efforts to realise his dreams of becoming a chef and restaurateur are doomed to fail. His rage at losing the possibility of envisaging any future, and capitalising on his potential, is conveyed through a moment of scorn and (insofar as he is still capable of it) aggression in the last part of *Les Témoins*, when he is at the end stage of his illness. The film depicts Adrien returning from work with a prepared meal to be reheated in the microwave oven. Would-be chef Manu asks what it is. On hearing that it is 'daube provençale', he angrily takes the brown unguent on the plate into his hand and crushes it there, reminding us of his own culinary expertise by detailing to Adrien at length the *correct* way of preparing this dish, before announcing that he will not be eating the food Adrien has brought home.

As with the ghost of Pierre in *Les Roseaux sauvages*, the iconography of *Les Témoins* departs from a broadly realist (even naturalistic) aesthetic in order to underline the tragedy of an energetic young man extinguished, a life brimming with promise and potentiality wasted.[4] In the scene late in the film that takes place at Christmas time, when Adrien invites Julie and Sarah to dinner with himself and the dying Manu (who is now being cared for by Adrien at home), Manu and Sarah find themselves together alone after Adrien takes Julie to Créteil, where she is performing. A lingering medium shot shows the two of them in profile in the dining room, sitting in silence opposite one another, the dining table separating them. Manu asks Sarah if 'je vous fais peur?' When she answers no, he asks her to accompany him into the sitting room, where a roaring open fire awaits. In the next sequence, they are stood facing each other, either side of the hearth. At this point, as the framing tightens to allow the view of his face to dominate the screen, Manu is photographed in a way that departs from contemporary idiom, using chiaroscuro techniques that (not for the first time in this film) recall a much older artistic tradition.[5] Dimly lit in warm colours by the fire in the grate, Manu's face is shown in close-up using a shallow focus, ensuring that the back of Sarah's head and jaw, on the darkened left of the frame, now become blurry and indistinct to the viewer; the right of the frame too is lost to darkness, save one or two coloured points of light emanating from the Christmas tree in the background. Light from the fire beneath illuminates the lower part of Manu's face, with a play of light and shadow traversing his nose, mouth and chin. With the optical priority settling on Manu's face, the multiple lesions spread across his cheeks (a characteristic symptom of AIDS) are now highly visible, as reflected firelight from the right-hand side shows them in relief. Without the clear AIDS context, this could equally be a depiction of the leprosy to which Manu had likened AIDS earlier in the film.

If this depiction of Manu, like 1980s Western discourses of AIDS in Simon Watney's contemporaneous analysis, 'returns us to a premodern vision of the body, according to which heresy and sin are held to be scored in the features of their voluntary subjects by punitive and admonitory manifestations of disease' (Watney 1993: 204), then it does so in order to challenge that discourse which it evokes.[6] Manu asks Sarah to kiss him, which she chastely and very gently does, on his lips, in a visible and tangible sign of her recognition of him as a human being, and as a man who already has a special shared intimacy with her, since Mehdi has been a lover to them both. As Éric Costeix notes (2008: 71–2), it is during this sequence that Manu hands on to Sarah the task of telling his story – thus securing the onward transmission of his testimony, as well as providing her with a newfound sense of purpose (up until this point, there have been repeated references in the film to her writer's block). Her kiss takes on a special significance against the backdrop of a historical moment which (as *Les Témoins* reminds us) sees people with AIDS denied the sensation of ordinary everyday physical contact. Connoting respect, compassion, reconciliation and the possibility of a partial transcendence, this kiss is replete with rich significance on an affective level. This is emphasised by the moment of tension introduced immediately before it comes, as the non-diegetic refrain being unobtrusively played on stringed instruments during this sequence halts immediately after Manu's request to be kissed by Sarah, as if doubtfully awaiting her response. With its emotional intensity, and timeless iconography, this sequence offers a counterpoint to the sight of a haunted Mme Alvarez in the hospital, destroyed by guilt following Pierre's assassination. It is through this portrayal of Sarah that Téchiné perhaps most clearly exposes to us his vision of harmonious and empathetic dealings between the young and their elders, based on solidarity and mutual respect. It is not, however, a vision always realised in Téchiné's cinema, which often casts a critical eye on intergenerational relations instead.

The example of Mme Alvarez is not an isolated one in Téchiné's films. As a cinema often dedicated to the exploration of adolescence, Téchiné's work regularly indicts adults, and more particularly the institutions they set up and serve, for their failure to safeguard and support children and young people. Dependent on adults throughout the initial stages of their life, the young, as Owen's poem implies, lack the power to be in control of their destinies, being subordinate to the regulation and command of adults, and required to comply with the regimes for organising everyday life – be it in school, at the workplace, in battle – that adults conceive and sustain, and which have adults at the helm. Unlike children and adolescents, who are not yet old enough to have attained the capability for self-sufficiency, adults who have established themselves in life have the capacity (even if only to a quite limited extent) to make at least minor material changes to the well-being of young people who fall either directly or indirectly under their care. Mme Alvarez and Sarah, who struggles to reconcile herself to motherhood, represent obvious studies of women who wrestle with this duty of care. M. Cassagne in *Les Roseaux sauvages*, the gay man who can offer no solace or advice to François as he struggles to come to terms with his homosexuality, is a similar character. Yet Téchiné's harshest treatment is not directed at individual adult protagonists in their very human struggles, which are often depicted sympathetically.

Téchiné's cinema of adolescence instead, in a Truffaldian echo, reserves its most vehement denunciations for those institutions (and those adults who blindly serve them) which operate to the severe detriment of young people, heedless of the damage their consolidated power wreaks on young lives.[7] It is these institutions which make martyrs of Manu in *Les Témoins* and Pierre in *Les Roseaux sauvages*. In *Les Roseaux sauvages*, the condemnations are channelled through the bitter voice of Henri, who rails against the then President de Gaulle (as we have seen), and also against the indifference to *pieds-noirs* that he perceives in Mme Alvarez, the French Communist Party and the metropolitan French generally. Unlike the martyred Pierre, Henri will ultimately find solace, but it comes from his young peers (particularly Maïté), not the older generation.

It is in *Les Témoins*, however, that Téchiné's attack against malign institutions is most strenuously developed. It is levelled chiefly against the forces of law and order, and at Medhi, who embodies them. The context of the AIDS epidemic is crucial here. As Mehdi's harassment of sex-worker

Sandra indicates (and his warnings to Manu and Julie, once he discovers their association with her), the police response to the AIDS outbreak is to clamp down and criminalise those that have already been driven underground for engaging in marginalised sexual behaviours – chiefly, homosexuality and prostitution. Mehdi's direct implication in these activities, as a police officer who is bisexual, is the cause of repeated heated arguments with Adrien. As a doctor, Adrien realises the urgent need to undertake preventative awareness-raising campaigns about AIDS amongst exactly those marginalised groups whom the police are driving away from beneficial contacts with the medical institution that Adrien represents in the film. Mehdi, who is unable to comprehend the testimonial urge motivating Sarah to complete and publish his ex-lover Manu's memoirs after his death, also apparently cannot understand the destructive impact that his police work has on efforts to prevent the further spread of AIDS: an impact that risks being counted in lost young lives. Adrien's revenge, in Téchiné's fictional story, is to obstruct Mehdi in his desperate efforts to be allowed to see Manu one last time before he dies. Fictional elements notwithstanding, it is the autobiographical quality of *Les Témoins*'s narrative, and the authenticity of its representations of these conflicts between medical and juridical institutions, that adds particular resonance in this case to Téchiné's exposure of the cavalier disregard of the institutions of civil society for the interests of the young people whom they are supposed to protect.[8]

In this essay, I have suggested that Téchiné's cinema of adolescence has a distinctive quality deriving from the filmmaker's commitment to exploring the condition of youth whilst locating these youthful experiences in precise historical contexts. The fact that Téchiné, inspired by his own personal history, returns to moments of great collective trauma in these films is another notable feature of his filmmaking. The choice to evoke traumatic episodes of the French national past in his cinematic treatments of young people on the threshold of adulthood and independence generates a particular kind of meditation on the future possibilities that the young can look forward to in their lives. It begs the question of what kind of world the young will inherit from their elders who are the custodians of that world, for the possibilities that are (or are not) available to youth depend on what material conditions hold sway in their environment as they come of age. Téchiné's films celebrate the potential and the energy that the young bring into the world, but they also demonstrate acute awareness of the eventuality that this potential never has a chance to blossom, and young lives will end up needlessly and avoidably wasted. The threats that Téchiné's cinema of adolescence identifies to the youthful birthright that is the process of becoming are the man-made peril of war, and also the disease of AIDS, which *Les Témoins* reveals also to be a man-made disaster, not purely an epidemiological one. Both *Les Roseaux sauvages* and *Les Témoins* testify to the way that young lives have, as a matter of record, ended up prematurely snuffed out for preventable reasons, rooted in decisions taken collectively by their elders, who are the gatekeepers to the political establishment and the institutions of civil society. Exceptional individuals – like Sarah and Adrien in *Les Témoins*, or M. Morelli, the supply teacher in *Les Roseaux sauvages* – may well prove sympathetic and supportive to the priorities of the needs of the young. However, drawing on his own experience, Téchiné seems overall to find a world in which, too often, the interests and well-being of the younger generation have been neglected or even consciously sacrificed by the older generations that wield power over the young, including the power of life and death, and consider their lives expendable. It is for that reason that I have suggested that to refer to Téchiné's 'cinema of adolescence' might be a misnomer, because his depictions of the young reveal how intertwined their fates are with the decisions and conduct of their elders. In consequence, intergenerational relations are characteristically an important component in Téchiné's films about youth.

Thus Téchiné, now well on the way to becoming a veteran director, sides with the young; and on behalf of the young, his cinema betrays a suspicion of institutions. One of these institutions is the discourse of testimony itself. This discourse becomes especially suspect if used hypocritically (as in the case of Pierre Bartolo, Serge's brother in *Les Roseaux sauvages*) to mythologise at a funeral, manufacturing a military hero out of a deserter who did not support the military institution which he had only unwillingly entered. Testimonial discourse, however, becomes especially harmful when it recognises grievable deaths, but ignores those who are killed by an unprecedented viral epidemic, who find themselves instead marginalised and stigmatised by the dehumanising discourses on AIDS that spread like a second wave of contagion. If in *Les Témoins* the exploration of the discoveries and desires of a young gay man feel more urgent, driven and affectively charged than the equivalent exploration in *Les Roseaux sauvages*, it is because the exploration of the subjectivity of a gay youth is never so important as it is against the backdrop of a discursive climate that would deny his very humanity.

Notes

1. This approach to AIDS testimony echoes a tendency identified in American cultural production (Hallas 2009: 9–11), but has also drawn criticism (Pratt 2008: 250–63).

2. Alain Ménil recalls how AIDS, before it was officially named, was known as the 'cancer gay' or the stigmatising 'maladie des 4H' – referring to homosexual men as one of the four categories of people (alongside 'les Haïtiens, les héroïnomanes et les hémophiles') predominantly found amongst those having contracted the disease (Ménil 1997: 36, n. 17).
3. Nick Rees-Roberts (2008: 105) remarks on the trope of martyrdom in French visual culture of AIDS.
4. See Costeix (2008: 18–20 and *passim*), for a reading of Téchiné in relation to naturalism and realism. I qualify Téchiné's aesthetic as 'broadly realist' for, as Costeix shows, his *mise en scène* is carefully constructed to draw on complementary and opposing elements in nature in order to create a logic at the aesthetic level expressive of the substantial concerns of his films. In *Les Témoins*, perhaps this is most apparent through Téchiné's symbolic use of colour, which clearly deviates from a classical realist mode of filmmaking.
5. Such an allusion is present in the shot previously mentioned of Manu and Sarah photographed in profile in Adrien's dining room: as they sit facing each other, we see on the wall behind them, just above and in-between their heads, a still-life painting depicting fruit against a dark background, executed in a style commonly found in seventeenth-century art.
6. Watney does not give details of the premodern disease(s) he has in mind, but leprosy (the disease with which Manu compares AIDS in *Les Témoins*) is one possibility – the symptoms of leprosy are also visible on the skin. Medieval French literature attests that lepers were outcasts from society, forced to live away from the community. Leprosy was considered in those times to be a sexually transmitted disease and thus was associated with the sin of lust. (See, for example, the depiction of lepers in Béroul's (1989) *Roman de Tristan*.) I am grateful to Fionnùala Sinclair for discussing medieval understandings of leprosy with me.
7. I have in mind especially Truffaut's *Les 400 coups* (1959), a landmark representation of adolescence in French cinema.
8. See Martel (2000: 351) for an account of police action in 1984–5 to close down Parisian nightclubs reputed as sites for sexual encounters between men.

Works Cited

Béroul [12th century] (1989), *Le Roman de Tristan*, in Daniel Lacroix and Philippe Walter (eds), *Tristan et Iseut: Les poèmes français; la saga norroise*, Paris: Livre de poche, pp. 21–231.

Butler, Judith (2009), *Frames of War: When is Life Grievable?*, London: Verso.

Costeix, Éric (2008), *André Téchiné: Le paysage transfiguré*, Paris: L'Harmattan.

Everett, Wendy (1999), 'Film at the Crossroads: *Les Roseaux sauvages* (Téchiné, 1994)', in Phil Powrie (ed.), *French Cinema in the 1990s: Continuity and Difference*, Oxford: Oxford University Press, pp. 47–57.

Hallas, Roger (2009), *Reframing Bodies: AIDS, Bearing Witness and the Queer Moving Image*, Durham, NC: Duke University Press.
Marshall, Bill (2007), *André Téchiné*, Manchester: Manchester University Press.
Martel, Frédéric (2000), *Le Rose et le noir: les homosexuels en France depuis 1968*, 2nd edn, Paris: Éditions du Seuil.
Ménil, Alain (1997), *Sain(t)s et saufs: sida: une épidémie de l'interprétation*, Paris: Belles lettres.
Owen, Wilfred (2013), 'Anthem for Doomed Youth', in Wilfred Owen, *The Complete Poems and Fragments*, ed. Jon Stallworthy, revised edn, London: Chatto & Windus, vol. 1, p. 96.
Pratt, Murray (2008), 'Forgetting to Remember Now and Then: AIDS, Memory and Homosexuality in André Téchiné's *Les Témoins* (2007)', *Australian Journal of French Studies*, 45:3, pp. 250–63.
Rees-Roberts, Nick (2008), *French Queer Cinema*, Edinburgh: Edinburgh University Press.
Schoonover, Karl and Rosalind Galt (2016), *Queer Cinema in the World*, Durham, NC: Duke University Press.
Téchiné, André (2004), 'Entretien avec André Téchiné', in *Les Roseaux sauvages*, dir. André Téchiné, Studio Canal (DVD).
Téchiné, André (2007), 'André Téchiné à propos du film *Les Témoins*', in *Les Témoins*, dir. André Téchiné, UGC (DVD).
Téchiné, André (2016), '"Quand on a 17 ans": André Téchiné porté par l'élan de la jeunesse', *Télérama*, 29 March, <https://www.telerama.fr/cinema/quand-on-a-17-ans-andre-techine-porte-par-l-elan-de-la-jeunesse,139926.php> (last accessed 23 August 2018).
Watney, Simon [1987] (1993), 'The Spectacle of AIDS', in Henry Abelove, Michèle Aina Barale and David Halperin (eds), *The Lesbian and Gay Studies Reader*, New York: Routledge, pp. 202–11.

Films

Caché, film, directed by Michael Haneke. France, Austria, Germany, Italy: Les Films du Losange, 2005
J'embrasse pas, film, directed by André Téchiné. France: Bac Films, 1991.
Les Égarés, film, directed by André Téchiné. France: Mars Distribution, 2004.
Les Roseaux sauvages, film, directed by André Téchiné. France: Studio Canal (DVD), 2004.
Les Témoins, film, directed by André Téchiné. France: UGC (DVD), 2007.

CHAPTER 13

'Je veux promouvoir le vivre-ensemble': Youth and Friendship in *L'Auberge espagnole*, *Les Poupées russes* and *Casse-tête chinois*

Ben McCann

> When you're 25, you're finishing your studies, you have that kind of free spirit about trying things. When you're 30, you're trying to start to be serious. Then when you're 40, you ask: Where am I now? I'm not young anymore, but I'm not old. (Cédric Klapisch, in Hynes 2014).

> Friendship . . . is a kind of virtue, or implies virtue, and it is also most necessary for living. (Book VIII, Aristotle 1934)

Cédric Klapisch, Friendship and Coming of Age in French Cinema

It is generally acknowledged that the release of Eric Rochant's *Un monde sans pitié* in 1989 and Christian Vincent's *La Discrète* a year later heralded the arrival of 'le jeune cinéma français', and with it an increasing emphasis in French cinema on the figure of the adolescent. David Vasse describes the on-screen adolescent in this post-1990s period as 'ce personnage brut, objet parfait d'inadaptation volontaire ou résignée à un monde qu'il ne reconnaît pas conforme à ses désirs' (2008: 99). Several French directors fixed their gaze on youth culture and intimate coming-of-age stories as a means of examining the hardships and uncertainties of adolescence in a fast-changing Hexagon.[1] Those diverse films included Mathieu Kassovitz's *La Haine* (1995), Bruno Dumont's *La Vie de Jésus* (1997), Erick Zonca's *La Vie rêvée des anges* (1998) and Noémie Lvovsky's *La Vie ne me fait pas peur* (1999). Other similar stories have since grappled for our attention: Ismaël Ferroukhi's *Le Grand Voyage* (2004) via Catherine Breillat's harrowing *36 Fillette* (1988) and *À ma sœur!* (2001), Sébastien Lifshitz's *Presque rien* (2000) and *Plein sud* (2007) and Thomas Cailley's *Les Combattants* (2014). Céline Sciamma's *Bande de filles* (2014) recounts how sixteen-year-old Marieme (Karidja Touré) must navigate her unsettling transition into adulthood while at the same time struggle against the institutional inequities and disadvantages of being black and living in the underprivileged *banlieues* of outer Paris. These films and many others never idealise the transition between youth and adulthood; instead, they focus on the hazards of youth and pose universal questions of identity, self-actualisation and subject formation.[2]

These coming-of-age films often deal with the struggle of daily existence against the wider economic and social changes wrought by globalisation – themes of poverty, migration, unemployment and the disintegration of the family unit are often recurring background factors. The double-edged nature of globalisation often comes into play too – on the one hand, France's new generation of young people are more mobile, more economically independent and less in thrall to institutional impediments than ever before, but on the other, they constitute a new body of European citizens unsure about job opportunities, financial comfort and domestic stability. As they contend with the unpredictabilities of neo-liberal economic imperatives and ever-fluid concepts of nationhood, identity and multiculturalism, the adolescent is often cast as France's 'hope for the future'; an optimistic, utopian safety valve that releases the pressure of previous generations and their current social struggles.

Cédric Klapisch has, for nearly three decades, inhabited this thriving, youth-centred ecosystem. Back in 1997, Claude-Marie Trémois tagged Klapisch as 'le plus humaniste [et] le plus libre' (p. 151) of a new breed of French filmmakers. Trémois noted how Klapisch's early films consistently mined the same thematic seam: 'les rapports entre les gens . . . [c]omment ils se perçoivent, comment ils se supportent – ou ne se supportent pas –, comment ils communiquent' (p. 151). Similarly, in 2018, *Variety* noted how Klapisch 'crafts vibrant, lived-in movies brimming with characters who feel well-rounded enough (flaws and all) to exist in the real world' (Debruge 2018). From the start of his career, Klapisch's films have frequently explored these group dynamics, whether in the context of a department store (*Riens du tout* (1992)), a high school (*Le Péril jeune* (1994)), a Parisian neighbourhood (*Chacun cherche son chat* (1996)) or six characters in a restaurant (*Un Air de famille* (1996)). *Ce qui nous lie* (2017), his most recent work, portrays three siblings struggling to hold onto the family vineyard amid mounting financial pressures. Klapisch is preoccupied by familial affinities and group dynamics, and details in often poignant ways how these 'families', whether at home, at work or through friendship networks, overcome emotional and economic turmoil. On some occasions, these families splinter and separate; on others, they unite in spite of their differences. Moreover, each film depicts a 'family' under pressure, and features at their centre either young, coming-of-age protagonists, or, in the case of *Paris* (2008) and *Ma part du gâteau* (2011), more mature characters who exhibit a childlike naivety as they recall life's disappointments or roads not taken. In *Ce qui nous lie*, Klapisch uses the rhythms and rituals of the Beaune *vendange* to make broader comments on the importance of friendships: 'Avec mon cinéma, je veux promouvoir le vivre-ensemble. C'est important à une époque où chacun se replie sur soi et valorise la fausse amitié sur les réseaux sociaux' (Klapisch 2017). Friendship and a mutual common purpose become the adhesive that bonds together disparate social and cultural groups. His films feature scenes of eating, drinking, chatting in bars and in streets, visiting famous monuments, listening to music and making wine. These are not solitary activities, but become shared, reciprocal experiences that deepen and evolve over time.

Youthfulness courses through Klapisch's films and makes its way into his lively visual style. His touch is 'modern' in structure and form; the films incorporate pop-art colour schemes, voice-overs, digital effects, split screen imagery, sped-up footage, overlaid graphics and collage sequences. Cynthia Lucia has described this style as a 'vibrancy of pacing, production design, dialogue, and composition that fuses an overarching realist aesthetic with elements of high stylisation' (2009). Form and content tend to intersect, via the overlapping, multi-character narratives, 'world music' soundtrack, transnational casting and the restless flitting between story strands. These choices reflect Klapisch's ongoing engagement with the hyper-connected ramifications of contemporary society and the youthfulness of his central characters. While Klapisch's youthful protagonists are not subjected to the same traumatic life experiences that befall characters in, say, *La Haine* or *La Vie rêvée des anges*, the changes that do take place to them and around them are no less momentous.

In terms of showing how French/European youth lives today, Klapisch's most relevant work remains *L'Auberge espagnole* (2002) and its two sequels, *Les Poupées russes* (2005) and *Casse-tête chinois* (2013).[3] Mingling elements of romantic comedy, sitcom and social drama, the trilogy narrates a familiar set of 'youth' rituals – the move from university to 'the real world', the often convoluted personal, romantic and cultural encounters that ensue, and the moral, ethical and emotional troubles that typify that key biological and physiological developmental stage between adolescence and adulthood. The trilogy follows four friends – Xavier (Romain Duris), Wendy (Kelly Reilly), Isabelle (Cécile de France) and Martine (Audrey Tautou) – and traces their individual journeys over a period of fifteen years, taking in along the way the Erasmus student mobility programme and Europe's growing multicultural and polyglot citizens. Klapisch cleverly develops several core themes throughout the trilogy – alienation, the bitter-sweetness of love, the melancholy of youth, the putting away of childish things – and underpins his career-long preoccupation with the fraught relationship between individual and community and the importance of acceptance and tolerance.

The plot of the trilogy corresponds to the familiar rhythms of the coming-of-age genre (Klapisch has described *Auberge* as 'l'histoire d'un Français qui devient un étranger' (2002) and the trilogy more broadly as 'about someone who is writing his own life, and it is both his life and the way he writes about his life' (2014)). Put this way, *Auberge*, *Poupées* and *Casse-tête* are *Bildungsfilms*. The expression is of course borrowed from the German literary term *Bildungsroman*, meaning 'novel of formation'. In such novels, made popular during the Victorian era, the subject is 'the development of the protagonist's mind and character, as he passes from childhood through varied experiences – and usually through a spiritual crisis – into maturity and the recognition of his [*sic*] identity and role in the world' (Abrams 1981: 121). The protagonist's passage from childhood to adulthood is often arduous (physically, emotionally, spiritually) and they must often overcome some type of obstacle or traverse some form of moral or ethical crisis in order to develop into adulthood and gain wisdom. The *Bildungsroman/film* narrates the struggle between the rebellious inclinations of the individual and the conformist demands of society.

Xavier, Wendy, Isabelle and Martine each undergo a 'sentimental education'. The quartet grows and develops emotionally, learns lessons along the way, leaves adolescence behind, and enters a new, adult phase of their lives. During promotional interviews for *Auberge*, Klapisch often repeated his views on contemporary French youth:

> I think it [*Auberge*] speaks to the nature of things today. These students are searching for cohesion amid confusion, both the confusion of the world and the confusion of being in your 20s and still trying to figure out what you want, what you need, what you care about, and the difference between what you thought the world was like and what it's really like. (Klapisch, quoted in Anon. 2003)

At their heart, *Auberge*, *Poupées* and *Casse-tête* are subtle and complex 'youth films' that depict a new generation of upwardly mobile European citizens navigating a rapidly changing 'new Europe'. In *Auberge*, *Poupées* and *Casse-tête*, the formative experiences of young contemporary French citizens are brought to light in foreign spaces. According to Duris, the central theme of *Auberge* is '[f]ais ce dont tu as envie [et] ne laisse surtout pas les autres te dicter ta vie' (Mereu-Boulch 2002). The film thus follows a classic teen-movie philosophy: self-determination, stubbornness and anti-establishment posturing. Take Xavier. Though twenty-five in

Auberge, he seems to us still very immature, caught between biological drives and social pressures, and, as David Considine (1981) has observed when discussing the central figures in youth films, forever grappling 'with the world of his [*sic*] present and past in order to formulate the self that will emerge in the future' (p. 136). His process of formation, his transition from adolescence to adulthood and his 'becoming European'/'becoming global' takes place against the backdrop of some of Europe's most cosmopolitan cities before terminating in New York, the ultimate global melting pot. Throughout the trilogy, Xavier takes part in a range of rites of passage: studying, making new friends, learning to understand his parents, juggling lovers, learning to talk '*puta madre*' Spanish from locals in a bar, and appreciating that love and friendship can be found where and when it is least expected. Xavier is implicated in a double narrative of selfhood: one written *for* him by Klapisch, and one written *by* him about his times in Barcelona, London, Paris and New York. What happens to him in these different cities is decisive in carrying him towards a new stage of maturation.

Emerging Adults, Emerging Friendships

In her introduction to *Emerging Adulthood in a European Context*, Rita Žukauskien notes that the transition to adulthood nowadays may include 'finishing formal education, acquiring professional qualifications, getting a permanent job, establishing one's own household, and starting a family' (2016: 4). Such markers, to a greater or lesser extent, apply to Xavier's own development over the course of Klapisch's trilogy, but they are a long time coming. A year in Barcelona in *Auberge* is not nearly long enough. It takes much longer for Xavier to 'become adult'. Though no longer an adolescent at the start of *Auberge* (Xavier is not the same as Tomasi, the hedonistic teenager Duris played in Klapisch's earlier *Le Péril jeune*), he seems to deliberately choose to be jammed between youth and adulthood, immaturity and maturity. This makes his transition from adolescence to adulthood across the trilogy appear stubbornly stretched out. At one point in *Poupées*, Xavier admits, via voice-over: 'J'y connais rien à l'amour moi, je suis un égoïste, je ne pense qu'à ma gueule.' He recognises his clumsy, often demeaning treatment of women close to him, and so even though he defers traditional steps towards adulthood, he tries to make sense of his daily experiences within that wider move towards maturity.[4] The transition is a complex process, often involving multiple steps. In fact, Xavier's prolonged pathway from one status to another is typical of many young people at the start of the twenty-first century.

Žukauskien's term 'emerging adults' is borrowed from American psychologist Jeffrey Arnett. For Arnett, it is no longer useful to classify people in the eighteen to twenty-nine age bracket as adults because they have often not accepted traditional adult roles (work, marriage, children) by this point. Because young people are deferring such traditional adult markers, they in turn reflect much more on their own lives and achievements up to that point, experiment intensely with their 'in-between' status, and change their life choices (career, relationships, friendships) rapidly and regularly. This preference for a kind of liminal existence both distinct and separate from adolescence and adulthood means that young people are no longer compelled to follow the standardised paths of their parents, in part because those traditional life choices no longer guarantee economic stability or success. Arnett instead proposes the term 'emerging adult'; or a 'period of development bridging adolescence and young adulthood, during which young people are no longer adolescents but have not yet attained full adult status' (2004: 312).[5]

This 'emerging adult' model seems particularly apt for the characters in *Auberge*, *Poupées* and *Casse-tête*. The dynamics between Xavier, Wendy, Isabelle and Martine change and mutate as each character ages and moves through their individual coming-of-age rituals. Each are prone to reminisce about what happened to them in previous cities, and use this introspection as a catalyst towards a greater acceptance of their own conflicting identities and beliefs. Part of the pleasure of the trilogy is to see the long-haul individual trajectories made by familiar characters across an eleven-year period, and to see the physical changes in the actors who play them. It is the changing faces and bodies of the actors that lend an emotional and intimate heft to their changing, developing relationships and emotional attachments. Klapisch charts the physical transformations of the actors as well as their on-screen move from adolescent, to young adult, from 'thirty-something' to 'forty-something' and shows how the collectivist faithfulness of friends is a key factor in the construction of the masculine and feminine self, the navigating of the transition from youth to adult, and the establishment of bonds of self-esteem, trust and intimacy. *Poupées* and *Casse-tête* return a second and third time to these four 'emerging adults' to see whether their initial aspirations – both romantic and professional – have been fulfilled. It was no surprise to discover that the quartet of *Casse-tête*, pushing forty, was no less befuddled and baffled as their younger twenty-something selves a decade and a half earlier in *Auberge*.

The trilogy thus stands as an urgent plea for the cultivation of honest, open and transparent friendships that move beyond the transactional or pragmatic towards something virtuous, mutual and communal. Klapisch may well have Cicero's (1923) views of friendship in *Laelius de Amicitia* in mind as he plotted the trilogy's romantic and youthful imbroglios:

> Since happiness is our best and highest aim, we must . . . give our attention to virtue, without which we can obtain neither friendship nor any other desirable thing; . . . those who slight virtue and yet think that they have friends, perceive their mistake at last when some grievous misfortune forces them to put their friends to the test.[6]

Friendship in the Trilogy

There is a short scene in *Auberge* that in fact reveals much about friendship and youth culture. On his return to the Barcelona apartment after splitting up with Martine in Paris, Xavier is slumped on the sofa, watching a television programme about human towers. The tower, or *castell*, is an important part of Catalan culture, often performed in public spaces in front of thousands of spectators. *Castellers* arrange themselves into multiple levels, starting at the base with a mass of people, gradually rising up to ten levels, and topping out the tower with a small child. In 2010, such *castells* were recognised by the United Nations Educational, Scientific and Cultural Organization (UNESCO) as an integral part of Catalan cultural identity, 'transmitted from generation to generation and providing community members a sense of continuity, social cohesion and solidarity' (Massallé 2014). Watching on the sofa with Xavier are three other flatmates – Lars, Alessandro and Isabelle – each lost in their thoughts.

The focus on the *castell* here does not seem coincidental. Xavier, Lars and Isabelle have each just ended a relationship – Xavier with Martine, Lars with his partner, who has unexpectedly turned up in Barcelona with his baby, and Isabelle with her Belgian lover. The *castell* here serves as a useful metaphor for the developing friendships and shared emotional experiences of this moment between these friends on the sofa. The *castellers*' motto is *força, equilibri, valor i seny* (strength, balance, courage and common sense): the *castell* will rise or fall depending on robust foundations, good internal balance, the structural support of others, and the trust required to safely build the castell higher and higher. Likewise, for the 'Spanish apartment' to flourish requires mutual understanding and empathy. If the flatmates do not always display common sense, then that is perhaps the ultimate point that Klapisch is making here in his coming-of-age tale – the *castell*, with its solid internal structure, shared planning and support, and focus on trust, balance and harmony, resembles the familial dynamics of many of Klapisch's films. Sometimes they totter, or fall; other times, they build from the ground upwards, involving multiple members of a community.

This brings us to a significant treatise on friendship, Aristotle's *Nicomachean Ethics*. While he recognised the significance of 'accidental' friendships based principally on pleasure and convenience, the impermanence of these networks of friendships reduced their sustainability. Lacking depth and a solid foundation, such friendships lose their potential to thrive. Like the *castell*, friendships need a firm footing. Even if they do not know it at the time, the friends on the sofa are cultivating a far more long-lasting friendship.

According to DeVito (2007: 282), friendship is the expression of 'an interpersonal relationship between two persons that is mutually productive and is characterised by mutual positive regard'. DeVito outlines several aspects of friendship that date back to Aristotle, whose own definition of friendship remains the key starting point for philosophical and ethical reflections on the nature of friendships. In Books VIII and IX of *Nicomachean Ethics*, Aristotle (1934) anticipates many of the qualities and characteristics of friendship:

> And in poverty or any other misfortune men think friends are their only resource. Friends are an aid to the young, to guard them from error; to the elderly, to tend them, and to supplement their failing powers of action; to those in the prime of life, to assist them in noble deeds . . . for two are better able both to plan and to execute.

For Aristotle, the supreme good is happiness, and an affective and virtuous companionship is essential for a well-lived life. Subsequent studies of friendship (Hartup 1993; Bukowski et al. 1996; Rawlins 2009; Hojjat and Moyer 2016) all focus on these bonds of reciprocity as outlined by Aristotle, alongside varying degrees of tenderness, honesty, affection and resilience over time. Mendelson and Aboud (1999) listed the six purposes of friendship: stimulating companionship, help, intimacy, reliable alliance, self-validation and emotional security. All of these qualities course through Klapisch's trilogy, in particular the importance of reliable alliances and self-validation.[7]

Aristotle conceived of three types of friendship in *Nicomachean Ethics*: friendship based on utility, friendship based on pleasure and friendship based on goodness. Friends of utility 'do not love each other in themselves, but in so far as some benefit accrues to them from each other'; thus, a mutual benefit is gained from this relationship. Consequently, in a friendship of utility, 'men love their friend for their own good . . . and not as being the person loved, but as useful or agreeable'. This friendship changes according to circumstances – once the reasons for the original friendship disappears the friendship breaks down. Such friendships are common in young people and emerging adults who pursue the friendship to gain some form of advantage (acceptance, financial or emotional gain). The pleasure that people take from this form of friendship is mutually advantageous only as long as both parties achieve something in return. Friendships of pleasure are also appealing for young people, because, according to Aristotle,

> the young guide their lives by emotion, and for the most part pursue what is pleasant to themselves, and the object of the moment . . . hence they both form friendships and drop them quickly, since their affections alter with what gives them pleasure, and the tastes of youth change quickly.

As with the friendship of utility, friendships of pleasure are based not necessarily on the friend, but on the pleasure received from the friend. The final form of friendship outlined by Aristotle is the most desirable of the three. Aristotle's perfect friendship is based on goodness: 'it is those who desire the good of their friends for the friends' sake that are most truly friends, because each loves the other for what he is, and not for any incidental quality'. This friendship, unlike the other two, is intentional rather than accidental. It is a friendship that endures. Instead of temporary, transient relationships based on utility or pleasure, the friendship of the good is formed out of a long-standing appreciation of the virtues that the other party holds dear. It is the individual and the qualities that they bring to the friendship – however flawed – that provides the incentive for the friendship to last.

What becomes clear from Aristotle's classification is that the emerging adults in *Auberge*, *Poupées* and *Casse-tête* intersect with each type of friendship. Aristotle writes that '[f]riendships with foreigners are generally included in this class', which certainly applies to the trilogy. His friendship of utility resembles the dynamics of the Barcelona flat, with its Erasmus connections as the glue holding together the friendships, and its temporary bonds and forced intimacy in the shared flat as two of its principal characteristics. Aristotle continues by noting that friends of this kind 'do not indeed frequent each other's company much, for in some cases they are not even pleasing to each other, and therefore have no use for friendly intercourse unless they are mutually profitable'. Apart from Xavier, we learn very little about the other characters in *Auberge*. Instead, Klapisch gives each flatmate a series of vignettes to showcase their personality. Any differences that do exist are easily bridged and minor domestic skirmishes are quickly harmonised. Rents might be are raised, the power might be cut, relationships may break down, the bathroom plughole may be full of hair, but everything, for Klapisch, is easily reconcilable.

Aristotle notes that 'complaints and recriminations arise chiefly if not exclusively in utilitarian friendships'. Yet the apartment scenes in *Auberge* show that while differences do exist between the flatmates, they can ultimately be unified. Cohabitation serves as the catalyst for cooperation and understanding, suggests Klapisch. Europe's young, emerging adult generation may speak different languages and hold fast to different cultures, but the clashes that exist between the flatmate friends are all resolved. The flatmates, regardless of nationality, 'belong' to this friendship of utility, connected to their fellow *étrangers* through shared values and emotions. The European project through initiatives like Erasmus can accommodate, assimilate and integrate national cultures within the apartment while at the same time allowing individual tics, traits and national characteristics to come to the fore. Friendships form most easily when effort is reciprocated (Brueckner 2006). Friendships in the flat stem from these trade-offs, and are then nurtured over the course of time.

In *Auberge*, all the friends in Barcelona have learned a literal and figurative new language. They are comfortable spending time in local bars, and enter into a direct engagement with the city, its customs and above all the people who become their friends. On his final night in the city, Xavier is given a red T-shirt by the rest of the flatmates as a leaving gift, and Wendy cries. She, like the rest of the apartment, senses that something has ended. She does not know it yet, but for some, that comradeship will last longer than any of them can imagine. At the end of *Auberge*, the situation changes, the nature of the connection alters and the friends disperse. Xavier returns to Paris, breaks up with his girlfriend Martine and lights out for the territory, fulfilling a long-term desire to become a writer. The utilitarian nature of the Barcelona friendships is brought into sharp focus in the film's closing moments, as he flicks through photographs of his time in Spain. Finally, he declares now, it is all clear and simple:

> Je ne suis pas ça . . . Ni ça. Je ne suis plus ça. Ni ça. Ni ça. Ni ça. Ni ça. Mais je suis tout ça [looking down at the photos spread out on the floor]. Je suis lui, et lui, et lui aussi [image of Alessandro] et lui aussi [Tobias] et lui aussi [Lars]. Et je suis lui aussi [photograph of him as a child] . . . Je suis elle [Soledad], elle [Wendy], elle, et elle aussi [Isabelle] . . . Je suis français, espagnol, anglais, danois. Je ne suis pas un mais plusieurs. Je suis comme l'Europe, je suis tout ça. Je suis un vrai bordel.

These utilitarian friendships have allowed Xavier to mature, and reflect on the benefits of his cultural immersion experience in Barcelona. He is more conscious of his own individual identity, he has redefined his relationships with his mother and Martine, he has altered the course of his professional career and he is mindful of the deep cultural ties that exist between young friends from across Europe.

In *Poupées*, the Barcelona friends reunite at a wedding in St Petersburg. They represent a flourishing generation of pan-European citizens, and so by reuniting the four main characters plus a number of others from Barcelona in the 2005 sequel, Klapisch recaps one of his central themes – the durability of friendships. Subtly, the friendships in *Poupées* move from the utilitarian mode to the pleasurable. Such friendships are often common among young people who have not yet developed the maturity to move beyond seeking pleasure. They are often tenuous, and can quickly end. Xavier's friendships can now be characterised as pleasure without commitment, aligning to Aristotle's second model. Arnett has noted that 'emerging adults often explore a variety of possible life directions in love, work and worldviews' (2000: 469); in Xavier's case, his sexual rite of passage in Barcelona that began with the seduction of Anne-Sophie (Judith Godrèche), a married women he meets at the airport, has, by *Poupées*, become far more integral to his 'emerging adult' status. In *Auberge*, Xavier leaves Martine behind in Paris, and over the course of his year in Barcelona becomes increasingly sexually confident. It starts with the affair with Anne-Sophie, but he also struggles to conceal his romantic feelings towards Isabelle – which are only thwarted when she tells him that she is a lesbian. He ends his year in Barcelona tentatively beginning a relationship with Neus (Irene Montalà), a Spanish waitress. Earlier, Martine had told Xavier that his fantasy is 'la petite fille, bien gentille, avec la petite jupe et les joues toutes rouges'; in other words, a compliant, attractive version of a woman epitomised by Anne-Sophie. Second time around, he vacillates half-heartedly in Paris between shop assistant Kassia (Aïssa Maïga), model Celia (Lucy Gordon) and old flame Neus. As they work together in London, Xavier grows increasingly attracted to Wendy, and there are still feelings between him and Martine. These dilemmas about the unattainability of women in *Poupées*, and the need to find the 'right one', eventually lead Xavier to realise that imperfection may bring happiness, fulfilment and, crucially, friendship.[8] As per the archetypal plot points of the *Bildungsroman*, Xavier understands that the love of a decent, kind, loving woman can bring contentment. Xavier and Wendy reunite at the end of William's wedding, but not before we have seen an argument between Wendy and William's long-divorced parents after the ceremony.[9]

Xavier and Wendy's cautious union in *Poupées* suggests that while happiness and monogamy might only be transient, it is, for the moment at least, a romantic interlude based not on conflict but on reconciliation. It is a step away from the friendship of pleasure towards one based on goodness. By the time we see Xavier in *Casse-tête*, his single identity has kaleidoscoped into multiple variations: unformed in *Auberge*, emerging in *Poupées*, he is by now an author, husband, lover, father, son, French, European and American. The smile is still there: sometimes glib, sometime needy, sometimes sarcastic, as is the compelling blend of bohemian–bourgeois insouciance and live-by-the-seat-of-your-pants decision making. Towards the end of *Casse-tête*, Xavier sits in a New York subway station with Wendy, Isabelle and Martine. He listens, mutely, as they each tell him the sort of woman he needs:

> **Wendy:** Tu sais ce qu'il te faut? Une fille un peu fragile. Quelqu'un de genre timide qui t'adore et que tu puisses un peu manipuler.
> **Isabelle:** Il aime les speeds [*feisty chicks*].
> **Martine:** Enfin, il cache bien son jeu. Il lui faut un peu une costaude . . .
> **Wendy:** Oui, mais douce. Sinon, si elle est trop dure, il va flipper [*freak out*].
> **Martine:** Il lui faut surtout une fille sensible.
> **Isabelle:** Mais pas un pot de colle [*not too clingy*]. Ça va l'étouffer en deux secondes . . .
> **Wendy:** Il te faut un mix de nous trois!

Three friends reappear to assert their friendship once more, to each other, but especially to Xavier. For Aristotle, such friendship is

> naturally permanent, since it combines in itself all the attributes that friends ought to possess. All affection is based on good or on pleasure, either absolute or relative to the person who feels it, and is prompted by similarity of some sort; but this friendship possesses all these attributes in the friends themselves.

In other words, this kind of friendship combines the utilitarian and the pleasurable. Whereas those earlier, accidental friendships remained transitory, and therefore with their potential and sustainability lessened, the ideal friendship requires a solid and mutual foundation. For Klapisch's characters, who have moved from Barcelona to New York, via London, Paris and St Petersburg, the connective tissue of their friendships has been progressively strengthened along the way in the trilogy. Xavier et al. have endured mutual hardship, loss and sadness, but have always been present in each other's lives to offer the friendship of virtue, trust and non-judgementalism promoted by Aristotle. In the Aristotelian sense, true, 'good' friends must accept the other friend as they are, and no one would choose to live without friends even if they possessed all other 'good' things. This belief system has been sustained throughout the trilogy. They have taken time, but these are friendships that will last.

The Best Kind of Friendship?

Following in the tradition of many coming-of-age films, one of the most enduring aspects of *Auberge*, *Poupées* and *Casse-tête* is seeing how the Barcelona flatmates transition tentatively and messily into adulthood. For Klapisch, when it comes to friendship, idealism slowly gives way to pragmatism, utility to pleasure, and then to virtue. The quest for the ideal friendship – and as an ideal to pursue – amidst the sound and fury of contemporary, hyper-connected life remains a recurring theme for this most humanist of directors. As the trilogy unfurled, Xavier's love life became increasingly complicated. At the close of *Casse-tête*, Xavier realises that he loves Martine. He implores her to stay in New York so that he and their children might build a life together. She agrees. Not insignificantly, this new union will be forged in the New World, not the Old, amid the graffiti and urban fizz of Chinatown and not the *grands boulevards* of Paris. 'On va rester ici', Xavier tells Martine. He completes his novel, but his editor is not happy with the 'atroce happy end'. But Xavier is. He replies that 'quand le bonheur revient . . . il n'y a plus rien à raconter. Faut s'arrêter.' The 'good' friendship between Xavier and Martine leads to romantic fulfilment, unconditional love and a lasting partnership. It has taken more than fifteen years, but, as Aristotle (1934) reminds us, these special friendships demand time, since 'though the wish for friendship comes quickly, friendship does not'. Such a friendship, remarks Aristotle, is part of what constitutes *eudaimonia*, or the highest good for humans. The *eudaimon* life is founded upon self-sufficiency and self-fulfilment: 'We define something as self-sufficient not by reference to the 'self' alone. We do not mean a man who lives his life in isolation, but a man who also lives with parents, children, a wife, and friends and fellow citizens generally'. This seems an apt summation of Xavier at the end of the trilogy – he has, through the nourishing properties of the 'perfect' friendship, forged across time, space and memory, reached self-actualisation, fulfilment and an acceptance of his shortcomings. His kids will be fine. And so will he.

Notes

1. This focus on coming of age and friendship has a long tradition in French cinema, from François Truffaut's 'Antoine Doinel' pentalogy (filmed over twenty years with the same actor, Jean-Pierre Léaud) to Éric Rohmer's urbane comedies of the 1970s and 1980s dealing with people in their twenties, to Patrice Leconte's *Les Bronzés* trilogy (1978, 1979, 2006).

2. When *Sight and Sound* published a 'French cinema special' in their June 2015 edition, the front cover headline was 'Race, Youth and the Faces of the New French Cinema'.
3. Henceforth, *Auberge*, *Poupées* and *Casse-tête*.
4. As late as midway through *Casse-tête*, Isabelle is still telling Xavier: 'Il faut que tu fasses quelque chose, parce que tu vires con là' [i.e. 'deviens insupportable']. Some critics have read the trilogy as the coming of age of 'un con', and list Xavier's numerous infantile, egocentric faults as evidence. See, for example, Damien Leblanc (2018).
5. French psychoanalyst Tony Anatrella has termed these individuals 'adulescents' (1988, 2003). Neither adult nor adolescent, the adulescent is in transition, seeking to establish a new identity. According to Anatrella, these young adults willingly defer the transition to full adulthood, resort to childlike or regressive behaviour, and live in and for the present.
6. See Cicero (1923). Hegel and Erasmus visit Xavier in person in two fantasy sequences in *L'Auberge espagnole*, so why not Cicero?
7. Joseph Mai (2017) notes in his recent study of the director Robert Guédiguian that friendship in his films is often politically and ethically inflected. Guédiguian, like Klapisch, tends to work repeatedly with the same core group of actors, notably Ariane Ascaride (his wife), Gérard Meylan and Jean-Pierre Darroussin, and the conversations and interactions between them '[help] us develop and revise our way of looking at the world' (p. 13).
8. As one reviewer remarked, *Les Poupées russes* might just as easily have been called 'Lovers Without Borders' (Holden 2006).
9. It recalls a similar scene in Maurice Pialat's *Passe ton bac d'abord* (1978), in which the younger generation realise that their parents' generation are just as prone to infidelity and bickering.

Works Cited

Abrams, M. H. (1981), *A Glossary of Literary Terms*, 4th edn, New York: Holt, Rinehart & Winston.

Anatrella, T. (1988), *Interminables adolescences: les 12-30 ans, puberté, adolescence, postadolescence: une société adolescentrique*, Paris: Cerf/Cujas.

Anatrella, T. (2003), 'Les Adulescents', *Études*, 399:7, pp. 37–47.

Anon. (2003), '*L'Auberge espagnole*: About the Production', *Cinema.com*, <http://cinema.com/articles/2228/auberge-espagnole-l-about-the-production.phtml> (last accessed 12 March 2018).

Aristotle [*c.*350 BC] (1934), *Nicomachean Ethics*, Book VIII, <http://www.perseus.tufts.edu/hopper/text?doc=Perseus%3Atext%3A1999.01.0054%3Abekker%20page%3D1155a#note-link3> (last accessed 8 May 2018).

Arnett, J. J. (2000), 'Emerging Adulthood: A Theory of Development from the Late Teens through the Twenties', *American Psychologist*, 55:5, pp. 469–80.

Arnett, J. J. (2004), *Emerging Adulthood: The Winding Road from the Late Teens through the Twenties*, Oxford: Oxford University Press.

Brueckner, J. K. (2006), 'Friendship Networks', *Journal of Regional Science*, 46:5, pp. 847–65.

Bukowski, W. M., A. F. Newcomb and W. W. Hartup (eds) (1996), *The Company They Keep: Friendship in Childhood and Adolescence*, New York: Cambridge University Press.

Cicero [44 BC] (1923), *Laelius de Amicitia [On Friendship]*, <https://www.loebclassics.com/view/marcus_tullius_cicero-de_amicitia/1923/pb_LCL154.191.xml?readMode=rectom> (last accessed 8 May 2018).

Considine, D. (1981), 'The Cinema of Adolescence', *Journal of Popular Film and Television*, 9:3, pp. 123–36.

Debruge, P. (2018), '*Back to Burgundy*', *Variety*, 23 March, <https://variety.com/2018/film/reviews/back-to-burgundy-review-1202735543/> (last accessed 26 September 2018).

DeVito, J. A. (2007), *The Interpersonal Communication Book*, Upper Saddle River, NJ: Pearson.

Hartup, W. (1993), 'Adolescents and Their Friends', *New Directions for Child and Adolescent Development*, 60, pp. 3–22.

Hojjat, M. and A. Moyer (2016), *The Psychology of Friendship*, Oxford: Oxford University Press.

Holden, S. (2006), 'In *Russian Dolls*, Some Continuing Adventures of Europe's Young Suave Set', *The New York Times*, 10 May, <http://www.nytimes.com/2006/05/10/movies/10doll.html> (last accessed 31 December 2017).

Hynes, E. (2014), 'Bonding through Time, on Film and in Life', *The New York Times*, 15 May, <https://www.nytimes.com/2014/05/18/movies/cedric-klapisch-returns-to-4-characters-in-chinese-puzzle.html> (last accessed 25 August 2018).

Klapisch, C. (2002), 'Interview with Bérénice Balta', *Cinelive*, June 2000 [*sic*], <http://www.Cédricklapisch.com/itw/auberge_cinelive_juin2000.html> (last accessed 12 July 2017).

Klapisch, C. (2014), 'Feeling the Pull of New York', Interview with Richard Mowe, *Eye For Film*, 16 June, <http://www.eyeforfilm.co.uk/feature/2014-06-16-interview-with-cedric-klapisch-about-chinese-puzzle-feature-story-by-richard-mowe> (last accessed 26 September 2018).

Klapisch, C. (2017), 'Cédric Klapisch : "Avec mon cinéma, je veux promouvoir le vivre--ensemble"', Interview with Barbara Théate, *Journal du Dimanche*, 13 June, <https://www.lejdd.fr/culture/cinema/cedric-klapisch-avec-mon-cinema-je-veux-promouvoir-le-vivre-ensemble-3358940> (last accessed 26 September 2018).

Leblanc, D. (2018), '*L'Auberge espagnole*: la trilogie de Klapisch est-elle l'histoire d'un petit con?', *Première*, 20 June, <http://www.premiere.fr/Cinema/L-Auberge-espagnole-la-trilogie-de-Klapisch-est-elle-l-histoire-d-un-petit-con> (last accessed 26 September 2018).

Lucia, C. (2009), 'The Many Faces of Paris: An Interview with Cédric Klapisch', *Cinéaste*, 35:1, <https://www.cineaste.com/winter2009/the-many-faces-of-paris-an-interview-with-cdric-klapisch/> (last accessed 1 February 2018).
Mai, J. (2017), *Robert Guédiguian*, Manchester: Manchester University Press.
Massallé, L. (2014), 'Strength, Balance, Courage and Common Sense', *Barcelona Cultural News*, 16 November, <https://barcelonaculturalnews.wordpress.com/2014/11/16/strength-balance-courage-and-common-sense/> (last accessed 2 August 2017).
Mendelson, M. J. and F. E. Aboud (1999), 'Measuring Friendship Quality in Late Adolescents and Young Adults: McGill Friendship Questionnaires', *Canadian Journal of Behavioural Science/Revue canadienne des sciences du comportement*, 31:2, pp. 130–2.
Mereu-Boulch, L. (2002), '*L'auberge espagnole*', *France-Soir*, 19 June, n.p.
Rawlins, W. (2009), *The Compass of Friendship: Narratives, Identities, and Dialogues*, Los Angeles and London: SAGE.
Trémois, C.-M. (1997), *Les Enfants de la liberté: le jeune cinéma français des années 90*, Paris: Éditions du Seuil.
Vasse, D. (2008), *Le Nouvel Âge du cinéma d'auteur français*, Paris: Klincksieck.
Žukauskien, R. (2016), 'The Experience of Being an Emergent Adult in Europe', in R. Žukauskien (ed.), *Emerging Adulthood in a European Context*, New York: Routledge, pp. 3–16.

CHAPTER 14

Catherine Breillat's Maiden Trilogy
Juliette Feyel

Most of Catherine Breillat's fame as a director stems from her cinematic explorations of the singularity of female experience and the quest for gendered identity. This topic has fascinated her for a long time, addressing it as she did in her very first novel when she was seventeen: *A Man for the Asking* (*L'Homme facile*, 1967) and again in her latest one: *Pornocracy* (*Pornocratie*, 2001). An anecdote she likes to recount is her meeting with director Roberto Rossellini when she was preparing her very first film, aged twenty-seven. When Rossellini inquired about what a woman could add to the vision of adolescent girls in cinema, Breillat replied: 'The point of view of shame. No man can address this because *you* men impose it upon us and *we* carry the shame' (Vassé 2006: 25). With such an interest in female sexual identity, Breillat could hardly avoid addressing female adolescence and offering her cinematic representation of what it is for a given subject to become a woman in relation to the cultural representations, discourses and fantasies attached to it. Three films have been devoted to the topic so far: *Une Vraie jeune fille* (*A Real Young Girl*, 1976), *36 Fillette* (*Virgin*, 1988) and *Fat Girl* (2001; known in French as *À ma soeur!* even if the director considers the English title better). Each movie introduces the audience to a pubescent girl's viewpoint during a summer vacation and is pervaded by an atmosphere of oppressive heat, boredom and confinement; the movies also describe these girls' first attempts at escaping reality through imagination or actual experiments with the opposite sex. The filmmaker admitted drawing much from her own personal experience to write the scripts (Clouzot 2004: 9) so that, to a certain extent, her films may provide the viewer with a sense of Frenchness. Indeed, when Breillat was a girl, 'youth culture' had not fully penetrated French society.[1] Although the three films are set in different time periods, it appears that Breillat, born in the late 1940s, remained very much influenced by her upbringing in a lower middle-class provincial background, a decade before contraception was legalised in France. It could be objected that there are changes in terms of social classes and time periods between each film; Alice's parents live in a remote rural area where they own a cultivated land and a sawmill in the late 1950s (*Une Vraie jeune fille*); Lili's father is a small shop owner who takes his family to one of the crowded camping resorts in southern France in the 1980s (*36 Fillette*); Elena and Anaïs's parents, in the late 1990s, appear more upper-class for the father flies back to Paris to supervise the employees of his company, letting his wife and daughters lock the holiday house and drive home by themselves (*Fat Girl*). Notwithstanding such differences, the mentalities remain the same and the panicked reactions of the parents facing their daughters' developing sexuality do not differ at all. The three plots seem to be firmly aligned with Breillat's own biography, and she even went as far as using a song that she wrote when she was twelve for the soundtrack of *Fat Girl*.

Firstly, the chapter will address how adolescent girls are subjugated in various ways both by their bodies and the social gaze weighing upon them. We will then investigate the strategies at their disposal to regain autonomy, and explain the function of masochistic fantasies for a girl's struggle toward emancipation. Ultimately, the goal of this chapter will be to parallel the films' tropes with Breillat's own testimonies on her life to demonstrate that these coming-of-age stories can also be read as a coming-of-age ritual for the director herself.

The young girl, in Breillat's films, exemplifies how being a woman is an alienating experience. Like other female characters in Breillat's universe, the young girl experiences a symbolic divide. This idea has been put forward by Breillat in numerous novels, films and interviews. One of its most successful renderings is the vision displayed in one of the scenes of her film *Romance* (1999). In this scene, Marie (Caroline Ducey) is depicted among other women, lying on an operating table, her body separated by a wall between two symmetric rooms. While her upper body is in a white, sanitised hall symbolic of the platonic, disembodied relationship that she has with Paul (Sagamore Stévenin), her bare pelvis lies in a darkened backroom, her legs spread apart and available for a group of naked, anonymous men. Marie carries the name of the Virgin and, to remain pure in the eyes of her husband, she represses her sexual instincts. The idea is also developed in the dialogues of *Anatomy of Hell* (2004), when the female character (Amira Casar) addresses the taboo surrounding menses, exposing it as another patriarchal strategy to curse the female body. Breillat believes that every woman is initiated into physical awareness through a primordial identification of her body with shame; a woman is taught to consider her lower parts with disgust because they are constructed culturally as a cause of sin and depreciation (Vassé 2006: 30–2).

Focusing on Breillat's maiden trilogy, it is therefore possible to discern what she regards as being the specificity of a teenage girl's experience in contrast with that of a mature woman. As can be expected from teen movies, Breillat's films address the physiological and psychological changes undergone by teenagers, the discovery of sexual desire, and the need to emancipate from parents' control. But one of Breillat's characteristics is to cast curvy-shaped young women rather than slim, child-like nymphets. The part of Alice, the fifteen-year-old heroine of *Une Vraie jeune fille*, was given to twenty-two-year-old actress Charlotte Alexandra. The camera lingers on the blatant discrepancy between the teenager's oversized breasts and curvaceous hips and the pleated skirt, tight buttoned-up blouse, and full white cotton briefs of her schoolgirl uniform. Breillat herself remembers how she felt as an adolescent, as she thought she had received a 'monstrous' body (Clouzot 2004: 16) that did not feel like hers anymore. In *Une Vraie jeune fille*, Alice returns home after a year spent away at a boarding school. A scene shows her as she clumsily jostles her mother while trying to pass through the door at the same time; within a few months, the teenager has lost the capacity to assess the space filled by her own body. Breillat does not conceive puberty as a gradual transition, but instead as a sudden dissonance between physical metamorphosis and self-awareness. Teenagers are depicted as clumsy because the mental representation they have of their own body has not yet adapted to its new volume, shape and appearance.

Puberty seems to happen overnight and looks as surprising for the girl as for the people around her. Becoming a woman is also to receive one's identity from others. Breillat's cinematography dramatises the experience of becoming a woman as an alienating process because it is not something that spontaneously comes from the subject, but rather emanates from others. From the girl's viewpoint, her body is suddenly noticed and perceived as sexually attractive. As if she were illustrating Simone de Beauvoir's *The Second Sex* (1989) which states that a woman is labelled as such through the designation made by others, Breillat particularly insists on the girls' feelings of alienation and subjective dissociation between their self-image and their 'being-for-others'. Although Breillat's heroines feel unchanged, they have no choice but to accept that their physical metamorphosis brings about a different status. Alice in *Une Vraie jeune fille* usually speaks in the mawkish falsetto of a little girl while she is seen curling up on her daddy's lap. The incestuous overtones of such a scene generate discomfort for the viewer, and that reaction is shared by the mother who states that Alice has become too old for that kind of behaviour. Both father and daughter immediately retort in indignation that this cannot be wrong given their family bond; however, as he realises that he is enjoying fondling his daughter a little too much, the father suddenly exclaims 'you are built like a woman!' The statement reappears in one of Alice's fantasies, when she imagines an older man sleazily whispering these very words to her ear. Ultimately, Alice's struggle toward self-awareness is summed up by the lyrics of the summer hit that resonates throughout the film like a leitmotif: 'tell me, tell me . . . am I a woman or a little girl?'

In Breillat's films, the girls' bodies have come to a level of maturity that is not matched by their emotional development. In *Une Vraie jeune fille*, although Alice borrows her mother's lipstick to flirt and seduce men at the fun fair, her misfortune with an exhibitionist proves her lack of experience and control over men's reactions. Similarly, Lili (*36 Fillette*) appears genuinely distraught when she realises that Bertrand (Olivier Parnière) wants to be much more than just a friend. Breillat has repeatedly stated in interviews that she suffered from a precocious puberty; as a coming-of-age woman she perceived her new body as a 'burden' (Clouzot 2004: 16) and had the impression of being a 'ticking time bomb' (Vassé 2006: 13).

Given the shame related to the pubescent female body, Alice's statement in front of her mirror, '*Je n'aime pas me voir autrement que par petits morceaux*', which Haylett Bryan (2016) translated as 'I only like seeing myself in small bits', could also be rendered as 'I can only *bear myself* in small bits'. The disgust she feels when seeing her face and lower parts reflected in one piece leads to her subsequent throwing up. In a voice-over, Alice later affirms that she cannot accept the 'proximity of [her] face and vagina', implying firstly the essential lack of integrity of the young female's self-image and, secondly, that she has internalised the social stigma surrounding female genitalia. *Une Vraie jeune fille* sheds light on the girl's difficulty to identify with a body that is already stigmatised, for it is simultaneously sexualised and denied as such: 'You're a whore!' her mother says, noticing her daughter's womanly shapes enhanced by a red and black bikini. It is, however, the mother who gives her daughter a red-coloured bicycle, a symbol of freedom that allows the girl to escape the confinement of the family household and explore her fantasies. Looking at hens greedily feeding on the offal of another hen, Alice's mother cannot help but underline their stupidity, while the scene draws an interesting parallel with her own attitude as a repressive woman toward a younger one. Becoming a woman also means facing contradictory injunctions from the girl's first role model. The same can be said of Lili's mother who alternates between blaming her daughter for having a date and later exhorting her to socialise with the neighbour's son, Bertrand, because 'at least, he is the same age'. In *Fat Girl* the unsympathetic mother is faced with her own contradictions when Elena cries: 'Did you ask your father for permission [when you had sex for the first time]?'

Worst of all, the teenager must discover, often at her own expense, that being a woman implies that her body is not hers anymore; the most intimate part of it – the hymen – has become a public matter. The three films insist on the fact that a girl's virginity is the property of her family. In a society where virginity determines a maiden's value and is the guarantee of an economic exchange between families, fathers and brothers have the right to monitor the intimacy of a girl. Alice's father explains that he must lock her up for her own good, that she is a 'danger to herself' because 'girls who give themselves, once they've given themselves, they have nothing left'. In *36 Fillette*, Lili's older brother, Jipé, clumsily takes it upon himself to go and visit Maurice, dressed in a soldier's uniform and with the intention to 'smash his face' which he believes will restore his sister's honour. In *Fat Girl* the whole family interrupts their holiday to hide away from public shame after Elena's disgrace. On the way home, Elena is told that her father will have her examined by a doctor because 'he has the right to' whether she wants it or not. The adolescent can only sarcastically retort, indignant: 'then why not publish it in the newspaper?!' The most intimate part of the girl's body is by no means something that she is to keep for herself, as it is instead a matter of gossip, rumours and comment around the entire community. As Anaïs sums it up: 'virginity is something disgusting'.

So, what can girls do to regain freedom, given how constrained they are? It must also be pointed that in Breillat's universe, men are all depicted as predators and, as such, are perceived as women's enemies. This is particularly true when men are portrayed approaching young, inexperienced girls whose virginity represents a tantalising trophy. This stance on men originates in the libertine literary tradition, a reference Breillat regularly returns to, as the filmmaker's casting reveals her interest in Don Juan types. When she cast Hiram Keller for the part of Jim in *Une Vraie jeune fille*, the actor had already been internationally praised for his ambiguous, faun-like good looks in Fellini's *Satyricon* (1969). Libero de Rienzo, who plays the Italian seducer in *Fat Girl*, has an accent that is a deliberate nod to the cliché of the Latin lover while his slightly asymmetric smile gives him a sarcastic, sneaky expression, which is precisely why she chose him for the part.[2] As for Étienne Chicot, who plays the middle-aged playboy in *36 Fillette*, Breillat wrote lines for him such as: 'A car is like a woman, you must like it fast. And seek to change it at any price', or 'Never put your knob three times into the same hole. Better you thump a goat, it still knows you at least.' These libertine, cynical and dangerous male archetypes are recurrent characters in most of Breillat's films. Fernando chats Elena into giving herself to him in all possible ways by promising to marry her. Moreover, it is suggested in *Une Vraie jeune fille* that men prey on women as a result of male competition. Alice's mother repeats to her husband that he feels threatened by younger men, and his adulterous affair is presented as his need to prove he is still vigorous and powerful. And whilst Alice assumes that Jim is not interested in her because she is 'too young', the film shows that the young man has kept his distance with her as long as he remained a loyal employee of her father. He begins to make advances to Alice only after the boss has refused to pay him a fair wage. The young man is already engaged to a girl of his age, who shares his home. Yet, his eagerness to join Alice at night despite all the risks involved, because she promised to give him her virginity, implies that his desire for the girl is intertwined with his need to take revenge on her father.

The economic dimension related to the question of girls' virginity is indeed a key theme in Breillat's cinema. She illustrates how the only viable path set out by parents and society is marriage. In *Fat Girl*, Elena is her parents' favourite child because she fully embraces this social norm. A scene in which she introduces her boyfriend to her family depicts the young couple as a replica of the one formed by Elena's parents; they have the same physical appearance and behaviour. While the two men are seen discussing career and money, the two women are watchful about what they eat, while anxious to provide their respective partners with the proper amount of food. Further on, when Fernando offers Elena a ring stolen from his mother as a pledge of his love, Elena respects the parental norm and the traditional bourgeois part given to wives by accepting it. She believes that she is being the perfect daughter, which allows her to be scornful and cruel toward her younger sibling who, having refused to endorse the same ideal, is unanimously regarded as a failure. Yet, the film turns out to be bitterly ironic; Elena is conned by a grown-up man and subsequently accused by the man's mother of stealing a precious ring. In addition to this, Elena's parents treat her like a criminal, because her disgrace brings dishonour onto the entire family. Finally, her younger sister Anaïs is slapped in the face for failing in her role as a chaperon and protector of the family's reputation. *Fat Girl* ends up exposing the bourgeois upbringing of the maidens as a trap and a maelstrom of contradictory injunctions since, no matter what girls are attempting, they will never be able to escape their alienated fate as subjugated beings.

In Breillat's films, teenage heroines also face a double-bind that requires them to be remarkably resourceful. On the one hand, they feel the urge to lose their virginity, in order to access the status of women and thereby free themselves. On the other hand, they must find a way of doing so without being submitted to the disgrace and shame involved by losing their virginity.

Lili's strategy in *36 Fillette* is different from Elena's. She practices what was called 'flirting' in 1950s France, and that meant agreeing to everything except having sexual intercourse. While *Fat Girl* exposes the hypocrisy of such practices in a society that focuses solely on the integrity of a girl's hymen and absurdly turns a blind eye on extreme practices such as sodomy and fellatio – as they supposedly do not question a girl's alleged purity – the heroine of *36 Fillette* exploits this loophole in a much more cunning way and keeps it to her advantage. The film stages Lili's shifting attitude toward forty-year-old playboy Maurice (Étienne Chicot). One moment she brutally abuses him until he loses his temper and starts showing signs of disinterest while, at another time, she simpers in a caressing voice to regain his attention. While teasing Maurice with the promise of losing her virginity to him, she always changes her mind at the last minute but keeps rekindling his desire by conceding certain liberties. Realising that he has been making a fool of, Maurice eventually capitulates and retreats. However, Lili's victory is incomplete; the film demonstrates the essential dead end of the 'flirt' strategy since the virgin is either conned or, if she cons the libertine, she cannot obtain what she was seeking.

In the same film, Lili ends up opting for another strategy, one that could be called the *femme fatale* option. Finding a young man who is more naïve than her, Lili gets him to have intercourse with her and, as soon as the act is over, she scornfully rejects him. Realising that it was her fist time, the credulous young man exclaims: 'you must love me then!' to which she retorts 'idiot!' and the final shot of the film freezes on her beaming, triumphant smile. The same tactic is used by Alice in one of her recurring daydream scenarios. After she has had sex with Jim among the dunes – an abstract, fantasised place where anything is possible – she abruptly orders him to leave. It is a way of showing him that she has only used him to be rid of the burden of her virginity. She refuses to display any pleasure in the sexual act, so she can save face and be spared the humiliation of being 'obtained' if she refused to consent to it; she thus avoided falling into the trap of the romantic illusion used as a lure by male libertines.

In *Une Vraie jeune fille*, Alice uses her imagination to conjure up a diversity of masochistic scenarios where Jim submits and abuses her. The contrast between her daydreams and the reality of their affair is striking. In reality, 'Jim' no longer appears as the quiet, mysterious, *homme fatal* of Alice's fantasies. Discovering his pay-slip in her father's desk, Alice notes that 'In fact his name was Pierre-Evariste Renard', a rather banal name[3] that creates an anti-climax by comparison to the idealised American dream Alice builds around him. Alice symbolically challenges the young man to transgress a barrier of protection around her bedroom. She entices him to walk the 'path of the boars', a path where, she knows, her father has laid fatal traps. The next morning, when the young man is found dead, while everyone screams and laments in horror, Alice remains indifferent. She has managed to avert the sacrifice of the virgin, which would have signed her defeat. Blood has been shed but she remains triumphant and unscathed.

Although extremely controversial, the rape scene at the end of *Fat Girl* can be interpreted as another expression of the *femme fatale* strategy that I have been discussing. It seems at first problematic to display a scene in which an adult coerces a thirteen-year-old girl into violent, non-consenting sex. It is indeed shocking to be faced with a scene in which Anaïs is taken to the woods by a beast-like, hairy and mysterious man, thrown down, gagged with her own panties and, what is worse, is shown wrapping her arms around his neck instead of trying to push him away. The British Board of Film Classification required this scene to be cut from the UK DVD release version.

However, as Douglas Keesey (2010) reminds us, Anaïs's solitary moments in the film are punctuated by her little sing-song telling us that, instead of a prince charming, she is waiting for the coming of an 'animal . . . a werewolf'. Therefore, this allows us to interpret the strange, unrealistic rape scene as a wish-fulfilling fantasy of her own in a moment when the whole family's attention is entirely focused on the shame and misery brought about by their favourite daughter. Keesey argues that, by being the instigator of this personal scenario, Anaïs manages to rise above 'traumatic gender differences' (Keesey 2010: 104) by means of identifying with both the rapist and the victim, the sadistic male and the masochistic female; in other words, the fantasy enables her to deconstruct gender stereotypes and thus become an empowered subject. Another article sheds an interesting light on the scene (Maddock and Krisjansen 2003). The critics' starting point is the fact that Breillat, confined by her parents as a teenager, found an outlet in reading Surrealistic authors such as Lautréamont, Breton, Klossowski and Bataille, as well as in the works of the artist Magritte who famously painted *The Rape* (1934). The critics argue that the rape fantasy is an expression of rage against the utilitarian, bourgeois, patriarchal order in which the young girl was brought up and a means of achieving sovereignty. Keesey, Maddock and Krisjansen attempt in various ways to demonstrate that filming a rape fantasy in the case of Breillat does not aim at satisfying the 'male gaze' (Mulvey 1999). On the contrary, these critics consider such a scene to be a means of surmounting patriarchal definitions imposed upon the female subject.

Going back to the teenage girl's double-bind that I described earlier, I would argue that the rape fantasy, as it takes place in *Fat Girl*, may also play another role: that of making possible the fact of losing one's virginity without losing one's purity and honour. Breillat's own words tend to confirm this when she says that because girls are 'brought up to be decent, rape is the only way to enact their desire for a man' (Keesey 2010: 102). Anaïs's words in the opening scene are very telling in this regard:

> When I meet a man I love, I'd want to be already broken in so that he doesn't think our first time together matters. I'd want my first time to be with a nobody. I don't want a guy bragging he had me first. Guys are so sick in their mind about that. (My translation)

Besides, Anaïs relishes imagining role plays where she, like a female Don Juan, shares her favours between several lovers, arguing with one of them that he should be glad she is sexually experienced because, as she puts it, 'girls aren't like soap; love doesn't wear them out'. In the lyrics of her sing-song, Anaïs also presents herself as a 'piece of raw meat' exposed on a windowsill for 'crows' to come and peck at. From this perspective, we can almost imagine that Anaïs is calling rape down upon herself, which, in her imagination, is to be the secret agent of her deflowering and her release from alienation while, at the same time, offering her the means of escaping the disgrace that comes upon naive girls who credulously buy the romantic lie. The end of the film offers a reversed hierarchy between the sisters: Elena has become the disgraced daughter, whereas Anaïs is treated with the greatest respect and compassion by police officers. Anaïs has now become the centre of attention and can proudly look at the entire world with defiance. Thus, the rape fantasy is a strategy for the coming-of-age *femme fatale* to regain control over her body and defeat the man's attempts at subduing her because she transforms him into an animal, a disposable tool, an object.

Like two witches, Alice and Anaïs manage to gain self-mastery through the power of their imagination. The power of fantasy, where the victim turns into the active author of the scenario, thus appears as the ultimate way of achieving a sense of freedom just like young Breillat fought her way into adulthood and found agency through writing and directing. Moreover, Breillat is famous for granting very little, if any, autonomy to her collaborators and actors. In interviews (Clouzot 2004), Breillat discloses some aspects of her relationship with actors. For example, when helping an actress find the right pose, gesture or gaze in a scene, she usually interacts with her by playing the part of the male character, the actor being asked to step aside. This is to say that, when directing actresses, she helps them by encouraging their passive response to another character's active initiative; female actors are asked to play the part of victims. This masochistic stance that is exclusively directed toward female characters has long been discussed by critics (Wilson 2001; Vasse 2004).

In contrast, she reserves a very different part to male actors; the director has staged herself in *Sex is Comedy* (2002). The film appears to be the making of *Fat Girl* and shows the sadistic ways in which the female director, played by Anne Parillaud, deals with male actors. A rather long scene dwells on Grégoire Colin's discomfort when trying on a phallic prosthesis for a sex scene. The filmmaker heavily insists on the fact that the prosthesis is 'more beautiful' than the actor's real genitals because it has a straight shape. These words echo those of Breillat herself when she recalls an anecdote during the filming of *Parfait Amour!* (*Perfect Love*, 1996). She told actor Francis Renaud that 'he was only a sexual object; not because he was an actor but for his pretty arse' (Clouzot 2004: 145). Such a statement reverses the common gendered hierarchy, as the male body is now the one being reified by the female gaze. Breillat's professional relationship with Étienne Chicot, the lead in *36 Fillette*, was no more harmonious, according to her own recollection: 'An actor needs to be masochistic... I admit I was mean to him... he wanted me to humiliate him. It was either me or him' (Clouzot 2004: 144). From these anecdotes that Breillat regularly brings up and acknowledges as being part of the artistic process of her films, it seems that conquering autonomy for the female subject as filmmaker involves symbolically confiscating the phallus from its bearer in order to give it to the female character who, in the last instance, is the one who gains power. Presenting the female character as a victim is simply an illusion whose role is merely to lure the male libertine and force him to make a mistake. In the end, he will be defeated by being treated like a tool, a means of emancipation for the coming-of-age maid, and then disposed of, or simply annihilated, erased and punished for his attempt at soiling the virgin girl since, for a man, castration is the ultimate means of imposing disgrace upon him. Stories of how Breillat as a filmmaker symbolically castrated her actors echo visual and thematic tropes in her films, such as worms being cut into pieces, humiliated and assassinated lovers, betrayed fathers, cheated husbands, and so forth.

Breillat's maiden trilogy brings to the fore many aspects of the process of becoming a woman. Drawing inspiration from her own experience, Breillat depicts adolescence as the experience of a brutal physical change. While teenagers' biological metamorphosis is an obvious transitional phase,

Breillat's films explore the specificity of girls' experience. Notwithstanding how they perceive themselves nor their level of psychological maturity, they are declared adults in the most abrupt manner. From the moment a man envisions her as an object of desire, the girl switches from one social status to another without any rite of passage. No longer a child inhabiting her own imaginary world, a girl is given no choice but to submit to her family's economic strategies. Breillat's maiden films address in a very explicit way the link between sexuality and transactions between adult men, showing that virgins are forced to be the unwilling keepers of their family's reputation and honour. Such an anthropological analysis is not new, but filming it from the girl's point of view is extremely uncommon. Having analysed the tropes in each film pointing at this topic, we then examined the strategies invented by each teenage girl. This has led us to reassess the well-documented and controversial issue of the rape fantasy in Breillat's cinema. We have argued that although female characters look like victims at a diegetic level, they use their body to lure and trap male predators through a cinematic fantasy, giving the female subject full control over the situation. And that is why, in Breillat's trilogy on adolescent girls, the girls who succeed in becoming powerful women are those who manage to become successful dreamers, creators, stage-directors and scenarists, just like in Breillat's own coming-of-age success story.

Notes

1. According to historian Mathias Bernard (2006), *Rebel Without a Cause* (1955) and Françoise Sagan's novel *Bonjour tristesse* (1954) are two milestones in France regarding the rise of youth culture defined as a specific content of ideals and representations for teenagers. Previously, this age group had not been identified as an autonomous socio-economic demographic with its own cultural goods.
2. Noted by the director during a Q&A session at the *Cine-Excess*, International Film Conference, directors Alex Marlow-Mann and Xavier Mendik, Birmingham City University, UK, June 2016.
3. Note that 'Pierre-Evariste' is the forename of Gallois, a genius French mathematician, while 'Renard' (fox) connotes cleverness and cunningness. Did Breillat want to stress the sneakiness of this character? Or is he designated as the fox who will try to rob the farmer's chicks?

Works Cited

Bernard, Mathias (2006), 'La "culture jeune": Objet d'histoire?', *Siècles*, 24, pp. 89–98.

Breillat, Catherine (1967), *L'Homme facile*, Paris: C. Bourgeois.
Breillat, Catherine (2001), *Pornocratie: Récit*. Paris: Le Grand Livre du mois.
Clouzot, Claire (2004), *Catherine Breillat: Indécence et pureté*, Paris: Cahiers du cinéma.
De Beauvoir, Simone [1949] (1989), *The Second Sex*, New York: Vintage Books.
Haylett Bryan, Alice (2016), '"I Only Like Seeing Myself in Small Bits": Catherine Breillat's Reflections of the Female Body', A. Marlowe-Mann and X. Mendik (eds), *Cine-Excess*, e-journal, no. 2, <http://www.cine-excess.co.uk/catherine-breillats-reflections-of-the-female-body.html> (last accessed 12 July 2018).
Keesey, Douglas (2010), 'Split Identification: Representations of Rape in Gaspar Noé's *Irréversible* and Catherine Breillat's *À ma soeur!/Fat Girl*', *Studies in European Cinema*, 7:2, pp. 95–107.
Maddock, H. Trevor and Ivan Krisjansen (2003), 'Surrealist Poetics and the Cinema of Evil: The Significance of the Expression of Sovereignty in Catherine Breillat's *À ma sœur!*', *Studies in French Cinema*, 3:3, pp. 161–71.
Mulvey, Laura (1999), 'Visual Pleasure and Narrative Cinema', in L. Braudy and M. Cohen (eds), *Film Theory and Criticism: Introductory Readings*, New York: Oxford University Press, pp. 833–44.
Vassé, Claire (2006), *Corps amoureux. Entretiens avec Catherine Breillat*, Paris: Denoël.
Vasse, David (2004), *Catherine Breillat, un cinéma du rite et de la transgression*, Paris: Éditions Complexe et ARTE Éditions.
Wilson Emma (2001), 'Deforming Femininity: Catherine Breillat's *Romance*', in L. Mazdon (ed.), *France on Film: Reflections on Popular French Cinema*, London: Wallflower.

Films

36 Fillette [*Virgin/Junior Size 36*], film, directed by Catherine Breillat. France: Gaumont Distribution, 1988.
À ma soeur! [*Fat Girl*], film, directed by Catherine Breillat. France: Rezo Films, 2001.
Anatomie de l'enfer [*Anatomy of Hell*], film, directed by Catherine Breillat. France: Rezo Films, 2004.
Une vraie jeune fille [*A Real Young Girl*], film, directed by Catherine Breillat. France: Rezo Films, Pyramide International, Boomerang Production, 1976.

CHAPTER 15

Dismembering and Remembering Childhood in Bruno Dumont's *P'tit Quinquin*

Elizabeth Geary Keohane

I used to work with a telescope, now I work with a microscope. (Barnes 2016)

The French director Bruno Dumont makes the above comment in relation to a recent film of his, the black comedy *Ma Loute* (2016). Yet it can be said that the remark applies just as much to Dumont's first comic outing, *P'tit Quinquin* (2014), a mini-series he both directed and wrote. Initially comprising four episodes/chapters, *P'tit Quinquin* was also shown as a feature-length film at several prestigious international film festivals, premiering at Cannes.[1] This chapter focuses on the representation of childhood in Dumont's film, arguing that he presents a nuanced take on the figure of the child not least because he calls into question the motives and actions of adult characters by foregrounding their exploration of childhood. Dumont's telescope-to-microscope analogy aptly describes his focus on the local in *P'tit Quinquin*, alongside his meticulous dissection of the village's inhabitants (indeed, bodies do not always remain intact in the film, as we will see). The entire village – from seashore to building sites – ends up being pathologically examined through Dumont's searching and inquisitive lens. The film focuses on a group of young children who live on the Côte d'Opale in the Boulogne region of France, particularly on one boy, the eponymous P'tit Quinquin. The nickname derives from a regional lullaby, *quinquin* meaning child in Picard. The film's title not only underlines the centrality of the child, then, but evokes an infinitely transferrable label of youth by suggesting any child or all children or, indeed, anyone who chooses to identify as or act like a child, as much as the particular character who bears this nickname.

The film's cast of child characters is joined by two hapless detectives from the *gendarmerie* who investigate a series of gruesome murders and mysterious deaths in the village – the delightfully eccentric Captain Van der Weyden, and his often pensive right-hand man, Lieutenant Carpentier. Though ostensibly framed as a rural murder mystery, the film frequently focuses on the youngsters as they visit the central crime scenes and ponder what these murders might reveal to them about adulthood and the community at large. The disposal of each murder victim (most end up consumed by farm animals) is seemingly staged by the killer(s) to create shockwaves that will reverberate throughout the community, and the recovery of many of the victims is often refracted through the children's perception of their surroundings. This refractive process helps Dumont to develop a bleaker, more irreverent take on childhood, one where the child-like quality of innocence is repeatedly called into question, and eventually quashed as part of the director's subtle yet no less despairing critique of small-town French society. The child protagonists of *P'tit Quinquin* have a knowing, world-weary manner, and like to play at being the adult. At once sensitive and resistant to the social and economic changes that are taking place in their community, they are often, just like many of the adults in the local area, racist, homophobic, vulgar and distrustful of authority. Yet the haplessness and ineptitude of the adult characters who mill around them, though mostly played to great comic effect in the film, also serve to emphasise the precocity and ultimate poignancy of the children's ostensible knowingness.

In a July 2015 interview with *The Guardian*, Dumont puts forward his view that a more nuanced understanding of childhood is necessary in film. He addresses the moral ambiguity of the children in *P'tit Quinquin* by highlighting that they should not be viewed as any different from adults when it comes to their capacity for emotional extremes:

> That's the power of humanity ... An extraordinary capacity for love, and an extraordinary force of aggression. Children are the same. That's the sort of thing that worries the civilised viewer, who would prefer those things to be separated out. People want a character to be all good or all bad, not both – but that's what the truth is. (Romney 2015)

Dumont's comments shed light on his recasting of child characters not as paragons of innocence or the unsullied moral centre of the film, but as key players in this small-town society, just as capable as adults of victimising those around them. Dumont does not offer an apology for the children's behaviour whenever it is unsavoury (as is frequently the case). Rather, his is a quest for a more accurate and comprehensive representation of the child. In the introduction to her 2010 text *The Child in Film: Tears, Fears and Fairy Tales*, Karen Lury writes that 'the child and childhood, and indeed children themselves, occupy a situation in which they are "other": other to the supposedly rational, civilised, "grown up" human animal that is the adult' (Lury 2010: 1). Dumont deliberately disrupts and reins in this othering process, preferring instead to show us that children more often than not absorb and replicate the ways of adults, and in fact reflect the behaviour and attitudes of the adults around them. Thus, at various points in the film, we see P'tit Quinquin cursing and making obscene gestures, smoking, spouting racist and homophobic abuse, and displaying violent tendencies (picking fistfights; throwing firecrackers at tourists and family members alike). In many of these endeavours he is supported by local adults, such as the sexton who willingly shares a cigarette with him as they lean against the church wall, and P'tit Quinquin's own father (one of the brothers Lebleu), who has evidently fostered a dislike of the *gendarmerie* – and authority in general – in his son. In an early scene, P'tit Quinquin snivels in front of Van der Weyden to avoid being further reprimanded for having flouted the road use code. Yet once the camera switches to the father's point of view, we see that P'tit Quinquin is making an obscene gesture behind his back, thus negating his apologetic stance towards the detectives, and sending a clear message to his father that he is in no way actually respecting their authority (Figure 15.1). Once the police depart, we see that the father immediately displays a disrespectful attitude towards them, calling them 'connards' – his attitude therefore immediately mirrors – and is more than likely the source of – P'tit Quinquin's own approach to the police. While for once Van der Weyden seems to be duped by P'tit Quinquin's guile here, it will be seen that the shrewd detective frequently reserves just as much suspicion for children and their motives as he does adults, and is not afraid to voice his criticism of the younger generation.

Figure 15.1 P'tit Quinquin slyly shows his dislike of the *gendarmerie*.

In drawing out and foregrounding the ambivalence at the heart of his child characters, it will be seen that Dumont then uses his young protagonists as a basis to explore thorny questions concerning French identity (the uncomfortable interactions between migrant children and the mostly racist native French children), the pitfalls of provincial life (isolation, insularity and secretiveness, amongst others), and the construction of masculinity and femininity (we might think of P'tit Quinquin's constant attempts to act in a 'macho' way around his sweetheart and neighbour, Ève, and on a more sinister level, the misogynistic and racist undertones to the murders that overshadow the community).

Yet it is not just through Dumont's young protagonists or puerile adults that the notion of the child comes to the fore. I will put forward the idea that Dumont frequently employs a subtle narrative technique where the camera offers a take on an adult situation through the eyes of the child protagonists, for instance, their encounter with a helicopter in an early scene. Alongside several moments of this nature in the narrative, the tone and pace of the film also mirror the sometimes joyful and generally unapologetic idleness of the children's summer holidays – the time frame of the film. Indeed, the murder investigation itself seems to be largely informed by the laidback rhythm of endless waiting around and the constant risk of being thwarted by uncooperative adults – elements that together in fact characterise the children's day-to-day existence as played out in the film. It will therefore be my contention that Dumont's film is not only one about children, but one which uses the motif of childhood to shape both its narrative techniques and style. In addition to this, I wish to explore Dumont's use of young actors with physical and learning difficulties, before moving on to a discussion of the way the young girl who acts as the moral centre of the film is represented. I shall proceed by addressing the topics outlined above under four headings: 'Inner Child', 'Through the Eyes of a Child', '(Dis)abling Prejudice', and 'Child Star/Child Sacrifice'.

Inner Child

Throughout the film, the main adult characters frequently display a childish sense of humour and youthful zest for life, and end up revealing and even pursuing childhood ambitions. Visiting P'tit Quinquin's father on his sprawling farm in order to question him about the recent murders, Van der Weyden admires the white horse which the farmer is tending. Van der Weyden then arranges to mount the animal to fulfil his childhood dream, for he has never before sat astride a horse. Rather than an image of a questing knight, riding in to save the day, Van der Weyden is presented to us in this scene as an affable ageing man who is tentatively fulfilling his long-held ambition (moreover, the mounting of the horse is itself played to excellent comic effect). As he gingerly makes his way across the field on his mount, followed closely by Carpentier, Van der Weyden's face conveys the joyful enthusiasm of a small child. Perhaps surprisingly, pressing detective work and even the highly suspicious nature of the farmer's relationship with some of the murder victims are cast to one side as Van der Weyden allows himself to enjoy the simple connection he is forging with the placid animal.

The inclusion of a lengthy corpsing sequence by the actors who play the priests at the first murder victim's funeral is a notable early moment in the film. Mirth overwhelms them as they break character and are egged on by P'tit Quinquin in his role as dysfunctional altar boy. The comic and decidedly jarring effect of this sequence, coupled with P'tit Quinquin's unbridled delight at their mockery, suggests a childlike appraisal of and resistance towards respecting the component parts of a religious ritual.[2] The act of corpsing by the priest characters is representative of many adult characters in the film, who openly embrace their inner child by engaging in a particular activity, or by choosing to behave in a certain way. After the burial, as if to compensate for their decided lack of solemnity in the church, the priests declare to Van der Weyden that children are the only hope for our increasingly bleak society, and place their hands on P'tit Quinquin's head (emphasising once again, just as the title does, that he stands in for *all* children) (Figure 15.2). Van der Weyden remains unconvinced, however, furrowing his brow at the beatific expression P'tit Quinquin duly adopts (Figure 15.3) (he will later say to a group of veterans at the local Bastille

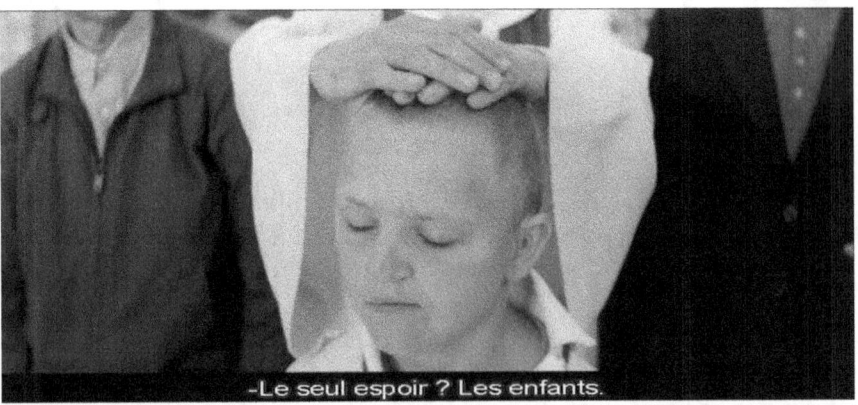

Figure 15.2 One of the priests lays his hands on P'tit Quinquin.

Figure 15.3 Van der Weyden shows a flicker of disapproval at the laying of hands.

Day celebrations that today's children will also go on to wage war, predicting their refusal to learn from the mistakes of the past).

Similarly abandoning himself to the irresistible urge for childlike fun, the usually careful Carpentier decides to throw caution to the wind during the investigation, and does car tricks along an empty country road, driving the small vehicle at speed on its side (Figure 15.4). As one meant to uphold the law as part of his occupation, this transgression while on the job echoes the irresponsible and irrepressible laughter of the two priests as they break the solemnity of the funeral mass held for the first victim. It also shows us that even the most grounded adults are not inured to their inner child, which may break out at unexpected moments, especially when tempted by seemingly irresistible opportunities.

Figure 15.4 Carpentier does tricks in the police car.

If these scenes of haplessness and professional ineptitude are played with tenderness or to great comic effect in the film, they also serve by extension to *elevate* further the status of children in *P'tit Quinquin*, or at least bring the adults and children closer together. This is emphasised by the fact that it is the children who are often among the first to arrive on crime scenes (often coinciding with the detectives), and who, for instance, discover the secret passageway at the *blockhaus* (where the partial remains of the first victim are recovered inside a dead cow). While in general P'tit Quinquin and his band of friends would appear to show little respect for authority, be it parental, religious or that of the *gendarmerie*, it is perhaps even more likely that they genuinely see themselves on the same level as the adults surrounding them. Certainly, the ineptitude of certain adults, whether on a professional or personal level, would lead the children to think themselves to be just as capable of handling even particularly threatening situations. This is perhaps emphasised by the solemn yet resigned faces of the children as they happen on the shooting scene later in the film. Young Mohammed Bhiri, who was previously deemed a threat to P'tit Quinquin's assertions of masculinity because he attempts to court young girls in the village and successfully steals an old grenade from P'tit Quinquin in front of Ève, has been pushed to the brink by the racist abuse he has suffered at the hands of the locals. Instead of showing fear in the face of imminent danger and the injury or death of someone their own age, the children display an almost world-weary acceptance of the likely outcome. When Mohammed dies, and is brought out in the Captain's arms, the children are not spared the sight of the erstwhile victim of their bullying lying dead. The resigned expressions of the children are given an acutely sinister edge by ghoulish face paint which draws together the colours of the French flag, red, white and blue (Figure 15.5). This serves as a distorted reflection of the tricolour that hangs out of the window in the Bhiri household, clearly displayed when Mohammed threatens to shoot (Figure 15.6). The juxtaposition of the two combinations of red, white and blue here seems first of all to convey a deformation of the principles of the Republic – *liberté, égalité, fraternité* – on the part of P'tit Quinquin and his friends, as symbolised by their eerie face paint. This contrasts with the pristine flag hanging under Mohammed's window. His anguished cries of isolation and desperate actions suggest that he has *not* experienced what the tricolour in principle had promised him. It can then be said that Dumont allows the children themselves, whether it be through their bodies or acts, to serve as the canvas upon which the racial and xenophobic tensions arguably prevalent in French society are illustrated.

Figure 15.5 The children gather at the scene of the Bhiri shooting as it unfolds.

Figure 15.6 Mohammed points a gun out of the window of the Bhiri household.

Through the Eyes of a Child

In an early scene in the film, a helicopter flies perilously and almost improbably close to P'tit Quinquin and his friends as they dawdle on the beach. The close encounter between the helicopter and the children occurs as it makes its way to an inland assignment; the helicopter momentarily swoops lower and lower to hover directly over the children, without landing (Figure 15.7). In framing the helicopter and the children so close

Figure 15.7 The helicopter swoops down to hover over the children.

together, the noise of the blades almost drowning out their shouts, the camera manages to impart to us, in an exaggerated fashion, an almost childlike take on the thrill of seeing a helicopter fly so close overhead. The children are delighted, and race to the scene to which the helicopter has been deployed (the *blockhaus*, to haul out the dead cow). This marks the beginning of their interest in the murderous wave that sweeps over the village.

If the camera seems to adopt a childlike take in the above instance, it is also necessary to consider the extent to which a child's understanding of film can be said to inflect Dumont's narrative. The figure of Ch'tiderman (Figure 15.8) (a pun on Spiderman and *ch'ti*, the word used for a native

Figure 15.8 Ch'tiderman.

of north-east France) bursts onto the scene in the latter stages of *P'tit Quinquin* – at a juncture when we feel there might be a pressing need for a local hero to rise up against such wanton criminality. Played by a child whom we never seen unmasked, but who is quickly identified as Ève's cousin Guy, we see him try – and usually fail – to display superhuman feats, such as scaling walls unaided (notwithstanding one surprisingly successful attempt to get traction on an outhouse wall). Dumont engages here with the tropes of blockbuster superhero movies as a child would perhaps understand them: the unquestionable ability to defy gravity, and impress any onlookers in so doing. The name Ch'tiderman is shouted repeatedly by the child in a way that suggests he is attempting to create his own mythology. It also represents a fusion of the local and the international, whilst pointing towards the need to affirm that one is entering adulthood. If the superhero name displays aspirations to manhood in this way, then the emphasis on geographical location also reveals a certain pride in being bound to that area. Superheroes, though often associated with specific cities (for instance, Batman and Gotham; Spiderman and New York), are generally never *named* in accordance with the place they inhabit. Yet a local child taking on this mantle – and emphasising proudly his locale in choosing his own superhero identity – once again highlights the extent to which the children of *P'tit Quinquin* are attuned to, and responding to, what is happening around them.

Whilst the child's homemade mask and hapless attempts at heroics around the farmyard lend him a comical and even slapstick air, his appearance also brings to mind that of the mysterious motorcycle driver, who never reveals his face (Figure 15.9) – not even in church, where he keeps his balaclava on.

Figure 15.9 The mysterious *motard*.

The motorcyclist is married to one of the female victims (a Madame Campin who is later found dead on the beach), who is found to be having an affair with Lebleu, the second victim. When Van der Weyden scans the faces of the mourners at the first victim's funeral (that of Lebleu's wife), he eyeballs the motorcyclist, but does not ultimately approach him. While the motorcyclist appears to be a far more menacing figure, one whose sinister silence marks every scene in which he appears, the facelessness and masked identity of both Ch'tiderman and the motorcyclist bind them together as outsiders, placed somewhat on the margins of any gathering precisely because we are never in a position to recognise their faces. And yet they are both accepted into village society despite their relative anonymity; one trying and failing to resemble a superhero, and the other the potential perpetrator of these crimes, flying under the radar. Indeed, together Ch'tiderman and the *motard* represent the struggle between children and adults as it plays out in the film: the child trying in vain to assert his own identity, and attempting in his behaviour to resist the rules imposed by adults, yet ending up creating an appearance that in fact mirrors that of those adults who would seem to share his motivation to transgress boundaries.

(Dis)abling Prejudice

Young male characters with disabilities, physical deformities or learning difficulties are used in Dumont's film to convey certain truths that other characters tend to hide or purposefully evade (a striking example is the farmhand with learning difficulties and a severe speech impediment, who repeatedly corrects the TV news reporter's use of words as she attempts to sensationalise Lebleu's death). The lead character P'tit Quinquin, for instance, is disfigured by a cleft palate. In his choice of protagonists, Dumont can be seen as attempting to normalise physical ailments and imperfections for his viewers. In *La Vie de Jésus*, Dumont's 1997 directorial debut, the protagonist Freddy has frequent epileptic fits, and these are played out on-screen, rather than being merely alluded to by other characters.

Dumont's predilection for foregrounding characters with physical and mental challenges, along with his casting of disabled or impaired actors, uncovers his compulsion to reflect the make-up of society, and once again reveals the way he resists subjecting certain types of characters to an othering process. Dumont says:

> Cinema usually recruits people who are exceptionally beautiful – I like putting very ordinary people in the spotlight. Walk down any street, you'll see plenty of people who are pretty singular looking. People think that the kid who plays Quinquin looks weird, but he doesn't. Look around you, there are loads of kids like him. (Romney 2015)

Darren Hughes aptly describes this approach as Dumont turning 'to the arts in a democratic spirit, celebrating the "common people" in all of their rich complexity' (Hughes 2002). Indeed, Dumont has found that his use of actors of differing levels of physical capacity has instead garnered criticism rather than approval. When probed about his use of disabled actors, he responds:

> I have a clear conscience. Some people think I'm laughing at my actors. Others say, 'You must love those people a lot.' You have to decide whether or not you're looking at something that disturbs you. It's impossible to work with people you don't respect. The people I work with are actors, and I have their confidence. If I didn't, they wouldn't be there. (Romney 2015)

The accusation of somehow drawing comic value from his actors with impediments is certainly a misguided one; Dumont presents a sensitive, if realistic, portrayal of a range of disabilities. There is no sense of tokenism in his portrayal of disability – to pick up on the phrase used by Hughes, it is the 'rich complexity' of humankind that is foregrounded in his characters. Dumont capitalises on this complexity and potential opacity in the case of one of the more minor characters in *P'tit Quinquin*, the eponymous character's young uncle, Dany.

Towards the very end of the film, Dany is intimated to be the culprit of at least some of the heinous crimes that beset the community, though usually when we encounter him on-screen he prefers to spin himself round and round into a dizzying faint. In laying bare his fragile state, not least his precarious sense of balance, it is suggested that these impairments could not possibly allow him to commit such complex and physically demanding crimes alone, and that in questioning Dany, perhaps the wrong person has been suspected by the bumbling detectives. Yet in leaving us with a series of murders that, although unsolved, keep bringing us back to the homestead of P'tit Quinquin, Dumont is perhaps showing us that the real crime here is the way a society or community can condition children to adopt its attitudes and prejudices, carrying them on into the future. This is made clear by the closing scene where P'tit Quinquin (holding Ève protectively in a tight embrace), his father and Dany watch impassively in the courtyard as Van der Weyden, flanked by Carpentier, declares their farmstead to be the source of all this malice. P'tit Quinquin as a child protagonist is by no means a figure of hope or a potentially blank canvas, as we have seen, but a fully formed person whose attitude and behaviour have absorbed and already reflect society's ills, rather than offering any scope to resist or put an end to them. In *P'tit Quinquin*, unlike *La Vie de Jésus*, there is no redemptive moment at the end, no 'glimmer of light' as Dumont terms it

(Walsh 1997). Even though *P'tit Quinquin* is ostensibly a comedy, it leaves us with an even bleaker image of the community as a whole than the final scene of *La Vie de Jésus*, where the protagonist flees police custody and, in complete solitude, appears to contemplate his murderous actions in the light-filled meadows outside the town of Bailleul. In contrast to this stirring connection between man and the immensity of Nature, in the closing scene of *P'tit Quinquin* we are drawn into the claustrophobic courtyard of the Lebleu farmhouse – which instead foregrounds cultivation, man's attempted mastery and manipulation of his natural surroundings, and also the weight of interpersonal relationships, whether romantic (P'tit Quinquin and Ève), familial (two generations of the Lebleu family) or professional (Van der Weyden and Carpentier).

Child Star/Child Sacrifice

Aurélie is the older sister of Ève and lives with her family on the farm next to the one belonging to P'tit Quinquin's parents. She is seen to have considerable musical talent, singing at the funeral of the first victim, and then at the village auditions for a reality television talent show. Her kindness and compassion towards the immigrant boy Mohammed stand out because of the harsh way he is treated by others, primarily P'tit Quinquin.

Aurélie's tendency to stretch out her arms as she sings startles us in the medium shot that captures her performance on the village stage, where she is bathed in beatific light (Figure 15.11), the church rising above the other buildings in the background. Her stance suggests that of a saviour or prophet, attempting to impart an important message to

Figure 15.10 Aurélie sings at the first victim's funeral.

the village residents. This similarity is perhaps already evident in her first singing appearance, which takes place at the pulpit of the local church (Figure 15.10). The chorus of her party piece (a pop composition that is sung in English) reflects the whodunnit narrative that drives the film, and the detectives' search for the killer, as well as implying the complicity of the locals with any such perpetrator: 'Because I knew/It was you.' Aurélie's stance in the above scenes also prefigures the discovery of the body of Madame Campin, who trains the local majorettes (and, as previously mentioned, happens to be the lover of one of earlier male victims), propped up against a rock on the beach (Figure 15.12). When he arrives on the

Figure 15.11 Aurélie sings at the talent show heats.

Figure 15.12 One of the murder victims as she is found on the beach.

scene Van der Weyden immediately admires Madame Campin's beauty, and says that the tableau reminds him of a Flemish painting – 'ces grosses femmes à poil' (much later, he remembers the artist's name that had previously escaped him – Rubens). However, the woman's position is an ironic take on martyrdom, insofar as it also brings to mind any of the numerous paintings of the martyr Saint Sebastian (Figure 15.13) by artists such the Flemish painter Gerard Seghers (1591–1651).[3] A juxtaposition between the tableau of Madame Campin and the earlier framing of Aurélie can be detected.[4] While both seem to lean on religious imagery, in the instance of the woman on the beach, the victim is exposed to all and sundry in harsh daylight, rather than the beatific light (in fact a spotlight) reserved for the self-sacrificing figure of Aurélie. Rather than being set against the village, and arguably invested with a sense of belonging, the background for the victim on the beach is that of the cold grey sea, further underlining her isolation.

The death of the woman on the beach, if somehow the consequence of her extramarital transgressions, would seem to suggest moral outrage

Figure 15.13 *Saint Sebastian comforted by an Angel* (*c*.1630) by Gerard Seghers.

on the part of the killer (despite the victim's resemblance to a religious martyr). Yet any notion of general moral outrage is called into question by the gruesome death of Aurélie. When the young Mohammed dies in a shootout, it is initially intimated that Aurélie, upon hearing of his death, commits suicide by allowing herself to be eaten alive by the pigs on her parents' farm. Thus death begins to ensnare the children as well. Aurélie's demise first brings to mind the initial murder uncovered in the film, where most of the female victim's remains were found inside a dead cow. Her troubling death, however, means that, despite arguably representing the conscience of the film, she feels she has no other choice but to allow herself to be consumed by the malice and malaise that have swept over the village. However, it is Van der Weyden who suggests that there is what he deems an 'exterminateur' in the area, someone who is punishing Aurélie for being in some way complicit in the humiliation of Mohammed. Yet Aurélie's evident sense of guilt as she hunkers down among the pigs – the last time we see her – would seem to suggest self-sacrifice, or at least conveys the idea that she is perhaps overwhelmed by the pace and finality of recent events. In any case, the intimation that the pigs annihilate Aurélie as she abandons herself to them conjures up a powerful off-screen image of the way the evil pervading the village has the potential to overwhelm and extinguish any flicker of goodness. With Aurélie's death so directly impacting the group of child protagonists, it is evident that it signals a complete loss of innocence for them. The once-smiling Ève is now broken, and P'tit Quinquin's new role is to soothe and comfort her as they try to face Aurélie's death together. It becomes increasingly clear to the children that they too are not only privy to the evil in their midst, but potential victims of it.

Conclusion

In presenting us with a lengthy exposition of these gruesome crimes, and dissecting a variety of potential suspects, Dumont serves us up a whodunnit without ever telling us who actually *did* do it – a disruptive comic ploy in itself. However, beyond such flouting of genre conventions, Dumont has created in *P'tit Quinquin* a film that changes the way we might think about childhood in French cinema. In embroiling its child protagonists in the grisly murders that beset the village, the child in Dumont's universe ends up being as complicit in these events as any adult. Moreover, in stoking the inner child in key adult characters, and allowing this to be openly expressed, even at the expense of professionalism or discretion, Dumont asks us to reconsider the way children and adults interrelate. The tension in the film hinges on the following question which, like the whodunnit question, is perhaps never fully answered: can the children, in losing their innocence, truly be said to be *elevated* to adulthood, if adulthood itself at once means a wish to regress to childhood, and an irresponsible compulsion to transgress the bounds of morality?

Notes

1. A follow-up series, *Coincoin et les Z'inhumains*, was screened on Arte in September 2018.
2. John Caruana describes Dumont as 'an atheist who is haunted by religion', an obsession fully aired in this scene (Caruana 2014: 110).
3. Dumont references the figure of Christ in Flemish painting in a 1997 interview with David Walsh.
4. Dumont has long shown a predilection for alluding to Catholicism. We might also note the similarly ironic use of a reproduction of a Giotto painting depicting the raising of Lazarus in the hospital scene with the dying Cloclo in *La Vie de Jésus*.

Works Cited

Barnes, Henry (2016), '*Ma Loute* Director Bruno Dumont: "You can't make a 'European film"'', *The Guardian*, 13 May.

Caruana, John (2014), 'Bruno Dumont's Cinema: Nihilism and the Disintegration of the Christian Imaginary', in Costica Bradatan and Camil Ungureanu (eds), *Religion in Contemporary European Cinema: The Postsecular Constellation*, New York and Abingdon: Routledge, pp. 110–25.

Hughes, Darren (2002), 'Bruno Dumont's Bodies', *Senses of Cinema*, 19, <http://sensesofcinema.com/2002/feature-articles/dumont_bodies/> (last accessed 3 September 2018).

Lury, Karen (2010), *The Child in Film: Tears, Fears and Fairy Tales*, London: I. B. Tauris.

Romney, Jonathan (2015), 'Why France's God of Grim Made a Knockabout Clouseau-Style Comedy', *The Guardian*, 8 July.

Walsh, David (1997), 'Interview with Bruno Dumont, Director of *The Life of Jesus*', World Socialist Web Site, <http://zakka.dk/euroscreenwriters/interviews/bruno_dumont.htm> (last accessed 7 October 2016).

Films

La Vie de Jésus, film, directed by Bruno Dumont. France: 3B Productions, 1997.
L'Humanité, film, directed by Bruno Dumont. France: 3B Productions, 1999.
P'tit Quinquin, film, directed by Bruno Dumont. France: 3B Productions, 2014.

Index

Note: n indicates endnote; *italic* indicates illustration

abortion, 147–8
adolescence (adolescent), 18–31, 47, 48–9, 50, 51, 58, 82, 83, 86
adulescents, 219n
aesthetics, 181
affect, 25–6, 27
agency, 48, 52–3, 58, 17
Al Malik, Abd, 136–49
Algeria, 176
Aristotle, 213–17
  and *eudaimonia*, 218
  and *Nicomachean Ethics*, 213
Arnett, Jeffrey, 211, 216
Atran, Scott, 119, 122, 126–7
audience, 20
autoportrait, 164, 166
Azuelos, Lisa, 22, 23–4

Bande de filles, 120, 206–7
banlieue, 63–5, 73–7, 155, 167
banlieue film, 136–49
Bardot, Brigitte, 53–5
Barot, Emmanuel, 173
beauty culture, 95, 96
Belle de jour, 52
Berliner, Alain, 33, 34, 35, 38, 39, 40, 41, 44
beur film, 149
Bildungsfilm, 209
body, 223–5, 230–2
Bouhdiba, Abdelwahab, 99, 102, 111, 114
Bouzid, Nouri 115–35
breakdancing, 117, 120–2, 125, 127, 131
breaking character, 238
Breillat, Catherine, 69–70
Brickell, Chris, 34
Butler, Judith, 41, 69, 71–2

Cantet, Laurent, 152, 156–7, 159, 161, 163–4, 167
castration, 231
Les Chevaux de dieu, 128
chick flicks, 64
childhood, 33–44
Ch'tiderman, 242–4
Cicero, 212
cinéma du milieu, 62–3, 77
Cité des 4000, 142–3
cohabitation, 153
La Collectionneuse, 47, 54, 55;
  see also Eric Rohmer
colour, 140, 143–3
Cordier, Antony, 68–9

dance, 64, 67, 76
Davenas, Olivier, 64–5
de Beauvoir, Simone, 118
Deleuze, Gilles, 73–4, 77–8
delinquency, 140–2
depression, 177
disability, 244–6
diversity, 154, 156–7, 162, 164, 166
Ducastel, Olivier, 103, 105, 108, 110–11, 113–14
Dumont, Bruno, 234–50
  Coincoin et les Z'inhumains, 250n
  La Vie de Jésus, 244, 245–6, 250n
  Ma Loute, 234
  P'tit Quinquin, 234–50
Duschinsky, Robbie, 44

education, 152, 154, 156–7, 159, 167
Egloff, Karine, 65
election (presidential), 153, 155

'emerging adult', 210–11, 214–18
Entre les murs, 152, 154, 157–8, 160–1, 163–7
éphèbe, 109
Esposito, Claudia, 176
Être et avoir, 152, 154, 156–7, 159, 161, 164, 166
Europe, 152–3
Ezra, Elizabeth, 117

family, 34, 35, 36, 37, 40–4
fantasy, 222, 225, 228, 230, 232
fashion photograph, 91, 92, 93
femininity, 35, 39, 41, 43
feminism, 82, 87, 90, 91, 92, 93, 94, 95
femme fatale, 47, 50, 53–4, 56–7
Flemish painting, 248
fragmentation, 35
framing, 37, 38, 39, 40, 42, 43
France, 99–105, 108–14
freedom, 173, 176, 177–8, 179, 180, 181, 183
French 'coming-of-age' films, 206–7

gamine, 54; see also *jeune fille*
gay marriage, 184–5
gaze, 174, 180–1
  object of, 34–8, 42, 44
  of the character, 38–40
gender, 33–44
  categories, 34, 40–1
  determining, 34, 37
  dysphoria, 38
  embodiment, 34, 36–40
  essentialism, 40
  identity, 33–44
  nonconformity, 33, 41–3, 44
  panic, 33, 40, 42, 44
  performance, 34, 35–40, 43
  rehearsal, 34, 38, 39, 40
  reversal, 37
genre, 18–20
Ghorab-Volta, Zaïda, 138–9
girlhood, 82, 83, 85, 86, 89, 90, 93, 94
Girshick, Lori, 40, 44
Godard, Jean-Luc, 47, 52–3, 57

La Haine, 120, 140–1
Hansen-Løve, Mia, 81, 83, 85, 86, 88, 93
  Un Amour de jeunesse/Goodbye First Love, 81, 82, 88
  Le Père de mes enfants/Father of my Children, 81, 82, 88
  Tout est pardonné/All is Forgiven, 82, 89
heteronormativity, 34, 35, 40, 41, 44
heterosexual matrix, 41, 43–4
hip hop, 121, 131
Hollywood, 22–23
homosexuality, 174

identity, 47, 48–51, 52, 57–8, 175
immigrant/immigration, 153–6, 164, 169n, 174, 179
imperfect (tense), 160, 163
individuation, 63–6
integration, 153–5, 159, 163
Islam, 118–19, 122, 126, 129–30

jeune cinéma français, 206
jeune fille, 50, 53, 55, 56
Jeunesse dorée, 138–9
Jewish–Arab relations, 147

Karina, Anna, 53; see also *Vivre sa vie*
Kassovitz, Mathieu, 120, 140–1
Kechiche, Abdellatif, 21

La Courneuve, 142–3
love, 174–9, 180–5
Le Pen, Jean-Marie, 153

Ma Vie en rose, 33, 34–6, 38, 39–40, 41–4
Maghreb, 100–1, 103–4, 107, 109–14
Making Of, 115–35
Marivaux, Pierre Carlet de Chamblain de, 180
Martineau, Jacques, 99, 100–8, 110–14
masculinity, 38, 39, 41, 43–4, 123–5, 128, 137–8
Massad, Joseph, 100, 112, 114
maternal, 41–4
McRobbie, Angela, 87, 90, 91, 92, 93, 96
melancholy, 82, 83, 92, 93
migration, 174, 175–9
Morocco, 101, 107–8, 110, 112, 114
Mulvey, Laura, 75
multiculturalism, 155, 163–4, 167

Naficy, Hamid, 117
narrative, 182
nation, 174, 179
National Front, 153, 155
Nettlebeck, Colin, 174
New French Extremity movement, 47
New Wave, 48, 52–5, 57–8
North Africa, 99–100, 102, 108–9, 113, 115–16, 123, 132–3

Ohayon, Sylvie, 136–49

Papa Was Not a Rolling Stone, 139–49
paternal, 43
Philibert, Nicolas, 152–4, 157–9, 161, 167
Pialat, Maurice, 65
Picasso, Pablo, 131–3
Pinoteau, Claude, 23
polis, 173, 182
politics, 173–8, 180–5
postfeminism, 81, 90, 96

Prédal, René, 62
prostitute, 49, 52–3; *see also* prostitution
prostitution, 48, 50, 52–3
puberty, 224

Qu'Allah bénisse la France!, 139–46
Quillévéré, Katell, 21

racaille, 155
racism, 235, 236, 237, 240
radicalisation, 115, 118–20, 125–6, 128
Rampling, Charlotte, 51, 55
Rancière, Jacques, 173, 181
rape, 229–30
Ronsard, Pierre de, 177
registers (linguistic), 152, 163
religion, 66, 238, 246–9, 250n
Renold, Emma, 36, 40
republican, 154–7, 159, 166
Rimbaud, Arthur, 47, 56, 58
rites of passage, 47–9, 51–2, 55, 57–8
Rohmer, Éric, 47, 49, 54–5
Rowden, Terry, 117
Ruoff, Jeffrey, 123, 125–6, 128–9, 130

Saint Sebastian, 248
Sarkozy, Nicolas, 154–6
school, 36, 37, 40, 41, 44
Sciamma, Céline, 21, 26–8, 33, 34, 36, 38, 44, 120
Seghers, Gérard, 248
setting, 25
sex, 224, 228, 231
    biological, 33, 35, 37, 40
    –gender binary, 33, 40–1, 44
sexuality, 144–7
shame, 222, 223
shot-reverse-shot, 35, 36, 38, 39, 43–4

skirts, 95
slang, 161, 163
slasher, 67
social reality, 173, 175
spectator, 34, 37, 40
sport, 63, 68–72, 75–6

Taïa, Abdellah, 99, 100, 103–14
teen movie, 18–31
teen film, 83, 85, 86, 87
teen pic, 62–5, 68, 77
teenagers *see* adolescence
terrorism, 115, 119, 129
tomboy, 62, 70–3
Tomboy (film), 33, 34, 36–7, 38–9, 41, 43–4
transnational cinema, 117
trilogy, 81, 82, 83, 85, 87

Vadim, Roger, 53, 55
vamp, 54; *see also femme fatale*
Van Sant, Gus, 66
Vasse, David, 206
verlan, 163–4
violence, 74–5
virginity, 226–30
Vivre sa vie, 47, 52; *see also* Jean-Luc Godard
voices, 101, 102, 107, 110–11, 114

Waldron, Darren, 38
Westbrook, Laurel and Kristen Schilt, 34
Williams, Linda, 184

youth
    and globalisation, 117, 119, 120–1
    and rebellion, 115–16, 119, 126
    and unemployment, 115, 118–19

Žukauskien, Rita, 210–11

EU representative:
Easy Access System Europe
Mustamäe tee 50, 10621 Tallinn, Estonia
Gpsr.requests@easproject.com